THE SHAMEFUL TRADE

The Shameful Trade

F. George Kay

WHITE LION PUBLISHERS LIMITED
London, New York, Sydney and Toronto

First published in Great Britain
by Frederick Muller Ltd., 1967

Copyright © F. George Kay 1967

White Lion edition 1976

ISBN 7274 0037 1

Made and printed in Great Britain
for White Lion Publishers Limited
138 Park Lane, London W1Y 3DD
by Hendington Limited
Deadbrook Lane, Aldershot, Hampshire

Author's Note

The literature about the enslavement of the peoples of Africa is considerable. The long battle to abolish the slave trade and slavery was primarily a campaign of words, and a triumph for the dissemination of truth in a manner deserving a more honourable term than propaganda.

Wherever possible I have consulted the original and contemporary material. Where references do not appear in the text details of sources are given in chapter notes at the end of the book.

For the purpose of clarity for the modern reader today's names for towns and countries in Africa are given as well as the original descriptions.

I would like to express my gratitude for the help and advice generously provided by the staffs of the London Library and of the reference libraries of the cities of London, Bristol and Liverpool. Much material was obtained on my behalf by the library of the US Embassy in London. Special thanks are due to Colonel J. R. P. Montgomery, M.C., Secretary of the Anti-Slavery Society, for data on twentieth-century slavery and the action of the United Nations to investigate and end it.

F.G.K.

Illustrations
between pages 122-123

A fragment from *Histoire de Barbarie*. 1637, depicting tortures inflicted on Christian slaves (*Radio Times Hulton Picture Library*)

H.M.S. *Gorgon*, a British steam frigate of the East Coast Slaving Squadron (*National Maritime Museum*)

A slave-sale bill, 1829, posted in the West Indies to advertise a public auction (*Radio Times Hulton Picture Library*)

The Anti-Slavery Convention held in London, 1840 (*National Portrait Gallery*)

Slave chains brought from Africa by Dr. Livingstone (*Radio Times Hulton Picture Library*)

A captured Negro wearing a slave yoke (*Radio Times Hulton Picture Library*)

A section of an embarkation canoe (*Radio Times Hulton Picture Library*)

Cross-sections of a nineteenth-century slave ship (*Radio Times Hulton Picture Library*)

A typical slave-market scene in Cairo in the 1840s (*Radio Times Hulton Picture Library*)

H.M.S. *Brisk*, under the command of Rear-Admiral Sir Henry Keppel, engaging with the slave ship *The Sunny South* (*Radio Times Hulton Picture Library*)

A slave auction in Virginia, 1861 (*London Illustrated News*)

A slave-dhow run ashore to avoid capture by a patrol ship (*London Illustrated News*)

Some of the slave traders captured by the British in the 1880s (*Radio Times Hulton Picture Library*)

A slave chain-gang under the guard of a native soldier (*Radio Times Hulton Picture Library*)

The Nazir of Messeria, a former slave trader who fought in the Battle of Omdurman (*Paul Popper*)

Slaves clearing a road through the bush in South-West Africa (*Paul Popper*)

One

The purchase or capture of some fifty million human beings month in and month out for a period of four centuries was perhaps the greatest crime against humanity ever perpetrated by Christendom, not least because those responsible for the most part saw no moral evil in treating men, women, and children as merchandise.

Beside this tireless enterprise, the Nazi cremation camps and slave labour regiments pale into a brief and minor aberration of a civilised people. What is worse is that the African slave trade emerged during the Renaissance of Europe, continued during the development of the continent's scientific, cultural and religious freedom of thought and action, was regarded as a normal and essential facet of economic and political expansion, and died despite the efforts of seemingly reasonable and honourable men to protract its long and sorry existence.

Its real evil was the callous greed which its very ease of accomplishment engendered. The men who began it and expanded it were not boorish sub-humans. They were devout and enlightened men like Henry the Navigator.

They were brave and intelligent sailors who were ready to die for England's freedom. They were the imaginative pioneers who opened up a New World. The bizarre truth was that, in all Christian countries, and over hundreds of years, these men could see no sin in the slave trade.

Greed distorted man's natural desire to explore and build a home in a wilderness. Instead of colonising the limitless lands the navigators found beyond the gates of the Mediterranean they pillaged and exploited them. Sooner than accept that the dark-skinned peoples whose land it was were quite obviously members of the human family the Europeans classified them as articles of trade. Rather than heed the evidence of a divine or natural plan for mankind to live in his apportioned area of the earth they transported a population greater than any of their own individual nations from one continent to another.

The African slave trade was not, however, a sudden and bizarre development through the discovery of an enormous source of supply of human beings in Africa and a well nigh insatiable market for their services in the New World. In Europe the feudal system, with its principles of semi-servitude for men tied to one master, was by no means dead. The great entrepreneur republics of Italy—Venice, Florence, Genoa, Naples—grew rich by trading with countries in the Near and Middle East where slavery was normal. To the fifteenth- and sixteenth-century business man, and to his employees on trading expeditions, slavery was the usual situation in countries beyond Christendom. It was accepted as a characteristic feature of life for subjected pagan people. As strong an influence in favour of, or at least acquiescence to, slavery existed in Spain and Portugal where Moorish custom had left its mark, while close contacts with North Africa made slaves in house, shop, and workplace a familiar matter to thousands of people.

It might be a pagan custom, but it was not regarded as a primitive one which would automatically disappear with progress.

Slavery was originally a hesitant step forward in the march towards civilised existence. It was a humane substitution for general massacre after victory in war, and one may assume that the majority of the defeated people were glad enough to continue living in slavery when the alternative was death.

Always in early times there was the inference that the slave was a hostage. He retained some features of his previous social status, and a distinguished prisoner of war enjoyed better conditions in slavery than many of the low-born members of the conquering race. The hostage implication persists until today, and international agreement among "civilised" nations does in fact approve in time of war that rank and file troops should be put to work without pay, while officers are not expected to do anything. No twentieth-century humanitarian really objected to the Japanese putting allied military prisoners of war to work on railway construction: the objection was that they were inadequately fed and subjected to inordinately long hours of labour. They—and the enemy prisoners working in

2

Britain, Canada, and the USA—were, of course, slaves. Their condition of slavery had no end, beyond the fortuitous and undated termination of hostilities. Like the Negro slave on a plantation, such modern war prisoners undoubtedly paid for their keep—and possibly yielded a profit for the employer, or slave master.

Only when nations developed economically and militarily were slaves regarded as a cheap and easily obtained labour force. Thereupon wars for political ends of gaining further territory sometimes changed to forays simply to obtain slave labour. The economic wealth and military power of all the ancient empires of the Middle East were based on the mass enslavement of men with physical strength to work for the captor. This proved more profitable than enslaving the defeated for the purpose of indemnity and ransom. Without such worker-slaves the great temples of Assyria and Babylon and the pyramids and tombs of Egypt would never have been constructed, nor of course, the massive architecture of these supreme masters of enslavement, the Aztecs, Toltecs, and Incas.

The city states of Greece brought about a revolution in thought and in methods of government, but they did not question the essential contribution of slaves to civilisation. The privilege of Athenian citizenship made for delightful living, but behind every citizen were slaves to feed him, house him, and protect him. The higher the status of an Athenian the less he could participate in any kind of useful activity, least of all in business, commerce, or industry. As a result, all the service industries were run by slaves, and most manufacturing enterprises were both slave-run and slave-managed. The police force, tax-collecting organisation, and many of the banks were in the hands of slaves. There is a record of a banker bequeathing his bank and his widow to his favourite slave—an enlightened attitude to a slave not imitated in the Christian era.

To what extent slaves contributed to the peerless arts and crafts of ancient Greece can never be accurately assessed, for slaves did not ordinarily gain personal fame for their creative work. But in the case of vase painting, where names were frequently included in the design, it is clear that very often only the master potter was a free citizen; the detail work was carried out by slaves or freed slaves.

The number of slaves in Athens in the fifth century BC has been estimated at 365,000. Even if this figure is a great exaggeration, the slave population must have been far greater than that of free citizens. No matter how poor a family might be it enjoyed the benefits of the work of at least one slave. The cost of a slave obviously varied according to the supplies yielded by successful battles. But one example from 416 BC indicates that a boy slave could be obtained for seventy-two drachmae (about £18). The slave was one reason why an Athenian family remained poor. There was literally no work available for a labourer or unskilled artisan who was a free man. Demosthenes, as a child, used to visit the two factories his family owned. His father took no part in the actual running of the business, nor were there free citizens on the staff. One factory, making arms, employed thirty-two slaves; the other, making beds, was run by twenty slaves.

The presence of slaves from their childhood blinded even the Athenian intellectuals to the basic injustice of the slavery. It is true that Zeno, founder of the Stoic school, condemned slavery, but his followers rejected his view, and preferred that of Aristotle, who believed that slavery was a natural condition of life for some races, if not by instinct, then certainly by the accident of birth. And all the idealism of Plato was insufficient for him to envisage a perfect state in which slavery was non-existent.

The genius of the Athenian character, with its tolerance, objectivity, and humanity, minimised the baleful effects of slavery. The huge population of slaves could have been a constant menace to political stability if they had not been decently treated; it was illegal to strike a slave in public, and no restrictions were imposed on slaves acquiring property. Nor did Athens have a vast empire and huge urban populations of the kind in which slavery, with its degradation of any kind of work and the depression of the consumer market, slowly and inevitably produces economic recession.

That situation eventually occurred in Rome, where there was a copy of the slave system of Athens, adapted to serve a great military power. This was in dangerous contrast to the Athenian situation, which was mainly commercial. Like the well-born Athenian, the aristocratic Roman could devote

4

himself only to the arts, politics and military service, both involving considerable expenditure.

No Roman senator could, by law, be involved in trade. No Roman citizen could serve in the army unless he equipped himself with arms and had the money to maintain himself during military service, and Rome was almost always at war, calling on her citizens to be on interminable and expensive campaigns.

The families who had founded the Roman state were steadily impoverished by this need to finance their sons for military duty. Lands were mortgaged to obtain the money, and inevitably the money-lenders took over the property, so that gradually the well-run mixed farms which had fed the young empire were inefficiently run by slaves put to work by the absentee financial tycoons, or more usually the lands were rationalised in large units and put down to grazing. The result was a decrease in food supplies and a drying-up of the source of an officer class to inspire the army. The facile solution was to capture still more slaves who had to be fed and who ran still more farms badly. Food had to be grown in distant colonies and transported to Rome at enormous cost. And all the time the urban population, largely consisting of unemployed, had to be pacified with the notorious "bread and circuses".

The potential danger of a vast slave population was, of course, obvious to any thinking Roman. The way to minimise that danger presented a dilemma. Humane treatment was one method, and without doubt the average Roman slave on household duties lived better than he would have done if he had never been taken from his barbarian community. These slaves were cooks, housekeepers, children's tutors, doctors, accountants, and private secretaries; they could earn a wage (*peculium*), and enlightened families did not refer to them as slaves but as dependants (*clientes*).

But those slaves employed by the state were harshly treated. The attitude was that if a slave was not asleep he had to be working, and in the mines, quarries, and on fortification construction there might be a policy of deliberately working them to exhaustion and death as the cheapest method of getting the work done. In the circus slaves were treated on the same standard as the animals. Slaves were sold in groups for training in gladiatorial combat, and when a thousand of them broke

5

out of the training camp where all too obviously the tuition was a preparation for death, the authorities executed them on crucifixes standing on either side of the entire length of the Appian Way as a lesson to others.

Neither a comfortable private job nor brutalised suppression in state employment could for ever stifle the restlessness of Rome's slave population. They caught a glimpse of their power when the Italian tribes, disenfranchised but pressed into military service which was little different from complete slavery, revolted in 90 BC and nearly destroyed the Roman Empire. Soon afterwards organised slave revolts on a large scale broke out in Sicily. Cataline and Spartacus proved that slaves could become military leaders able to challenge Roman might and would be put down only with great difficulty. Ruthless dictatorship was the only solution Rome could discover.

The cult of Christianity proved a spiritual force of greater effectiveness than the physical one of slaves in revolt. Christianity was, of course, in Rome a secretive religion making an immense appeal to the downtrodden. The early Christians, however, tended to accept the concept of brotherly love, without distinction between freeman and slave, as a situation in some future kingdom, either the heavenly one after death or a mortal one after some worldly revolution. That slavery was an established, immutable custom was not really questioned: the converted Roman aristocrat might treat his own converted slave as his equal, and take the step to free him from bondage. But he did not envisage the city in which he lived being run without slaves even if it turned Christian. The New Testament uses slave terms to make its points—"bought with a price", "Redeemer" and so on, which is an indication of the attitude that slavery was a worldly evil to be endured rather than destroyed.

In her death throes Rome gave her slaves a status very close to completely full citizenship. But the change was made too late. Rome's slaves, as an enslaved population always will, were ready to ally themselves with their master's foes; they could have no patriotic loyalty to the nation which had enslaved them; they were the willing dupes of every agitator; they had nothing to lose by change.

All Europe had known what it was to be enslaved by Rome. The memory instilled a loathing of the degradation of the system which, allied with the precepts of Christianity, abolished pure slavery among the nations emerging from the ruins of the empire. But it was replaced with a close copy of the semi-slavery, semi-freedom which Rome had belatedly instituted, with full Roman citizens in many trades—notably those connected with food production—legally forced to work for life in their individual trades. The compromise based on this deceptive status became the serfdom of medieval Europe, which has lasted until modern times. The serf was merely a slave with certain tenuous privileges. He was as much a part of the medieval manor as the trees and barns which surrounded the lord's home. He was transferred to new ownership when the manor changed hands. He could not leave without the lord's permission. But he owned some property, under restriction, and his personal life was more or less his own concern. He could within limits choose when he carried out his bond work, though from birth to death he was in bondage.

The Black Death was the serf's liberator. De-population in Europe enabled him to bargain for his services. He could get good money for his own produce and use that money to buy off his lord. In England he discovered that he could ignore laws about remaining on an estate with impunity. He could dare to select where he wanted to live and what sort of work he did without much risk of punishment.

Forebodings of disaster through this freedom proved groundless. The free man, as craftsman, artisan or hired labourer, proved to be a far better worker than the serf. He learned skills under the impetus of competition, and the same rivalry forced him to try new methods. Freedom for all men was proved to be a profitable policy. Ordinary labour attained a dignity it had never previously enjoyed.

Possibly this lesson on the practical advantages of free, paid workmen was as forceful as any moral attitude to the evil of slavery in the centuries which followed. Never, in Europe's almost continual warfare, did the major European powers resort to slavery as a form of reparation and punishment of the vanquished European adversary. Not even Hitler dared impose complete servitude on nations which he considered basically Aryan (i.e. Western European). His slave labour forces were allegedly of Asiatic origin: Poles, Russians, gypsies, and so forth. Manpower from Western countries was at least ostensibly paid, if forced to work, in constructional organisations like that of Todt.

The West European attitude to slavery, as all right for non-Aryan or non-Christian peoples, typified in this century by the Nazi theories about it, has for at least fifteen hundred years been affected by this superior–inferior race theory. Slavery was the facile idea of Athenian philosophy to solve an economic problem, and Athenian democracy permanently affected Europe's social system.

As always, diligent search of the Bible could produce an excuse for an acquiescent attitude to slavery. The eighteenth-century merchant, seeking a reason why his personal prosperity should not be jeopardised by freeing black human beings from servitude, piously quoted Noah's comment in Genesis: "Cursed be Canaan; a servant of servants shall he be unto his brethren." Whatever reason Noah had for cursing his grandson it is highly improbable that it was on account of the colour of his skin, and at least he was accepted as a brother human.

Thus enslavement in modern times by the predominant white nations of Western Europe has always necessitated two basic factors: the potential slave had to be non-Christian and he had to be non-white. If, as contemporary legends strongly suggested, the pioneer explorers of the African coastline and coastal belt had met the fabled Christian monarch Prester John deep in the African rain forest and found his millions of Negro subjects worshipping the true God it is extremely unlikely that the African slave trade would ever have started; similarly, it would not have occurred had the inhabitants of the newly explored continent displayed white skins and hairy faces like the explorers who descended on them.

But the Africans who gladly came out in their canoes and offered a welcome in the coastal villages were brown or black; they were half-naked; they had never heard of Jesus Christ. They were as novel in appearance as the animals around them —and far more valuable commercially. A mere handful of enterprising, simple-minded men exchanged their European merchandise for African products. Human beings, ivory, gold, parrots, spices—they were much the same. The original and perhaps understandable transaction which involved taking back some of the local products, alive or lifeless, was not in itself an unforgivable evil; the human beings on board were

8

among the souvenirs to embellish a fairy-tale story of lands beyond the horizon.

But it sowed the seeds of the most degrading activity which mankind ever conceived and persisted in following for century after century in the name of trade.

The custom of savage and primitive communities, the policy of states on the threshold of modern civilisation, were quickly transformed into a ruthless international business. The debauchery of the Negro in his native land was indeed the ultimate of the curse on Canaan. It also brought a heavier curse on the white races which persists to this day and is only now extracting its toll in racial hostility.

The mass servitude of the black races of Africa has created racial hostility of a type quite different from that between white nations and brown or yellow peoples. Indians and Chinese are still regarded as different rather than inferior. The colour problem of today is really one of freedom versus slavery. On the one hand there is the Negro resenting the aura of inferiority with which a slave ancestry surrounds him; on the other is the uneasy conscience of the white man who feels shame about the past and has premonitions that the future may extract reparation unless he continues the suppressive acts which his ancestors pursued with such implacable efficiency.

Two

The continent which was to yield Europe such a profitable harvest of manpower at bargain rates was, of course, accepted by the empires of the ancient world in the Nile and the Euphrates valleys as the habitation of human beings extending to illimitable distances. But medieval Europe believed Africa to be a comparatively small outpost to the heat of hell at the edge of the world. Its barriers of inland desert and bordering ocean intimidated European exploration until the concept of a terrestrial globe turned it into something to be circumnavigated. Political expansion was out of the question. The races living across the Mediterranean on the northern zones of the continent were so numerous and warlike that no penetration beyond limited and costly campaigns such as the Crusades appeared feasible. Thus Africa, with its Nile Valley the cradle of human civilisation, the second largest continent of the globe, containing a quarter of the earth's land surface, was free from European invasion for centuries.

Balanced almost equally across the Equator, only the northern coastline of Africa lies more than thirty-five degrees from the Equator, and the climate makes it almost unbearable for the peoples of temperate Europe. Over most of the land mass, rainfall is seasonal and prolonged land travel without machines or carefully planned expeditions with beasts of burden imposs-ible. In the northern half, the gateway for Europe, the pre-vailing wind system creates a hot desert unequalled in extent anywhere else. Not many rivers are navigable for any great distance from their mouths. Natural harbours are scarce and the ocean swell pounding on the shores makes it difficult or impossible to land for hundreds of miles.

The man who was the unwitting founder of the African slave trade had no intention of gaining profit or power from the explorations he inspired and financed. Prince Henry the

Navigator never in fact navigated a ship, and his total experience of sailing was across the Straits of Gibraltar. But he was fascinated by the sea and by the potentialities of man to conquer it. When he was born in 1394 the most enterprising of sailors believed that no man dare risk passing beyond Cape Juby in the latitude of the Canaries because even at that point the sea ahead could be seen to be boiling (the effect was in fact the perpetual spray of the surf). By the time Henry attained manhood the danger line had dropped southwards a further two hundred miles—to Cape Bojador.

For twelve frustrating years Henry financed expeditions to pass Bojador. Some captains quailed when they reached it; others were beaten back by contrary winds and currents; a few died in the attempt. The general opinion was strengthened that beyond the cape lay a bottomless pit.

"You cannot meet there a peril so great that the hope of reward shall not be even greater," Henry told one of his explorers, Gil Eannes. "In truth I marvel at these misgivings which have possessed you all. I am astonished to think that you have them from the opinions of a few mariners . . . who do not know how to use a compass or read a chart."

Henry had encouraged the development of navigating instruments and studied every report and chart he could get hold of; he was impresssed by the fact that exploration of the Atlantic coastal waters of Africa had not progressed since pre-Christian times. The Carthaginians had probably sighted the Canaries in the fifth century BC and the Romans made a reconnaissance of them in 25 BC. The islands had been rediscovered by Lancelot Malocello in 1270, which had resulted in Genoese merchants despatching an expedition to them. It was never heard of again. Thereafter several expeditions had attempted to explore the region; most of the sailors were intimidated by the conditions and returned without extending the penetration southwards, but this did not prevent them writing glowing reports complete with maps. These accounts recorded sights of monsters along the coast and in the sea, and stressed the unendurable conditions of heat and storm.

In his palace built on the promontory of Cape St. Vincent Henry sifted the fact from the fiction. He became convinced that world's end was much more distant than the superstitious sailors believed. Just as Cape Juby had changed from a barrier to a landmark so Cape Bojador could become a stage on a far longer journey.

There has always been controversy as to Henry's motives in his preoccupation with oceanic exploration. The ostensible one is clearly that he had the very human desire to make discoveries and put his theories about world geography to the test. But he was also a deeply religious man. Like most Christian rules of the time, he accepted the legend that somewhere in Afro-Asia there was an immensely powerful priest-king named Prester John who ruled over all the world beyond the borders of Christendom, Islam, and the Mongol Empire. Prester John probably emerged as the result of stories about the ruler of Abyssinia. But the Papacy believed that Prester John was ruler of a domain far larger than Abyssinia, and a succession of Popes endeavoured to contact him. Henry wanted above all to meet the Papacy's wish. Moreover, he envisaged an alliance for war in which Prester John would attack on one side and Christian Europe on the other in one final glorious Crusade to destroy the infidel for ever.

This dream was a way of counteracting the despair which had swept Europe some two centuries earlier, when hopes of global peace had been rudely dashed. In 1221 Pope Honorious had announced that a monarch of unparalleled piety and majesty, King David, was reigning in the Indies and would soon crush the infidels of the Holy Land, thus linking Christian Europe and the East in one vast union of Christian peoples. The Pope was soon proved painfully wrong.

King David was Genghis Khan. His kingdom stretched from the Arctic snows to the Himalayas, from the Mediterranean to an ocean no European had ever seen. The great Khan, and his successors, Kublai and Tamberlane, continued to expand their territories by a policy of destruction and massacre on a scale never before known, and by 1453 Europe itself was menaced from the Mongol bastion at Constantinople. And long before this, Saladin had conquered Egypt, thereby controlling every trading route overland between the West and East.

Thus Europeans turned away from the East in frustrated fear. The Atlantic was an unknown ocean, but better the devil unknown than the devil all too obviously irrepressible. There was also gradual acceptance of the new theory that the world was round, and therefore the defences of the Moors and the

Mongols could be out-manoeuvred by sailing to their rear.

In the business world the practical need for the spices, silks and precious metals of the Indies encouraged the financing of expeditions. There was also the dream world of the sea which terror and forebodings about the land engendered. Somewhere in the Atlantic were the Islands of Delight, the Gardens of Enchantment, the Seven Cities, the fabled super-civilisation of Atlantis. Like galactic space in the mid-twentieth century, the Atlantic beckoned with a mixture of fear and hope. Henry added the attraction of the profit motive.

He realised that merchants and ship owners could be interested in his projects if he explained that the discovery of a sea route to the Indies would bring vast profits; there was also a more immediate prospect of reaching the gold trade passing through the great market city of Timbuktu, now isolated from Europe by the Moors.

Before Henry died in 1460 the squat but very seaworthy Portuguese caravels had nosed southwards round the treacherous shoals of Cape Bojador to the mouth of the Gambia river south of Cape Verde. They had discovered no powerful Christian monarch, no River of Gold, and no Gardens of Enchantment. But as well as some evidence of the expected riches in the shape of ivory, spices, and gold dust, they found another: black servants.

The first batch of slaves were unshipped at Lisbon in 1441 by a young explorer named Antam Goncalvez, commissioned by Henry to go trading for animal skins and oils. He penetrated to about twenty-five degrees north to the coast around Cape Bojador, and went ashore with nine men, his aim being to capture one prisoner so as to demonstrate to his employer the type of human being living in the area. They eventually chased a naked man leading a camel, and wounded him with a javelin. Soon afterwards they saw a group of people who were clearly planning to rescue their kinsman, and a little way apart a girl (who it turned out later was a slave). They grabbed the girl, and the group on the hill made off. The following night they attacked two encampments, killing four and taking ten captives. The skin colour of one of the prisoners was dark brown, in contrast to the blackness of the rest. He could talk an Arabic dialect and explained he was a minor chief, and that some of the other prisoners were slaves. Goncalvez put one woman prisoner and an Arab sailor ashore to let the natives know that ransom negotiations were possible. However, Goncalvez himself did not wait to hear the result and sailed back to Lisbon to hand over his trophies to his employer.

The traditional attitude to captives taken in honourable combat was followed in the case of this first import of sea-borne Africans. The chief, and two youths the chief said were of aristocratic birth, were apparently made guests of Henry's court and treated gently, being fitted out with Portuguese-style clothing befitting their rank. The chief had told Goncalvez that five or six Negroes would be handed over in exchange for himself and for the two youths if they could be taken back to Africa. This offer was subsequently changed to a definite one of ten Negroes for the three prisoners—with the encouraging suggestion that it would be better to convert ten prisoners to Christianity than the three already held. The chief insisted that he and the youths were Gentiles and therefore amenable to salvation. Nothing was said of the remaining prisoners who were presumably confirmed in their status as slaves and put to work. In an audience with Henry the chief recognised the evangelistic zeal of the monarch and was intelligent enough to sense the Prince's desire for other profitable opportunities. The chief promised that the Negroes he would provide in exchange for himself and his companions would have a wide knowledge of the interior of Africa, of the possible whereabouts of Prester John, and of the route to the Indies.

The offer was enticing and Goncalvez was ordered to take his captives back. After the ship reached the Cape Bojador area the chief betook himself off and was never seen again, but after a week's waiting in the mouth of the Gambia river a deputation arrived and exchanged ten Negroes for the two youths, who were shipped back to Portugal, the precursor of regular deliveries.

The arrival of these small groups of African captives aroused great excitement in Lisbon, and no little envy of those who were the first to have black servants in their homes. The eventual result was the growth of expeditions with a main purpose of catching natives. Bands of armed men chased any group they could find, killing those who resisted, whether man, woman or child. The white man quickly became an enemy in the eyes of people who had approached them with kindly curiosity.

14

Henry expected to receive a fifth of all merchandise brought back from the expeditions he organised. Division of the slaves was a delicate matter because of the variation in quality according to age and sex. The prisoners stood the passage to Portugal badly, and one captain, Lancarote, put in a plea to his royal master that it would be best to get the Negroes out of the holds as quickly as possible, herd them in a field outside the city gates, divide them into five groups and let Henry choose the group he wanted without delay. This became the normal practice.

It was the custom to offer the best specimen for domestic work with the church authorities or forcibly to convert some little boy to Catholicism by putting him in a monastic order for life. This sort of action stifled whatever qualms anyone felt about enslaving persons taken by force.

Some idea of the mental outlook of the age is forthcoming from the chronicler Gomes Eannes de Azurata who interrupted his account of the Guinea explorations to offer up an explanatory prayer on the reason for his pity for the captives: "I pray Thee that my tears may not wrong my conscience, for it is not their religion but their humanity that maketh mine eyes to weep in pity for their sufferings. . . ."

The fate of these slaves was not too bad if they survived the change of climate and diet. One fortunate fact was that none of them was apparently of the Islamic faith, and they readily agreed to be baptised. As household slaves they were treated in the same way as Portuguese serfs. Male children were trained in craft work, and in time were encouraged to marry slave girls of their own race. The employers were empowered to act as parents as regards the marriage portion, which indicates that these early slaves were able to earn some sort of wage.

The excuse made so often in later years that the slave of a European employer enjoyed a higher standard of living than he ever did in his native land was made with some justification in fifteenth-century Portugal. Those Africans who adapted themselves were evidently happy, and made no attempt to escape from bondage. Their virtues were quoted by Eannes de Azurata as obedience, absence of malice, a disinclination for lechery, and a fervour for Christian beliefs. He also mentions the Negro's love of bright colours and finery: "They collected rags and pieces of material and sewed them to their clothes to embellish them."

Many references to these early captives stress the blackness of their skin, but free pure-blood Negroes did not inhabit the areas penetrated by Portuguese mariners prior to 1445, when the Senegal tribes became potential victims. The first few hundred prisoners shipped to Portugal must have been Arabs, Moors and possibly some Moorish-Negro mixtures in this area at the ultimate extent of Arab trading influences. If the captives were indeed ebony black they must have been already enslaved after purchase or capture further south and in the interior of Africa.

Slavery was therefore not a brand new evil inflicted on Africa by the pioneering Portuguese explorers. The hinterland of the western area of Africa which the mariners opened for European trade was at the time largely under the influence of Islam, the actual control and political affiliations with the tribes and nations naturally being stronger in the interior than on the coast. The sinews which bound the parts together were the caravan routes across the Sahara, then probably not quite such an arid barrier or so extensive as today.

The major trading centre was Timbuktu "on the northern banks of a great river" which was believed by Europeans who heard of it to be the Nile. Beyond this river (the Niger) lived black people who had resources in diamonds and gold, the most valuable of the numerous commodities sold in the Timbuktu markets. Originally the richest and most powerful nation among these black people lived in Ghana.

Bias clouds every objective assessment of the social and political standards of the true African races prior to European colonisation. Lack of written records enables almost any desired theory to be put forward—from a dismissal of the peoples of an entire continent as primitive savages to claims that they had achieved a type of civilisation which compared favourably with any in Europe.

The truth seems to lie in the centre. Some nations did achieve power and a high standard of civilisation, but none of the miniature empires lasted very long; they quickly grew soft and fell to an invader.

Probably the only country in the west of Africa which did attain real stability for a considerable period was Ghana, still untouched, of course, by Henry's navigators. It had become a cohesive nation by the fourth century AD and its influences extended along the Atlantic seaboard as well as enjoying treaties or conquest over groups as far as the Sahara to create a considerable empire.

Arab traders brought back many tales of the fantastic wealth of the kings of Ghana, with the usual accounts of a thousand horses in the royal stables, each animal with its retinue of slaves to look after it, luxurious palaces of enormous size, and so on. The symbol of monarchy in Ghana was a nugget of gold, stated in early Arabic accounts to weigh thirty pounds and enlarged as the legend was retold until it weighed a ton, when Egyptian dealers were supposed to have bought it and melted it down for transport.

Ghana's capital city, Koumbi, had Moslem and pagan communities living in harmony, and both in size and civilisation the city apparently compared favourably with any town in medieval Europe. Ghana prospered by trade, enjoying a seemingly inexhaustible supply of gold, ivory, diamonds and skins. Such wealth inevitably invited attack, and in 1076—a date as important in West Africa's history as 1066 in England—Afric-Arabic tribes attacked the country. Ghana was able to put an army of 200,000 in the field, but was quickly defeated and the country broke up under the invasion of many tribes— the Ashanti, Fanti, and Akim among them.

Farther east another powerful and wealthy nation grew up in Nigeria. With the break up of Ghana Nigeria became the great trading nation, and its city of Kano, with its encircling walls eleven miles long, was then regarded by the Arab caravan merchants as the most important marketing centre apart from Timbuktu. The people of Kano embraced the Muslim faith as a result of Arab contacts, but they were true Negroes, very black and very tall. Unlike the people of Ghana who dealt almost entirely in raw materials, the Nigerians were skilful craftsmen. Their textiles and leather products, dyed with an indigo colour famous throughout the Arab world, were eagerly sought. Equally well known were the silversmiths who worked with the leather craftsmen to make saddlery of pliant leather dyed in many colours and beautifully inlaid with silver embellishments. The Nigerians, like the Ghanians, relied on slaves to maintain their economy.

But West Africa's domestic serfdom was guarded by traditional rights and laws. Slavery was a usual punishment for a crime which did not justify execution. It was the alternative to paying a fine. Slaves could marry and they could own property. A slave could buy a slave for himself and no cordon existed preventing contact with free men; marriage between the children of a slave and those of his owner were quite usual. The greatest evil was perhaps the ancient world-wide custom of a slave being regarded as his owner's substitute; he could thus be imprisoned for his master's crime, and he was sometimes sacrificed when his master died and was buried with him.

The sale of slaves outside the community was rare; the movement of slaves occurred only as the result of the capture of prisoners of war. It can therefore be readily understood that the arrival of the Portuguese with their desire to obtain a few slaves did not cause consternation as the news filtered back to the marketing centres of the Arab mercantile system. The peoples living on the coast in the zone penetrated by Europe in the mid-fifteenth century were on the fringe of the highly civilised areas; they were the weaker tribes and were fair game for exploitation by the more stable nations prospering within the Arab zone of commercial activity.

Very quickly the Portuguese desire to obtain slaves brought about a degeneracy among all the African people involved in trade contacts with the expeditions. Gold, spices and ivory yielded only a reasonable profit: such merchandise was available in other markets and both buyer and seller knew the real market value. But the price of a human being had no such rational figure. The African merchant regarded the profit as unbelievably good; the Portuguese rejoiced in a ridiculously good bargain.

The *Chronica de Guine* records that as early as 1448 nearly a thousand slaves had been carried to Portugal—partly from the Barbary coast and partly from Guinea. Andalusian and Castilian merchants were told by their Portuguese colleagues that the profits were anything from 500 to 700 per cent on a healthy male slave. In the Gambia area the tribal chiefs bartered slaves for a few brass rings, leather shields and coloured baskets. Even better was the idea of putting in at the Canaries, picking up a load of cowrie shells, and exchanging a basketful of them for a slave, the seller threading the shells on a cord and displaying them as a symbol of wealth. Farther north, where running costs were less because of the comparative ease of the voyage, eighteen "blackamoors" could be exchanged for one horse in 1455.

Prince Henry did issue specific instructions that Negroes must not be kidnapped by members of the expeditions he authorised; the orders were to trade peacefully. However, permits for expeditions were usually granted to the highest bidder, and the price could be partially paid at the end of the enterprise in cash or kind: Henry knew perfectly well that "kind" meant slaves, even though his courtiers always evaded giving their master all the details of the commercial results or the methods used to attain them, and instead stressed the value of the charting and geographical reports.

It has been estimated that after the initial import into Portugal of slaves as novelties the trade settled down to an average annual intake of 750 slaves. Then it dropped to around five hundred, largely because the supply in a period of tribal stability along the coast began to dry up.

Three developments were to alter the situation completely. The first was the extension of the exploration into the Gulf of Guinea where the true Negro peoples lived in vast numbers. The second was the frantic competition created when other nations risked infringing the Portuguese monopoly of trade and exploration along the African coast. The third was the discovery of America and the development of plantations in the New World. From a minor evil not so very different from the enslavement customs of the Arab merchants and the more powerful African nations the slave trade moved inevitably towards a moral disaster for the West and an incurable economic and political catastrophe for Africa.

Three

From the time that Prince Henry's explorers had returned with the first trading trophies from lands beyond Ceuta the Portuguese did their best to maintain a monopoly of trade. Charts were secret, and sometimes deliberately drawn inaccurately. But secrecy about such an important discovery was impossible. Genoese sailors were among the crews of the exploring Portuguese caravels. Some of the Negro slaves taken to Lisbon were bought by Andalusian merchants and questioned about their origin. Lastly, some Portuguese merchants, exasperated by exclusion from the enterprises farmed out by Prince Henry, sought financiers in Castile who might be ready to fit out ships. In 1454 a Castilian expedition did in fact sail on a trading voyage to Guinea. It was attacked by Portuguese vessels as it returned, and one ship was captured. The others reached Cadiz safely, proving that the stories of wonderful trading opportunities were true.

John II of Castile lodged a protest with Alfonso V of Portugal about the attack on Castilian ships and took the opportunity to claim that Castile had the exclusive rights of sailing the ocean washing the Guinea coast, threatening war if the infringements continued. John's claim was based on a papal bull said to have been issued by Pope Martin V prior to 1431.

This claim created a crisis because Prince Henry was operating on a patent granted by King Alfonso which gave Henry a monopoly of exploration and trade south of Cape Bojador, this making the exclusive right a matter of national prestige as well as a commercial facility. The risk of war lessened on the death of John II in 1455, and in the same year Pope Nicholas V issued a bull granting to the King of Portugal, his heirs and those of Prince Henry, all "provinces, islands, harbours, places and seas whatsoever already acquired, or come to be acquired, from Cape Bojador and Cape Nam southwards".

Nicholas's successor, Calixtus III, issued another bull in 1456 extending the rights through "all Guinea and past the southern shores to the Indies" and apportioning those rights to the Order of Christ in Portugal, which meant in effect giving a monopoly to Prince Henry, who was head of the order. By this time trade was very lucrative, and the slave traffic was contributing a not inconsiderable proportion of the profits. Over a period of four years Portuguese merchants enjoyed a monopoly never seriously jeopardised, but after Prince Henry's death in 1460 the Portuguese impetus to explore still further disappeared, and King Alfonso directed the national energies into preparation for a confrontation with Castile and in developing trade with North Africa across the Mediterranean.

However, merchants who had enjoyed prosperity under Prince Henry's inspiration did not remain inactive. In 1469 a Lisbon merchant, Fernao Gomez, obtained a five year grant for trading in Guinea beyond Sierra Leone, with the stipulation that his captains had to increase the voyaging distance by one hundred leagues a year. The result for Gomez was that he opened up areas yielding pepper and gold in large quantities, the latter from a place he called Samma (Takoradi). The supplies of gold, pepper and ivory were so great that Gomez was apparently not greatly interested in slaving, and the stipulations periodically issued by the King to ensure his share of Gomez's profits do not mention slaves among the imports.

War broke out between Portugal and the newly allied kingdom of Castile and Aragon in May, 1475, the ostensible reason being a dispute on the rights of succession but in fact was the culmination of rivalry for the African trade. For years Portugal had been steadily losing the battle to keep out interlopers from Castile. The areas where the Negro chiefs normally met the Portuguese ships were well guarded, with the result that non-Portuguese captains had to drop anchor elsewhere. Such haphazard visits did not produce the collections of gold, spices and ivory the visitors hoped to find all ready for a trading transaction, but there were plenty of natives to be bought or captured. In the year war broke out three Castilian caravels anchored in the mouth of the Gambia river and the local chief, believing them to be Portuguese ready to trade in the customarily honest manner, went aboard one of the ships with his relatives. They were all promptly made prisoner, and a landing party rushed ashore and grabbed 140 of his subjects who were standing innocently on the shore awaiting their chief's return with gifts. This was the system of slave trading which was to prove not only the most profitable, but in areas uncontrolled by the Portuguese, the easiest. The news of profits being made by Spanish slavers aroused the avarice of other maritime nations.

Thus, by the end of the fifteenth century the Atlantic seaboard of Africa became the battle area where Europe's powers manoeuvred to obtain supremacy in trade and maritime communication. The world had been proved round and no longer did the overland exchanges with eastern Mediterranean nations give entrepreneur states like Venice, Florence, and Genoa the fabulous profits they had enjoyed for so long.

In the background of this undeclared war was the magnet of the New World. In vain did Spain and Portugal attempt to enforce the divinely bestowed monopoly of colonisation. Their resistance declined in importance, and the two most powerful maritime nations of Western Europe, England and the Netherlands, emerged as the pioneers and as implacable enemies, with France an aggravating subsidiary adventurer.

The people of Africa remained a source of wealth as slaves, but expeditions were no longer simply trading enterprises. They had political impetus, and wars between African tribes, hitherto accidentally convenient as a means of negotiating supplies of prisoners, were deliberately fomented not solely to get prisoners but to weaken the power of Portugal.

In addition to government backing of political intrigue along the African coast the purchase or capture of slaves became an essential policy of expansion of imperial power. The Tudor monarchs had always been agreeably co-operative in financing any sort of dubious enterprise which would show a profit, and indeed the traditional English system of overseas trading meant that royal patronage was vital for the success and even for the very existence of an enterprise beyond the shores of the realm.

Penetration into the seas off Africa and development of trade with the nations on the coast was a matter of prestige for a nation which had lost its possessions in Europe but was feeling a sense of national cohesion and independence under Henry

VIII. Not least of the ambitions engendered was the desire to emulate the successes of the French in infringing the Iberian monopolies, confirmed by the series of papal bulls promulgated in 1493.

French sailors of Brittany and Normandy, financed by a wealthy merchant of Dieppe, Jean Ango, and protected by letters of marque from King Francis I, had begun a massive onslaught on the Guinea trade. They plundered loaded Portuguese ships in preference to risking a clash with the Portuguese land-based forces at the forts, sited more to ward off European interlopers than to intimidate the Africans, but as the French restricted their operations to the Cape Verde area, where sources of slaves had by then been almost exhausted, there is no indication that slaving was the main French objective.

The French successes were well known in the west country ports of England, and the result was that William Hawkins fitted out expeditions for Guinea between 1530 and 1533. He was in fact as much interested in trade with Brazil as with Africa, but adopted the most feasible route by dropping down to ten degrees north of the Equator, touching at Sierra Leone for food, water, and some ivory, before sailing west. The demand for workers among the Brazilian settlers may have sown an idea in Hawkins's mind, though there is no evidence that he transported slaves on any of his voyages in the period 1530–3. It was a project that he later discussed with his son, John, a boy born while his father was on his Brazil voyages.

After this series of expeditions by William Hawkins there are no precise details of English expeditions for several years. The enormous profits obtainable had declined. Gold and ivory amassed over many decades had been exhausted, and current yields were modest and expensive. The only really inexhaustible supply of trade was the slave, though the territories opened on the Equator and beyond did not offer such plentiful supplies of human beings as the country to the north of the Gulf of Guinea. Portugal did her best to conceal the dimensions of the demand for slaves in her New World colonies, and she devised strict controls. The monarchy expected a royalty on every captive, the price of a slave was regulated, and attempts were made to enforce routing of Negroes via Portugal so that the King benefited from freight duties. This complicated system involved needless expense in time and money, and increased the casualty rates among Negroes. A compromise arrangement developed. Slaves bought on the African mainland were shipped to the island of Sao Tomé, some two hundred miles off the coast. There they were graded and collected into large groups before transfer to the Volta river zone where the Lisbon-bound ships awaited favourable weather.

Sao Tomé started as a slave marshalling area in 1485 when colonists were given special privileges by the Portuguese crown, which, however, excluded trading in gold. The best alternative was slaves. Early in the sixteenth century sugar was planted and mills constructed, and soon three hundred slaves were at work in the plantations, the first large scale employment of African serfs by European masters in African territory. The lucrative business which developed in slaves and sugar—the trade being open to all nations who exchanged manufactures and foodstuffs for the island's sugar and slaves—resulted in the crown taking over the revenue by 1522, the concessions being farmed out. Many of the white residents were Jews, the offer of exile on Sao Tomé being the best that Jews living in Portugal at a time of vicious campaigns against their religion and freedom could hope for; their numbers were increased by the despatch of criminals from the homeland, and Sao Tomé was a useful compromise between Portugal and Africa as a home for the half-breeds becoming fairly numerous by the beginning of the sixteenth century. These two groups were the most cruel and ruthless. Their treatment of slaves fomented unrest, and there were several large-scale revolts. They built up to real trouble and in 1536 John III sent an armed expedition to intimidate the slaves into permanent submission. A good many escaped and lived as outlaws in the densely thicketed hills in the southern area of the island. In 1574 the plantation slaves rose in well-organised attacks with these outlaws, burning farms and killing the occupants. A good many of the planters who survived decided life would be better across the Atlantic on the Brazilian plantations. This marked the decline of Sao Tomé both as a slave collecting centre and a sugar producing island.

General progress in navigation and the entry of other nations into the slave trade made the eventual decline of such Portuguese merchandising centres inevitable. Portugal had enjoyed almost a century of monopoly before real competition turned the slave trade into an international free-for-all.

The superstitions about supernatural dangers were completely dead. Renegade Portuguese pilots were ready to sell their services to the highest bidder. Maps, charts and accurate reports were in circulation throughout Europe. In England, France, and the Netherlands sailors were ready to man the ships and business men to finance them. Most of these adventurers had slaving in mind as an item of trading, though not invariably the principal one.

The vices of brutality and greed which produced a successful slave captain were not so different from the virtues of courage and enterprise which were essential for a ship's master on a passage to Africa. The three-masted merchant vessels of the period were able to make headway against an adverse wind (a vast improvement on the typical merchant ship at the beginning of the fourteenth century) but they were slow, clumsy to handle, and "beamy" in relation to their length of keel, which made them dangerous in heavy weather. Making a journey out and back of more than four thousand miles was no routine activity for sailors who rarely went out of European coastal waters.

Rounding Cape Bojador was the major test. Crews, unaccustomed to ocean voyages, liked to hug the coast as much as possible. To do so on the North-west African coast courted disaster. Reefs and currents made it essential for a ship to stand out to sea. When this was done the sea current moving steadily from the Straits of Gibraltar towards the Canaries aided the prevailing winds for a good run to Sierra Leone. There the Guinea Current flows eastwards into the gulf, except at the turn of year. For the return passage ships had to steer due west, well away from the mainland, to locate the Equatorial Current, after which the south-west winds could be picked up for the run back to Europe.

Merchants had to bear in mind the seasonal changes in winds and currents if an expedition was to succeed. In addition it was advisable to avoid landfall in the tropical zone between May and September, when the rainy season made disease rampant among the crews, and traffic in goods and slaves with the interior decreased. Ships therefore left Europe in the autumn and expected to get back by May at the latest. With fair weather and correct navigation to pick up the currents the outward passage could be completed in two months. The return always took longer because of the greater distance involved in the wide sweep north-west in a great curve until Cape Verde confirmed the ship's position. Casualties among crews were frequent—by disease when only a proportion died and the ship successfully completed her passage, and all too often by maritime disaster when nothing was ever heard again of the vessel or the human beings aboard her.

In addition to reliable knowledge of the sailing route there had to be accurate information of the best areas for trade, with some healthy suspicions about the dangers of approaching the zones patrolled by the Portuguese. The trading coastline extended for eight thousand miles, and Guinea was an elastic term even for the central part of this distance.

Guinea was the usual description of the entire coastal area from the mouth of the river Senegal to the mouth of the river Congo. The vagueness of this description was restricted in contracts and trading instructions to "the land of Guinea", which was regarded as the zone between the river Senegal and the coast opposite Sherbro island (Sierra Leone).

Navigators and traders applied loosely descriptive terms to the principal commodities obtainable along particular stretches of coastline. They were traditional names based on pioneer trading; in all of them other products—which always included slaves—were available.

Running from north to south the first was the Gum Coast between Cape Blanco and the river Senegal. Large forests of gum-bearing trees lay to the north of the river. The people there were dark-skinned but Arab in appearance and by religion. Such slaves as they offered were captured from south of the Senegal where the Jalofo people lived, the most northerly of the true Negro races. Their origins are not definitely known. West African folklore suggests that the black races came from the east after crossing water. A picturesque theory is that they came from the lost continent of Lemuria in the Indian Ocean, travelling across the encroaching water. The water was more probably a lake, and the Negroes originated beyond the great lakes of Victoria and Tanganyika far to the south-east of their eventual settlements. What is certain is that the migration occurred before the ancient Egyptians began trading with West Africa to obtain gold.

The Jalofo people lived as a network of tribes, each with its own chief, and often at war with one another. At the time of

26

Portuguese exploration they were all reputedly paying tribute to a king named Mandimansa who lived well inland and was spoken of with such awe that the Portuguese once thought he might be Prester John.

Next came the Guinea coast, a good source of gold and some ivory. The principal inhabitants were the Mandiguas, a warrior tribe who quickly learned of the profits obtainable from slaves.

The (Pepper) Grain Coast stretched from the Sherbro river to Cape Palmas. The Portuguese called it the Mallaguetta Coast, after the species of pepper grains obtainable there, which were named after the tribe harvesting them. Mallaguetta was not a true pepper and lacked the flavour of Indian pepper. After Vasco da Gama opened up the sea route to India the value of the African pepper declined and the Grain Coast became of minor importance. Anchorage off the coast was difficult and dangerous, and the people were regarded as savage and treacherous.

The Ivory Coast (included by the Portuguese in the Grain Coast) extended from Cape Palmas to Cape Three Points. The Becuidos people of the area were famous as elephant hunters.

From Cape Three Points to the mouth of the river Volta was the Gold Coast, the source of the greatest wealth in Guinea. Its inshore seas were rich in fish, and the Portuguese attempted to consolidate their annexation by imposing dues on the native fishermen.

The Slave Coast extended from the Volta right round the Gulf of Guinea as far as the Portuguese settlement at Loango in Angola. The large marketing centre for slaves was at Benin (in Nigeria). Slaves were brought here from every part of Central and West Africa once the trade developed. In the interior a slave could be bought for a few brass bangles. He was sold to Negro merchants from Benin for gold which in turn was taken to the Volta area for sale to the Europeans. This internal trading necessitated slave porterage, and at times the demand for slaves to carry European trade goods to the interior for slave purchase was so great that a slave for sale at Benin fetched twice the price of a slave put up for sale to the Europeans.

The whole of this area was being explored by English seamen by the middle of the sixteenth century, and Negroes were being brought to England. Richard Hakluyt includes an account of

27

William Towerson who was on the Guinea coast in January, 1556. He invited an African on board, who demanded information as to the fate of "five taken away by Englishmen: we made him answer that they were in England well used, and were there kept till they could speak the language, and then they should be brought again to be a help to Englishmen in this country."

This sort of abduction was not unusual by English and European seamen who were trying to break the Portuguese monopoly. The aim was to learn African languages as well as to teach the Negroes a white man's language. They also wanted intelligence on Portuguese defences and trading methods. The Negroes thus more or less forcibly transported were not enslaved, and the promise to take them back was kept when possible. Towerson's second voyage in 1556–7 was a success when Africans gave them a great welcome after a couple of their tribe stepped out of the pinnace and described their happy adventures in London.

A few slaves had, however, arrived in England from Africa by this time. John Lok was in command of three ships which sailed in the autumn of 1554 on an expedition financed by five merchants. As well as gold and ivory he brought back "certain black slaves whereof some were tall and strong men and could well agree with our meats and drinks. The cold and moist air doth somewhat offend them."

These Negroes were clearly enslaved by the time of purchase. If Lok brought them for any purpose other than that of getting information about their country and its trade it would have been only to supply domestic servants for his employers, possibly as status symbols. Lok could not have been disturbed by any moral consideration: the men were slaves and with some reason —apart from the dangers of an unfamiliar environment—he could claim that a slave in a wealthy merchant's house in England had a better existence than in an African merchant's porterage train.

The increase in the number of English ships off Africa brought the inevitable protests from Portugal, as well as from Spain when a transatlantic passage was also involved. Sometimes the complaints were heeded, as for example as early as 1480 when Edward IV vetoed a large expedition being fitted out by London financiers. Under Queen Mary, married to Phillip of

Spain, a complete embargo was promulgated in December, 1555. As the voyages of Towerson and Lok indicate, little notice was taken of it. With Elizabeth I on the throne financiers conveniently adopted a pious policy and insisted that trading voyages to infringe the Portuguese–Spanish supremacy were an advancement of the Protestant religion. The Queen was quite ready to believe the expeditions were part of a holy war.

The beginnings of large-scale trading by England coincided with—and quickly aggravated—internal strife in West Africa. A century of Portuguese exploitation had completely dislocated the West African economy. News of the attractive merchandise from Europe and the wealth being amassed by tribes on the coast filtered back to the interior. In the middle of the sixteenth century a powerful nation, the Zimbas, began moving westwards from Central Africa. They were cannibals and warriors, and easily conquered the people on the coast from Ghana to Cameroon. One group penetrated as far as Sierra Leone where they made peace and settled down. Another group attempted to take over the Senegal area, were defeated by the Souzos, who then moved south-west and occupied the area on the banks of the Gambia river. The unfortunate victims fled in large numbers to the Portuguese forts and trading posts, were given sanctuary on Portuguese ships—and were then taken away to slavery. These wars thus produced temporary and localised prosperity for the slave trade, but ruined all other mercantile traffic.

This situation was in part the reason for the success of the expeditions of John Hawkins, one of Elizabethan England's "sea dogs" (he commanded the *Victory* against the Armada) and the real originator of the transatlantic slave trade for private gain.

As a boy he was inspired by stories told of the expeditions of his father, and he applied himself diligently both to seamanship and business knowledge. Early on he made contacts with Portuguese navigators from whom he learned about the sea routes and the Portuguese defences. From his father he had caught the dream of developing trade with America, and as a small child of seven he had met a Brazilian native chief William Hawkins brought to England in 1539 for the purpose of learning about the natural resources of South America.

The trading route of England–Africa–America–England was John Hawkins's brilliant idea to make a handsome profit from each leg of the voyage. Portugal and Spain were, of course, following much the same route for the reason that it was the easiest sailing itinerary, but as often they went through the awkward system of transferring slaves for the New World in their own countries instead of moving them direct, and they did not occupy their minds with arrangements to develop home exports and stimulate colonial trade.

John Hawkins was at first an honest and kindly man in his relations with the people at the trading posts. On a series of voyages to the Canaries he made many friends—and learned of the volume of slaves passing the islands en route to the New World. This information he gave to a group of London merchants. These men included his father-in-law, Benjamin Gonson, Treasurer of the Navy; Sir William Winter, Master of Naval Ordnance; Sir Lionel Duckett, later Lord Mayor of London; and Sir Thomas Lodge, a governor of the Muscovy Company. These distinguished persons were clearly in close contact with Queen Elizabeth, and she was happy to indicate her interest in Hawkins's project. He sailed in three ships, manned by a crew of a hundred; the smallest vessel was only forty tons. They left England in October, 1562, and in the Sierra Leone area attacked Portuguese and Spanish vessels, capturing "partly by the sword and partly by other means" three hundred Negroes. These Hawkins sold in Spanish New World possessions on a monetary scale averaging £20–£30 per slave. The merchandise he bought—ginger, sugar, and hides— was so plentiful that he had to buy two extra vessels to carry it. The entire enterprise took eleven months.

A year later he commanded a larger expedition of four ships and a force of 150 seamen. The principal object was to grab slaves, and stores of beans and peas to feed five hundred Negroes were stowed on board in the expectation of success. They sailed from Plymouth in October. By December they were seeking their quarry in the Cape Verde area, Hawkins sending armoured and armed parties ashore. They had "great pleasure to behold" the Africans fleeing from them, crying out and leaping in the air, mystified when pellets from the pursuers' arquebuses caused almost invisible but crippling wounds. This particular chase yielded no captives and Hawkins moved to the Sierra Leone coast. Here his armed bands went ashore, burning huts and capturing a few Negroes. Subsequently a pitched battle took place. Seven of Hawkins's force were killed and twenty-seven injured; only a few Negroes were taken alive.

Methodically more Negroes were captured and on January 29 Hawkins set sail for the West Indies with four hundred slaves. The ships were becalmed for a time, and later swept off course by storms so that landfall on the island of Dominica was not made till March 9. Thereafter Hawkins moved from port to port in the Caribbean down to Venezuela, having to battle against the ban on Spanish colonists purchasing slaves from strangers. Such was the demand, however, that Hawkins experienced little difficulty in making unofficial deals. The expedition put into Padstow, Cornwall, on September 20. Running expenses had been £4,990 plus the cost of cargo and the value of the ships. The rewards were 50,000 ducats in gold and some merchandise. Crew casualties numbered twenty. Fatalities among the slaves were not recorded.

The success of these voyages spurred Hawkins to envisage a major expedition backed both by his mercantile friends and by the State. Trade and the flag would be carried simultaneously into every corner of the expanding territories of the Old World and the New. Hawkins was a product of his age, but his attitude to the Negro as an article of trade was typical of all who followed his example—right down to the comfortable, civic dignitaries of Liverpool 350 years later, who fought tooth and nail to maintain a trade which they honestly believed to be as good for their King and Country as it was for their own pockets.

Hawkins lived in Devon but was constantly in London, and was, after his successful expeditions, well known in court circles because his Queen loved to have her sea dogs around her as well as her luxury-loving politicians. Hawkins perpetually talked of his dreams of a full-scale attack on the trade monopolies of Spain and Portugal.

His conversation eventually produced practical results. With the cautious approval of Elizabeth I, a group of wealthy merchants and influencial politicians began the organisation of an expedition to Guinea. They included Sir William Cecil, the Queen's Secretary and principal adviser; Benjamin Gonson, Treasurer of the Navy; and business men like Sir William Garrard, and Sir Lionel Duckett (later Lord Mayor of London). The inspiration for the scheme came from two Portuguese merchants, Andre Homem (or Gaspar Caldeira, as he occasionally called himself) and Antonio Luis. They were two of several merchant adventurers who had fallen foul of the circles round the Portuguese throne which intended to keep the Guinea trade to itself. Deprived of the chance to obtain Portuguese finance, the two men had searched around for promoters in other countries, first in France where they obtained capital for an expedition which met disaster from Portuguese retaliation, and then in Spain, where merchants considered the proposition financially risky and rejected the scheme.

Homem and Luis came to England. The Queen could not officially support them in a scheme infringing the rights of a friendly power, but she listened to their stories of unbelievable wealth in the fertile lands beyond Cape Verde with avidity. The upshot was a discreet order to Cecil to investigate the Portuguese renegades' proposition and if he were satisfied, to back it. With the financing and planning in good hands, the Queen turned to her well-loved young sailor, John Hawkins, for more information about Africa. Hawkins reminded her of the reasonable success of his previous expeditions, gave vivid accounts of the challenge of sailing in these unknown waters, and stressed that no expedition could succeed unless it was on a large scale. But he was ready to lead such an expedition and show his faith in the outcome by investing £2,000 of his own and his brother's money in it. This was, of course, a very large sum, and must have represented virtually all the wealth they had. With the plan endorsed by both the business men and her master mariner, the Queen was ready to risk a degree of personal involvement. She would loan two of her own ships, the *Jesus of Lubeck* and the *Minion*.

During the spring and summer of 1567 preparations were meticulously carried out. The two Royal vessels were berthed off the Tower of London. The hulls were repaired, stores and armament taken on board, and a crew selected. Meanwhile Hawkins had gone to Plymouth to prepare the private vessels for the expedition. One belonged to his brother and himself, the *William and John*; the others were the *Swallow*, the *Angel*, and *Judith*.

Both the *Jesus of Lubeck* and the *Minion* were more than twenty years old. The former, of seven hundred tons, was still a splendid vessel and formidably armed. The *Minion* had often been in tropical waters and her timbers were badly riddled with worm. But her size—three hundred tons—made her valuable for the human cargo Hawkins expected to pick up. The four other ships, based on Plymouth, were tiny. The *William and John* was of 150 tons, the *Swallow* one hundred tons, the *Angel* thirty-three tons, the *Judith* fifty tons.

Time was passing. It was essential to clear the Bay of Biscay before the first of the winter storms and to ensure fair conditions on arrival on the Guinea coast. Moreover, Hawkins was impatient to get away before the Queen had second thoughts. Sack after sack of dried beans had been loaded in London, and at Plymouth the local blacksmiths had been given orders to make scores of manacles and leg chains. Everything possible had been done to keep the production of these two commodities secret, because they signified slaving. As it was, the Spanish ambassador had his suspicisions and taxed the Queen with them. He had been assured that the expedition had nothing to do with trading in the Spanish possessions in the New World. Hawkins knew of the Queen's moodiness. She was liable, when brooding on the half-lies she had told the Spanish diplomat, abruptly to call the whole thing off.

But this time the Queen did not change her mind. Hawkins received the official God-speed for his expedition. The Queen's message, written by Cecil, confirmed her consent to a voyage to those areas of Africa which did not pay tribute to, nor were under the domination of, the King of Portugal, to load slaves for sale in the Spanish dominions of the Indies. Hawkins issued orders that the expedition would sail as soon as the wind was favourable. The Plymouth ships moved from the wharves and anchored alongside the Royal vessels in the Catwater, where they had arrived from London.

On October 2, 1567, the *Jesus* weighed anchor and led the squadron out to sea. On her forecastle were displayed two emblems—the Tudor dragons of Elizabeth and the bound Negro of Hawkins. The four hundred men who manned the ships waved to relatives and friends as they were standing on the grassy slopes of Plymouth Hoe.

Within twenty-four hours the ships were overtaken by a westerly gale—a cold, rain-filled storm from the North Atlantic. For four days and nights the ships ran before the wind, shipping heavy seas and suffering leaks from strained timbers. When the dawn of the fifth day broke the seas were still heavy but the wind had veered to the north and was blowing only moderately. It was possible for the lookouts in the *Jesus* to climb the four masts and search the horizon. There was no sign anywhere of the other five ships.

At midday a solitary sail was seen, the *Jesus* altered course, and came up with the *Angel*. A few nights later the *Judith* joined them. The three vessels sailed uneventfully to Teneriffe in the Canaries, carefully avoiding Madeira in case their presence should arouse the curiosity of the Portuguese naval ships always stationed there. Hawkins was able to obtain provisions and fresh water from the Spanish inhabitants, but he knew it would be unwise to tax their sense of hospitality for too long, in any event he had to search for his other ships. He found them in a bay of the neighbouring island of Gomera, battered but still seaworthy. On November 4 Hawkins led his squadron south-south-east for Cape Blanco.

He had added an abandoned Portuguese fishing boat to his squadron by the time he approached the estuary of the Senegal river. When Cape Verde was in sight Hawkins dropped anchor close to a suitable beach. Just before dawn on the following day he led a force of two hundred armed men ashore, his intention being to get five or six miles inland and burst on a village just as daylight came.

They found a village, but they had no knowledge of African wariness. Sentries had warned the villagers of the army of white men and the inhabitants had fled to the bush.

A group of seamen, looking for loot, stumbled on a few women and babies cowering in the undergrowth. They grabbed two or three women just as the peculiar shrilling noise of Africans at war echoed from every side. Several hundred Negroes ran forward, shooting arrows which had little effect on the well-protected English. Hawkins shouted to his men to attack, adding a warning that they should try to take prisoners instead of killing out of hand. But every time the Englishmen lunged forward the Africans melted away, re-forming in a shrilling circle when their adversaries paused for breath. It was futile to continue the assault and Hawkins withdrew when they had captured nine Negroes.

The action, which the sailors regarded as an amusing hunt, proved more costly then they imagined. The slight nicks some had received in arms or legs from the Negroes' arrows healed well enough—but the arrow heads had been tipped with poison. Eight men died from a form of tetanus.

The hostility of the Negroes of the area was obvious from the way they hovered along the tidal strip during the day. Hawkins realised that his quarry was more dangerous and cunning than he had expected. He moved south to the Gambia river, entering its wide estuary. There he persuaded a Frenchman, trading on the coast for gold and ivory and not for slaves, to join him. The Frenchman's ship was a captured Portuguese caravel of 150 tons. Hawkins renamed it *Grace of God* and put his young cousin, Francis Drake, in command of her. Another small French ship requested permission to join the expedition, so Hawkins was in command of a formidable squadron. This was satisfactory enough, but was not really helping to achieve the aims of a trading expedition. Nearly a month had passed since the coast of Africa had shimmered in the haze, and the only results were nine Negroes manacled in the hold of the *Jesus of Lubeck*.

Chivalry and honour had different standards in Elizabethan days than they had before or have had since. Hawkins' treacherous viciousness against the Negroes was not unique. He was prepared to practise the same sort of deception and unwarranted attack on anyone and anything foreign. As the Negroes were so cunning and elusive he considered the possibility of grabbing slaves already bought by somebody else. In the island-strewn area between the coast and the Bijagos Isles his scouting parties got a glimpse of a small fleet of Portuguese caravels. Hawkins guessed they were loading slaves to fulfil contracts for Spanish requirements. He waylaid a small Portuguese ship and persuaded (subsequently the Portuguese Government complained that Hawkins used torture) the captain to pilot him through the shoals and into the Cacheu river where the ships were tied up.

Hawkins sent one of his officers to confer with the Portuguese captains. A warning burst of gunfire let the deputation know that the ships were armed and ready. The leader of the deputation, a youngster of twenty-five named Robert Barrett and a relative of Hawkins, shouted that he came peacefully and wanted to buy slaves. The reply was another fusillade of shot. Barrett had some forty armed men with him, crammed into three small pinnaces. He decided to attack. Without waiting for a hand-to-hand battle, the Portuguese crews ran off. To

Barrett's chagrin the slave holds of the deserted ships were empty.

The victory had been unbelievably easy even if the loot was non-existent. It was obvious that the Portuguese had retired farther upstream where, as the captive Portuguese pilot explained, there was a village with a slave mart. Hawkins took three of his smaller vessels into the river, from which Barrett could draw two hundred reinforcements for an attack.

The men landed and followed the river bank trail inland. In half an hour they reached a village. It was deserted. The previous experience of a seemingly lifeless village should have served as a warning. It did not. The raiding party went around picking up pots and trinkets and setting fire to the huts. Suddenly the shrilling began. The Portuguese had rallied at least six thousand Negro warriors to help them in an attack on the interlopers. Yard by yard the English fought their way back along the trail. Halfway along they would have been ambushed by the Portuguese if it had not been for a relief party from the ships who drove off the ambush forces.

Hawkins was fortunate to get away without a major disaster to his force. He still had only nine slaves. He loitered around the area for some time, sending boats ashore, trading with a chief or two—and painfully increasing his slave quota to 150. The near-failure of the expedition—Hawkins was so preoccupied with the idea of slaving that he refused to consider trading for gold or ivory—resulted in his decision to go farther south than he or his father had ever been before. It meant the risk of being sighted by the Portuguese in their slaving stations along the coast of Sierra Leone, but there was no alternative if complete failure of the expedition was to be avoided.

The New Year brought better fortune. Off Sierra Leone a large canoe came out, propelled by a dozen rowers. In the middle sat two men. In halting Portuguese they asked Hawkins to help their chief in a local war. Victory would yield large numbers of prisoners. Hawkins agreed, expecting little more than a foray. But the enemy proved formidable. The enemy warriors numbered many thousands and they were well entrenched in their wooden-walled town. Fighting went on for several days. When the English firearms forced the enemy to give way, the Africans allied to the English went mad, killing indiscriminately and taking no prisoners. When Hawkins and his men tried to grab prisoners and lead them off unharmed their allies began attacking them as well. But Hawkins managed to round up 250 men, women and children, obtained at a cost of four of his men killed, and some forty-five wounded. That night the half-destroyed town glowed with innumerable fires as Hawkins's allies celebrated their victory by cooking the flesh of their dead adversaries. The promise of unlimited slaves turned out eventually to be a token delivery of sixty or so. Hawkins was insatiable in his desire for Negro prisoners and angry about being deceived. But time was flying by. He had, after all, more than four hundred Negroes below the hatches, which was to the best of his belief the biggest number ever carried in a non-Portuguese expedition. His ships sailed for the New World on February 7, 1568.

The slaves were kept mostly in the holds of the *Jesus* and the *Minion*. The air was foetid, not only from their own bodies but from the filth in the bilges, where sea water turned the gravel used as ballast into a tepid soup swarming with insect life.

Fifty-two days passed between the disappearance of the African coastline and first glimpse of the New World. Landfall was made on the island of Dominica in the Windward Islands, still maintaining a large population of Caribs who had learned how to deal with any careless European invader. But Hawkins badly needed fresh water, not least for the slaves who were sick with dysentery and from deficiencies in the diet of boiled beans. He had already lost many of the children and the women. He was ready to risk a battle with the Caribs in order to get fresh water if that would save his valuable cargo.

Armed landing parties took the casks ashore and a plentiful supply of water was obtained without trouble over two days. Hawkins then led his squadron towards the mainland of South America, having chosen the island of Margarita as his first place to trade. The waters off the island and its neighbours were rich in pearl-bearing oysters. Hawkins knew that there was an insatiable demand for slaves to work as divers. They were forced to dive thirty or forty feet to the sea bed and their brief existence was probably the most miserable of any slave in Spanish ownership, not excepting the metal mines of Peru.

The Spaniards on Margarita were formal but courteous. Hawkins was able to barter some slaves and goods for fresh meat and vegetables. He then sailed for a Spanish colony westwards along the coast (near Puerto Cabello in Venezuela) where he took his Negroes ashore for exercise. Officially the Spanish should not have traded in Negroes or manufactures with a heretic, but the sight of the slaves, ailing and weak as they were, aroused the cupidity of the inhabitants. Many were sold under cover of darkness. Rumour had it that more merchants were gathering in Valencia, but were too frightened to come to the coast. Hawkins sent a group of sixty fully armed men to interview the merchants—but the deals were disappointing because of the intimidation of the Spanish authorities to force their subjects to obey the law, and the time they had had to organise armed resistance to the English invaders. Hawkins deemed it advisable to clear out with fewer slaves sold than he had expected.

Visits of this kind to Spanish settlements, a mixture of formal overtures of friendship, displays of force, and clandestine sales of a few Negroes, became his customary policy. Hawkins's usual excuse for the need to trade in violation of Spanish legislation was that he needed just enough gold to pay his seamen. Always the threats left the Spanish colonists in no doubt as to the inadvisability of refusal to sell provisions and provide facilities for water collection. If they also profited from a few slaves for themselves then that brought good into an evil situation.

This was a cruel age, and Hawkins was a typical product of his age. In the accounts of Hakluyt and other contemporary writers the barbarous and perfidious actions of both the English and the Spanish are graphically described, usually with apologetic explanations of the unavoidable necessity involved.

The biggest sufferers, the Negroes, are mentioned only incidentally. Whatever codes of honour existed they did not apply to those with black skins. In a rampage around the settlement of Rio de la Hacha a Negro slave came to Hawkins for sanctuary. In return for freedom and protection he offered to show Hawkins where the King's fifth—the pearls and precious metals retained as the royal perquisite of the colony's trading— was hidden. Hawkins found the treasure, and he used it to force the authorities to trade with him. As a result he sold sixty slaves (said by the Spaniards to be "old men and infants at their mothers' breasts, and among them was not a slave worth anything at all"). To heal any animosity the local Spaniards might

38

feel because of the pillage, arson and looting of his seamen, Hawkins presented a few slaves as gifts—and handed over the Negro informant to whom he had promised protection and freedom. The man was executed by being cut up into sections.

Hawkins's cargo of Negroes went on suffering: there were still 150 slaves in the holds of his ships. It was then mid-June; they had been there since the beginning of the year.

More Negroes were sold at Santa Marta. Then Hawkins sailed on for Cartagena where he hoped to get rid of the final complement of fifty. But Cartagena was a strongly defended and populous town, and the usual methods of blackmailing the inhabitants into trading by firing a few cannon and sending armed parties ashore did not work.

Autumn was approaching and it was essential to start the homeward passage. Hawkins sailed north-west towards the Yucatan Channel in order to swing east past the western tip of Cuba and out through the Florida Channel into the Atlantic. He encountered bad weather during which the *Jesus* sprang so many leaks that she was almost abandoned. An ocean passage was clearly impossible without major repairs, and Hawkins eventually decided to take his battered squadron to San Juan de Ulua (near Veracruz, Mexico), the chief port through which the treasure of Central America flowed to Spain.

Hawkins had no choice but to seek refuge in this port. He chose an unfortunate time because a Spanish fleet was due to arrive to pick up treasure. The inevitable result, despite the fanatical battle which the English put up, was a disastrous end to the Hawkins expedition. Hawkins escaped in the *Minion* and Drake in the *Judith*, with such members of the crews of other ships who had not been battle casualties and had been able to reach the ships which were still seaworthy. Among the loot taken by the Spanish from the dismasted and riddled *Jesus* were seventeen slaves who had somehow survived the battle, manacled in the hold.

The overcrowded *Minion*, with two hundred men on board, almost immediately ran into a gale which lasted for a fortnight. Hawkins was forced to turn back to the Mexican shore in search of food and water. There he offered his men the choice of risking refuge in Spanish territory or the passage across the Atlantic in a leaky, under-provisioned ship. About a hundred men chose to go on shore. Some had second thoughts when the

39

boats took them shorewards through the pounding surf. They were flogged until they jumped overboard.

The *Minion* passed through the Florida Channel in November. The Atlantic crossing took nearly three months. There were twelve unsold slaves on the *Minion* when she fled from San Juan de Ulua. Obstinate to the last, Hawkins had refused to put them ashore with the crew members who did not want to make the Atlantic crossing, just in case he could find some port where he could sell them. Five of them quickly died of starvation at a time when the crew were suffering from scurvy. Only half of the crew were still alive when the *Minion*, seeking the first possible refuge, put in at the Spanish port of Pontevedra (north of Vigo). The Spaniards treated the survivors of an expedition which had, as news had already informed them, committed a series of unfriendly actions against their authority, kindly—too kindly. The ill-judged feasting of men suffering from prolonged starvation killed many more—leaving, according to one account, only fifteen men to take the *Minion* back to England. Twelve sailors from an English merchant ship in Vigo were put on board and the *Minion* headed north for England. She arrived at Plymouth on January 26, 1570. Drake had brought the *Judith* in a week earlier. No details of his passage across the Atlantic have survived, but his shortage of food would not have been so severe as he was not carrying so many men.

The trading profits from the expedition were 25,000 gold pesos, which were roughly £8,500. The valuation of the lost ships for a putative claim against Spain was fixed at £28,000. As a commercial enterprise, the Hawkins slaving voyage had obviously been disastrous. But as an experience from which lessons for the future could be learned it was invaluable. England, and notably the real patron of the enterprise, the Queen, noted that Spain, ostensibly a country bound in friendship by the ties of marriage with England, brooked no trespass on her trade on the Spanish Main. A challenge would in some future day be inevitable. Nor was Hawkins's defeat at San Juan de Ulua regarded as shameful (as indeed it was not). Weary and famished crews, manning ships almost falling apart, had challenged the impressive might of a Spanish treasure fleet and its attendant warships, and had been close to as great a triumph as they had achieved in the sallies on smaller Spanish colonies in the Caribbean. The Hawkins and Drake who had fled the Mexican coast were twenty years later to chase an Armada along the English Channel, using very similar tactics as those they had devised off the coast of America.

For the rumbustious, awakening England of Elizabeth I the voyage was therefore not a disaster to be forgotten, but an enterprise from which lessons should be learned. Across the Atlantic were potential customers anxious to hand over gold and silver, pearls and jewels, in undreamed-of quantities for the merchandise they needed. That merchandise was available in equally undreamed of quantities along the coast of Africa.

Only two rival powers offered any obstacle to English maritime enterprise in the slave trade. Portugal disliked interlopers in Africa; Spain claimed a monopoly of land in the New World. The challenge had been accepted by Hawkins in the name of his Queen.

To the modern reader the title of "father of the slave trade" which Hawkins had earned, is a term of opprobrium. For him, and for three centuries afterwards, it was an expression of admiration. Perhaps the kindest thing is to say that he could hardly have known better. He lived in an era where harsh attitudes were evidence of bravery. He sailed seas where rival seamen did not hesitate to sink a hostile ship and leave her crew to drown; boarding parties threw adversaries into the sea; officers might be given the privilege of capture and execution on land. The accounts by Hawkins and his seamen show no resentment at the treachery and viciousness of the Africans who fought to evade capture.

He was born in an England whose Queen had no compunction in having enemies beheaded. Death by hanging, drawing and quartering was the legal penalty for treason. Poisoners could be boiled to death. Minor crimes were punishable by mutilation—nose slitting, ear removal, hand amputation, and branding. It is in this context that Hawkins of the transatlantic slave trade has to be regarded. He was as avaricious as he was brave, but he cannot be regarded as a brute, even though he inaugurated a shameful trade with a monstrous degradation for all who participated in it.

Four

With the opening of the seventeenth century the two leading colonising nations—Spain and Portugal—ceased to enjoy supremacy in the New World and in the ocean approaches to it. Portugal herself had fallen under the suzerainty of Spain and was therefore both involved in Spain's wars in Europe and bereft of her independent control of her African outposts.

The great economic expansion of the emergent nations of Europe demanded two objectives: a share in the West African slave trade and a foothold in the New World. One activity could not yield the expected rewards without the other. Britain and France were already firmly, if illicitly, entrenched in the African market. Now they were joined by the Netherlands and Denmark; even Sweden and Brandenburg were testing the opportunities. Given the attitude that the Papal decrees about Portuguese rights to lands explored by Portuguese navigators were not valid, there was really no reason why every nation should not freely supply goods to African nations in areas only partially explored and exploited, though in fact, of course, the established market zones technically in Portugal's possession attracted the newcomers. The real profits came from slaves— and for these there had to be entry into the insatiable market for labourers across the Atlantic.

Spain had been compelled to abandon her claims to Columbus's discoveries. English colonisers had taken possession of part of Bermuda by 1609, and several other islands, including the Barbados, were under English control by 1625. Undefended and virtually unpopulated islands were being grabbed by French and Dutch expeditions wherever they could be found. For the sale of Negroes these islands were more important than the colonies of the mainland of America because of the development of Caribbean plantations. Not until well into the second half of the century did the development of the tobacco industry open a vast new market for African workers in the North American continent.

The only moral consideration was perhaps a lingering respect among the nations of the Reformation of the Papacy's bestowal of monopoly rights on the Portuguese, and this was with little difficulty changed into a political move of the temporal powers in the Vatican. As regards the moral factors involved in slave trading the Catholic Church was ready to quieten anyone's conscience.

A Portuguese priest, Father Sandoval, wrote to the rector of the Jesuit College at St. Paul de Loando (Luanda) in Angola in 1610 for a ruling on buying slaves. The reply was that the trade was legal, and he need have no scruples about it "because the Board of Conscience in Lisbon had investigated the moral and religious factors of slavery.

"Nor did the bishops who were in Sao Tomé, Cape Verde, and here in Loando—all learned and virtuous men—find fault with it . . . It is generally accepted that the owner who owns anything in good faith can sell it and that it can be bought . . . I declare that in the fairs where these Negroes are bought there are always a few who have been captured illegally because they were stolen or because the rulers of the land order them to be sold for offences so slight that they do not deserve captivity, but these are few in number and to seek among ten or twelve thousand who leave this port every year for a few who have been illegally captured is an impossibility, however careful the investigation that may be made."

Such a conscience-easing attitude was, as always, buttressed by the thought of saving the Negroes' souls: "And to lose so many souls as sail from here—out of whom many are saved—because some, impossible to recognise, have been captured illegally does not seem to be doing much service to God, for these are few and those who find salvation are many and legally captured."

Portugal and Spain in theory enforced the conversion of slaves to Christianity prior to shipment; the English and Dutch went through no such formality, and as a result the Council of the Inquisition drew the attention of the King of Spain to the perils of pagan slaves mixing with Catholic slaves on the plantations, asking that royal orders be issued to the colonies in the New World that the inquisitors exercised special vigilance against heretics and pagans among the slaves. Thus a slave in himself was not living proof of man's brutality to man; he was merely a visible shame if his soul had not been saved. Even among Protestant nations this attitude of the traditional fount of Christian law exerted a strong influence. It was perhaps the fundamental reason why Christian Europe perpetrated its vileness for so long.

The piratical, adventurous forays by well-armed seamen which had typified non-Portuguese activities in Africa during the sixteenth century were replaced in the succeeding one by respectable, nationally organised business enterprises. The Dutch formed the West India Company in 1621, with a monopoly in the African market and rights for economic development of Dutch lands in the Americas. It became a formidable competitor and helped to raise the Netherlands to the status of a world power.

The mercantile sense of the Dutch was both more realistic and conventional that that of their rivals. They did not regard every black-skinned African as a dupe or a quarry. They approached them as potential business friends. Their trading goods were of decent quality and available at a reasonable price. The result was that the loyalty of many coastal tribes towards their Portuguese masters quickly evaporated. In most areas of the Gold Coast, save in the immediate localities of the Portuguese factories, the Negroes resumed their territorial rights. Then in came the Dutch, offering a fair price for land on which to build store houses and forts. So strong did Dutch influence become that by 1637 they were able to organise an attack on the principal Portuguese fort in Africa, Elmina, seventy miles east of Cape Three Points on the Gold Coast. The Dutch made an alliance with the Negro forces. Together they drove out the Portuguese.

The Africans had no objection to the Dutch increasing Elmina's defences and building more forts because the new-comers made it clear that the defences were against rival Europeans and not to intimidate the African. The basic hatred of the coastal tribes was for the Portuguese. They were prepared to be friends with anyone who were enemies of Portugal. But France merely made sporadic expeditions and the English behaved in much the same way; in any event England was heavily involved in the Civil War. Permanent naval patrols or established strong points on the coast were not feasible.

At this period both the Danes and the Swedes made their attempts to get a share of the African trade. The inspiration came largely from Dutch merchants who thus hoped to break the monopoly of the Dutch West India Company. Their activities appear to have been concerned mainly with trading goods. Transport of slaves to the New World was not the main objective, although reports of transactions suggest that it was customary to take a handful of Negroes when native traders offered them.

England had a little earlier set the example for the Dutch company, which the Netherlands then studied and improved. The London enterprise was founded in 1618, three years before the Dutch company began operations, under the name of the Company of Adventurers of London Trading into Parts of Africa. The monopoly was granted by James I to the Earl of Warwick, who was interested in obtaining man-power for his farms in Virginia, though slaving does not appear to have been in the mind of the governor of the company, Sir William St. John.

Indeed, one of the company's captains, Richard Jobson, trading in the estuary of the Gambia river, was greatly put out when offered slaves by an African merchant.

"We were a people who did not deal in any such commodities," Jobson told him; "neither did we buy or sell one another, or any that had our own shape."

There was little room for decent principles like these in the African trade, and the company made losses on its expeditions, partly because even English merchants and captains ignored its monopolistic rights. It finally lost its privileges when Charles I granted a patent to a group of company merchants to trade in Guinea, Binney (Benin) and Angola. Under the Commonwealth, Parliament queried all royal monopolies, and the Guinea company's rights were transferred to a new group of merchants, but with a smaller area of monopoly, virtually the coast within sight of the island of Sherbro off Sierra Leone. The new company was no more fortunate than the one it replaced. Royalist adventurers as well as Dutch and Portuguese ships harried the company's sailors and trading posts. Heavy financial losses resulted in the activities being abandoned.

The East India Company also dabbled in the African trade at this time, and some slaves were bought, for domestic work and labouring in the company's Indian establishments; they were not numerous, but are an indication how the Negro was regarded as a slave for employment even in a country where cheap labour was readily available.

The stable enterprise which made England the leading slave-buying and slave-transporting nation was the Royal African Company, formed in 1672. It took over the assets of the earlier organisations and built some new forts, including one at Accra. At first it concentrated on buying gold, and in its first year of operation obtained enough to supply the Mint for the production of the first guineas. But supplies of gold were exhaustible; supplies of Negroes were endless. Though slaving was not the specified trading purpose of the Royal African Company, everyone financing it hoped and believed that it would be an integral feature of its commercial activities.

France tailed well behind England and the Netherlands in the development of her African trade. In the mid-seventeenth century most of the operations were still organised by the sea-faring families of Brittany and Normandy. These were the origins of an enterprise, the French Company of the West Indies, with trading plans for the over-exploited coast north of the Gambia river, though optimistically rights of monopoly were granted as far as the Cape of Good Hope. This company faded away after a few years. Enterprise after enterprise followed one another into ruin.

French colonists were starved of labour, despite efforts by one organisation, the Company of the Senegal, to build up its slaving activities. It carried Negroes to Marseilles for naval galleys as well as to the West Indies. But the supply was insufficient and French colonists had to buy Negroes wherever they could find them, and this meant from British and Dutch traders. The insistent demand resulted in further enterprises, at least one of which was financially supported by Louis XIV as a personal investment. John Barbot, agent-general of the Royal Company of Africa and Islands of America, wrote a graphic account of Guinea in 1682 as seen from the French angle. It is evident from his report that there was no need to capture slaves, the Negro merchants being only too eager to meet the demands in the course of trade.

"Those sold by the Blacks," John Barbot wrote, "are for the most part prisoners of war, taken either in fight or pursuit, or in the incursions they make into their enemies' territories; others stolen away by their own countrymen; and some there are who will sell their own children, kindred, or neighbours. . . .

"The kings are so absolute that upon any slight pretence of offences committed by their subjects they order them to be sold for slaves, without regard to rank or possession."

A cruel ruse mentioned by Barbot concerned the kidnapping of children. The custom was for parents to send their small children to the millet fields at sowing time and just prior to harvesting to scare off birds. Neighbours then grabbed these children and took them to the coast. In times of famine, and in the weeks prior to the harvest, Negroes willingly sold their own children and even, Barbot alleges, themselves, in order to get food. The prevailing price for a good slave was two ounces of gold.

Barbot believed that the most active slave trading was in Accra because the country in the vicinity was perpetually at war with its neighbours, the principal slave market being at Abonee. Friendly nations were allowed to bring slaves to that point, some thirty miles north of the coast, but no further, in order that the local dealers could act as middlemen and take the slaves on to the European buyers. The mark-up in the price at this stage was 100 per cent.

Treatment of the captives was more brutal than that inflicted by the Europeans. Barbot wrote: "These slaves are barbarously treated by their masters who subsist them poorly, and beat them inhumanly, as may be seen by the scabs and wounds on the bodies of many of them when they are sold to us. They scarce allow them the least rag to cover their nakedness which they also take off them when sold to Europeans and they always go bareheaded. The wives and children of slaves are also slaves to the master under whom they are married; and when they die they never bury them but cast out the bodies into some place to be devoured by birds or beasts of prey. This barbarous usage of those unfortunate wretches makes it appear that the fate of them that are bought, and transported from the coast to America, or other parts of the world, by Europeans is less deplorable than those who end their days in their native country; for aboard ship all possible care is taken to preserve and subsist them for the interest of the owners, and when sold in America the same motive ought to prevail with their masters to use them well that they may live the longer and do them more service. Not to mention the inestimable advantage they may reap of becoming Christians and saving their souls. . . ."

Barbot was, by the standards of his time and profession, a humane man. He speaks with disgust of the harsh treatment of slaves on the passage to America, mentioning that the English in particular lost great numbers—two, three and even four hundred out of the five hundred shipped.

He could be stirred with compassion. By coincidence he once bought over several days six Negroes who turned out to be mother, father, three sons and a daughter. He ordered that they be put together in the hold and better treated than the other slaves, and in Martinique was sufficiently disloyal to his employers to sell the family as a unit at a low price to a planter who promised to treat them well and let them live as a family, rather than making individual deals so as to obtain the best figure.

Such consideration for individual slaves was exceptional. By this time an efficient system had developed, whichever nation was involved, to process African natives into manacled serfs.

Compounds existed on the beach near the slave trading countries into which the slaves were herded, the African merchants having previously shaved all the hair so as to disguise the actual age of the slaves, while their bodies were rubbed with palm oil to give an appearance of sleekness and vitality. In the compound they were then stripped naked for medical examination. The most valuable merchandise was lighter in colour than the Negroes on the coast, and was considered stronger and more adaptable to work. These Negroes reputedly came from tribes at least six hundred miles inland and were cannibals—a fact which made them readily accept the widespread rumour that the Europeans were buying them to eat. The potential value of these warrior slaves in the American auction was somewhat minimised by the likelihood of trouble on board ship. They were prone to go berserk and kill their captors when they got the chance.

The ships' surgeons became expert in selecting strong slaves belonging to tribes which had gained a reputation as a supply source of good workers. They had also to make an accurate estimate of age despite the merchants' attempts to mislead them. Thirty-five was the maximum age for a first-class slave. Those who appeared older, or had defective eyes, teeth, or limbs, were graded as second rate. By this time, too, syphilis had been passed on to Africa by the European sailors. A special watch was kept for venereal sores which might be the source of contagion on board ship and in any event presaged a short life.

The slaves passed as fit and healthy were then branded on the breast with the purchasing company's mark. The reason for the branding was to prevent the Negro slave traders exchanging the approved slaves for unfit ones during the marshalling in the compounds preparatory to shipment and to settle disputes about ownership at the auctions in the West Indies.

Most of the west coast of Africa is poor in harbours, and embarkation of slaves was always a problem. Sometimes the canoes could not effect the transfer for a fortnight due to bad weather. During this time the European purchasing agent had to maintain the purchased slaves on behalf of the ship's captain. The diet was restricted to European-style bread and water at a cost, in the late seventeenth century, of twopence per day per slave, almost the same as the prison fare for criminals in England.

When shipment began the Negro merchants stood at the gate of the compound and took away the loin cloth from each slave. On board ship a piece of canvas was handed over as a replacement. Any slave lost during transit from shore to ship had to be replaced by the agent.

Food for the slaves consisted of yams and bananas when obtainable, as well as plantains (dried bananas) which the slaves liked best. To supplement the fruit millet and maize were bought when available. Of the European food supplied the natives would eat boiled horse beans (a form of broad bean) and European cereals in the form of a porridge.

A customary sight around an achored ship was the fins of sharks. By accident one or two slaves—and not improbably a member of the European crew—would invariably fall into the water before the ship weighed anchor. Sharks were said to follow slave ships right across the Atlantic, waiting for the bodies thrown overboard, daily in most cases.

On board all male slaves were put in irons, shackled in twos; women and children were usually battened down in the hold. It was alleged by some agents that the more brutal ships' masters cut off a leg or arm of any slave who attempted to jump overboard before the ship sailed, partly to restrain him and partly to terrify the others. This amputation was doubly terrifying to the Africans, for the religious belief of the Gold Coast slaves was that an after-life would not be possible if a limb were missing.

On the passage to America the slaves were brought up twice a day for food—at 10 a.m. and 4 p.m. The crew stood to arms at these times. The male slaves were assembled on the main deck where cannon could command them; the women on the quarter deck, and the children on the poop. After eating—a peckful of a porridge made from maize among ten slaves was a typical ration—each slave was marshalled for return to the hold, being given a pint of water as they shuffled past the water barrels.

Once out of sight of land the slaves were taken out of their shackles, the theory being that they would not attack the crew because of their own lack of knowledge of handling a sailing vessel. As captors have discovered before and since an effective method of control was to allow a few captives extra privileges if they agreed to act as informers and guards. Slaves from the coastal areas, who were aware that death in a stewpot was not the ultimate end of the ocean passage, were regarded as reliable lackeys for this job.

Thomas Phillips, master of the *Hannibal*, employed by the Royal African Company, left an account of his slave trading adventures between 1693–4, in which he said that thirty or forty Gold Coast Negroes were appointed overseers and guardians, to sleep among the slaves to prevent them quarrelling "as well to give us notice if they can discover any cabaling or plotting among them, which trust they will discharge with great diligence: they also take care to make the Negroes scrape the decks where they lodge every morning very clean, to eschew any distempers that may engender from filth and nastiness; when we constitute a guardian we give him a cat o'nine tails as a badge of his office, which he is not a little proud of, and will exercise with great authority."

Phillips was, comparatively speaking, a humane man. In fine weather he brought the slaves on deck for an hour or so every evening, encouraging them to dance and move around to music provided by the crew. This was not, of course, a move motivated solely by kindness but by the anxiety to curb mortality by maintaining physical fitness. Two or three slaves were dying daily even before the *Hannibal* stood out to sea. With a complement of seven hundred slaves on the manifest the vessel sailed for Sao Tomé, where she took on water, sugar, and rum. The passage from Sao Tomé to Barbados lasted from August 25 to November 4. Fourteen members of the crew and 320 slaves died. The latter loss was deeply regretted by the master, who was at pains to record that every death meant £10 lost by the Royal African Company and £10 10s. by the ship owners in freight charges.

The most common cause of death appears to have been dysentery, called the "white flux", but this may have been a tropical fever. It killed quickly and was virulently infectious, the crew catching it as readily as the Negroes crammed below decks. Another common disease Phillips of the *Hannibal* calls smallpox. This disease was by then very common in Africa wherever Europeans had penetrated. In the outbreak on the *Hannibal* it appears to have been a mild form of variola, or possibly chickenpox. Only twelve Negroes died from this disease, though a hundred at a time were covered with sores and suffered fever. The crew members moving among the victims to give them plenty of water to assuage the fever and palm oil to ease the pain of the pustules did not catch the disease. This may, of course, have been due to immunity from an attack of smallpox in previous years, a common enough situation when the disease was endemic in Britain.

Ships' masters conscientiously kept records of mortality, though the causes were inevitably vague. The log of the *James* for a voyage in 1675, during which fifty-three Negroes died, includes the following causes of death:

"Departed this life suddenly; departed this life of a fever; wasted to nothing and so died; received with a dropsy and departed this life of the same disease; miscarried and the child dead within her and rotten; fell into a consumption; died of a great swelling of his face and head; would not eat nor take anything; died of a flux; fell overboard; died of the cramp; very thin and weak when received."

Many deaths undoubtedly occurred simply because the Negroes lost all will to live; as many resulted from suicide. Great care had to be taken to stop slaves jumping overboard and sinking immediately, even though most of them could swim. The despair and terror were such that the captives often refused to eat even when foods with which they were familiar

51

were available. Barbot, stressing that he was by nature a compassionate man, mentions that he sometimes had to have the slaves' teeth broken in order that their mouths could be opened and food forced down their throats.

The Dutch claimed, and with some justification, that they managed the slaves during the Atlantic passage better than other nations. They provided three meals a day, and the amount of food, though not the kind or quality, was better than many a Negro had enjoyed in freedom; one of many disasters inflicted on Africa by the European market for slaves was that the time-honoured tradition among the larger tribes of storing grain and dried bananas after good harvests as an insurance against famine had been abandoned. Food surpluses fetched such good prices from the slaving agents on the coast that they were sold right after harvesting.

The hostility of both the English and the Dutch to the Portuguese was a reason why the latters' treatment of slaves was frequently condemned with pious protestation.

James Barbot, a relative of the slaver from whose account of Guinea extracts have been quoted earlier, claimed that Portuguese ships carried 650 or seven hundred slaves, men having to stand tied to posts, women lying in a narrow slit between decks, children crammed in the steerage, and pregnant women kept together in a cabin. James Barbot remarks on the fact that all the Portuguese slaves were christened before being taken aboard, it being a sin under pain of excommunication for the shippers if any unbaptised slave were landed in Portuguese colonies in the New World.

Suffering more severe than that endured by the bulk of slaves was the lot of the "contraband Negroes" almost universally carried on every ship. These were slaves purchased by members of the crew for their own profit and hidden wherever they could find a niche to tie them up. Usually the captain and officers were permitted to buy one or two slaves for their own as personal merchandise. This was an effort by the employers to curb illicit trade. All that happened, of course, was that the personal acquisitions of the officers increased by the permitted quota. "The captain's slaves never die" was a wry comment on the fact that he replaced casualties from the company's stocks in the hold. Some measure of the hideous hiding places in the bilges, behind timbers, in rope and sail lockers and so forth, in which the crew hid their living contraband, can be gleaned from the fact that the most diligent search by agents at the port of entry failed to discover all the living contraband. The only bright side of this branch of the traffic was that the number of slaves officially permitted to the officers lived better than the rest. They were fattened up and often taught a simple trade so as to enhance their price in the American market.

The mortality rate for captured Negroes can be gauged from the journal of the *Arthur*, a Gravesend vessel of the Royal African Company, logging details of her voyage between December 5, 1677, and May 25, 1678. She anchored off New Callabar (in the vicinity of Port Harcourt, Nigeria) after a two months' passage from the Medway. On the first day's trading the local chief sold a male Negro for thirty-six copper bars and a female for thirty. Soon there were numerous canoes bringing human merchandise, and anything from a couple to thirty Negroes were purchased at a time, the slaves being selected with care as regards health, and the age limits restricted from fourteen to thirty. Business was in fact so good that purchases had to be restricted until supplies of yams to feed the Negroes could be obtained.

Sickness had broken out on board by March 1. Some members of the crew were ill, and the captives bought at the outset, who had by then been in the holds for three weeks, "doe decay and grow leane, and some are sick". The master accepted such things as the inevitable result of life near the Equator. He was at pains to point out that the Negroes had as much food as they could eat, all the comforts possible, and no member of the crew was allowed to strike them.

By March 3 fatalities were occurring among both crew and slaves. Such medicines as were available were given to both white and black patients. But deaths continued, and by the middle of the month the master was pursuing the hapless policy of buying live replacements in an endeavour to maintain his quota. On March 27 the ship moved into tidal waters, and a muster was taken of the cargo. The total was 175 men, 135 women, nine boys, and ten girls. The ship then put out to sea. Three days later the ship's doctor died, and half a dozen of the crew were ill as well as some thirty Negroes. The passage to Barbados lasted until May 22. Deaths among the slaves totalled sixty-eight. The sick were given brandy and wine; the healthy got tobacco. When the yams proved to be spoiled the Negroes were given the same provisions as the crew. As soon as the master could buy food in Barbados the surviving slaves got fish, beans, and potatoes. But Negroes continued to wilt and die, and their sale as quickly as possible became an urgent matter. The ship had sold all her 265 survivors by May 31, an indication that demand, even for sickly Negroes, was brisk.

The actual prices obtained for the slaves was not a matter for the ship's master but for the company's agent. The average price was at this time £20 in British possessions in the West Indies, dropping to £16 or £17 for a weakly or very young slave. At the latter prices there was a good chance for a plantation owner to retrieve his investment if he could get a year's work out of his purchase; after that every slave represented at least £15 profit per year.

The company allegedly restricted supplies of slaves to keep up the price, and purchase from foreign shippers, who were ready to undercut to £14 per head, was illegal. Planters were at this early stage in the development of sugar and tobacco planting, unable to pay cash. They were given six months' credit or a year's credit—at high rates of interest.

Pleas from the planters to increase the supplies of slaves and so reduce the price fell on deaf ears in England. The Government regarded its control of the slave trade as of direct political and economic benefit. For one thing it was creating a large number of seamen experienced in transoceanic navigation and stimulating the shipbuilding industry to construct better vessels.

Almost spontaneously, the future of Britain's world-wide trading enterprises was being shaped by the situation created by African trading and New World colonisation.

The primary occupation of the colonisers on the Caribbean was sugar production. Sugar cane is believed to have originated in tropical Asia or the Pacific islands. It was for centuries one of the great trading commodities of the Arabs, and the Moors introduced it as a normal if luxurious item of the diet to Spain. When Portuguese colonists reached the Canaries and the Spaniards settled in the Caribbean they quickly realised that the climate was suitable for sugar cane, and it became the principal agricultural crop in both areas. In Elizabethan England sugar was a very costly imported luxury, most sweetening and preserving of foods being achieved with honey or spices. The British occupation of West Indian islands made it feasible to emulate the Spanish. Sugar cane was the most profitable crop, with methods of cultivation copied from the Spaniards. Inevitably the system of slave labour to work the plantations was followed, and many were thriving by 1640.

The yield was far in excess of local needs and was of course grown as an export commodity. Payment ultimately came from the consumer in Britain, but with the three-cornered routine of British manufactures for Africa, Negro slaves for the West Indies, and sugar for the home market the ramifications of business affected the entire economy of the country—and large profits were obtainable at every stage, principally because the key commodity—the Negro slave—was obtained at a very low price.

The principal kinds of trade goods used in the seventeenth century to buy slaves were weapons (including firearms), iron bars, and textiles. The exports of weapons, including arrow heads and knives, gave a much needed fillip to the trade of Sheffield craftsmen, who even then had a reputation for skill in tempering metal going back three centuries. The craftsmen had fallen on lean times by the start of the seventeenth century, when it was reported that a third of the 2,207 householders in the town were dependent on charity. Then improved techniques introduced by Flemish workmen resulted in the production of sharper and more durable knives, and trade began to revive just in time to meet the demands for African exports.

The iron-making industry was long established and wealthy, the London ironmongers enjoying a considerable export business. The bars were cast in bloomeries along Thames Street in the City and loaded straight on to Europe-bound ships at the adjoining wharves. Many of the galleons in the Armada were equipped with English-wrought cannon, a fact which Raleigh protested about in Parliament. By the time iron bars became useful items of the trade goods for Africa the industry was, however, approaching a supply crisis. Enormous areas in the south of England had been denuded of trees to keep the furnaces going. In Sussex, for example, 50,000 men were employed in felling timber and transporting it to the forges, of which there were more than sixty in the county. As an example of the timber consumption a forge at Lamberhurst, producing 260 tons of iron a year, needed 200,000 cords of timber to do so.

Ironfounders were compelled to move northwards and to seek other sources of fuel. Edward Lord Dudley took out a patent in 1620 for the manufacture of iron by using coal for smelting the ore, which then came into use as the method among the smiths of Dudley, one of the biggest iron-working towns in the Midlands. Hostility by the timber interests and the upheaval of the Civil War ruined the new enterprise. It was not until Abraham Darby began using coke at Coalbrookdale that the iron trade really began to produce all the iron that was needed to meet the demands of industry at home and the flourishing export trade.

Important as iron was in the African market where weapons and utensils of metal were prized as highly as precious metals, the really inexhaustible demand was for cloth. The textile industry received a fillip which was the overture to its subsequent growth during the industrial revolution. It was the earliest to benefit from overseas markets and was geared to the requirements of foreign customers by the time Hawkins was pioneering to Africa and the Caribbean. The industry was then based on domestic manufacture, the pivot being the clothier who bought the woven cloth from cottages, arranged supplies of wool from farms, and was prepared to finance both parties. Typical of the wealthy Tudor clothier was Peter Blundell, of Tiverton. His textile business provided him with a fortune equivalent to nearly half a million pounds in modern monetary terms.

Many clothiers then brought the weavers together under one roof. Sixteenth-century mills of this kind existed in Newbury, Oxford, Malmesbury, Lavenham, and Cirencester. These were the country's first factories. One at Newbury flourishing during the reign of Elizabeth employed fifty men to shear sheep, many children to sort the wool, and one hundred women to card it. Two hundred girls spun the yarn and four hundred men and boys carried out the weaving. A further 140 workmen were employed for fulling, dyeing and treating the nap.

Woollen cloth was the mainstay of the African trade, but cotton was also being used by the late seventeenth century. The craft was developed when refugees from Spanish domination in Flanders arrived after 1585, the raw cotton coming from the Middle East, imported by the Merchant Adventurers. Calico was also arriving from India. The cotton industry was centred on Manchester, an area free from restrictions imposed by the craft guilds in longer established towns which wanted to retain the monopoly of woollen and linen textiles.

No invention of any importance had contributed to textile production since the pre-Christian era, except possibly the spinning wheel introduced from Italy in the fourteenth century. The crafts therefore gave work to a very large number of people working on piece rates. By the middle of the seventeenth century these worked out at about 10s. per week for a wool weaver, which was at least as good a wage as he could earn in agriculture, though his wife and children had to assist him with the ancillary tasks if he was to earn this wage. This family responsibility for production was, of course, copied in the cotton industry when the factory system and mass production machinery were developed, the absence of skill depressing wages while output per worker soared, adding still more to the profitability of the mercantile interests.

The population increase in Britain was estimated from about 5 millions in Tudor times to $10\frac{1}{2}$ millions by the beginning of the nineteenth century. The increasing population within this period could only be fed by increased industrialisation. The agrarian revolution of the fifteenth century had changed England from a corn-growing country to a huge sheep farm. Improvements in agricultural techniques did not enhance food production till well into the eighteenth century. But the increased population had to be fed—and sugar, easily transported, not liable to deterioration during storage, a rich source of energy, provided the answer.

The cheapness of slave purchase in terms of manufactured goods may be appreciated from the Royal African Company's records. In 1676 the accounts of the *Sarah Bonaventure* of London, chartered by the company, shows that the purchase price of trade goods included linen cloth at 11s. per piece (about sixteen yards), woollen cloth 24s. per piece, and serge 42s. per piece. Iron bars cost 13s. 6d. per ton which worked out in bars at from 2s. to 6s. per bar, according to size. Muskets cost 8s. each.

Three lengths of good woollen cloth was a typical price for two slaves; thirty iron bars was considered a high price for one young and strong male slave. A slaver therefore could expect to buy a Negro at anything from 24s. to £9 (assuming the highest price and rate in iron bars).

The *Sarah Bonaventure* eventually shipped one hundred

57

Negroes—forty-six men, thirty-four women, and twenty children—across the Atlantic. One bill for food supplies for the Negroes, consisting principally of cereals, coconuts, yams and fruit, came to £21. Food stowed on board in England would at a generous estimate have doubled this figure. Thus the food for a slave on the voyage cost under 9s.

The price of a slave in actual transactions, as distinct from official or controlled prices, in the West Indies varied between £16 and £22. The theoretical gross profit during the eighteenth century therefore ranged from £7 to around £20 per slave delivered alive. This profit was always greater if payment for slaves was taken in sugar—a ruling rate being 2,400 lb. of sugar for a choice male slave—and the sugar was sold at a good profit on the English market, on the buying price which was the equivalent of 10s. per cwt.

Net profit was, of course, much less. Commissions had to be paid to agents and auctioneers; sometimes to the ship's captain. There were crew wages and food supplies, charter costs, harbour dues, and often a royalty to be paid to representatives of the Crown both at home and abroad. Credit had to be given to the planters. Then, of course, wastage of life was a serious source of loss. One estimate of the average mortality rate for slaves in the late seventeenth century was 27⅔ per cent.

However, on a shipload of four hundred slaves the net profit could hardly be less than £2,500, plus the gains on ancillary trading for gold, pepper, and skins, and the potential profit on the sale of sugar. With the good fortune of few fatalities, a speedy voyage, and an eager market in the Caribbean, the profits could be at least treble the minimum figure.

The English economy rapidly became independent on the export trade to Africa (and the Orient) and the sugar supplies from the New World. The currency which lubricated this traffic was the Negro slave. Once the trade had begun there was no turning back.

It is useless to condemn the moral outlook of the seventeenth century by contrasting it with the emancipation movements of the nineteenth. It is very doubtful whether the humane idealist would have beaten the practical politician with his lofty arguments if the labour force in the Americas had not been long established and had no chance whatever of returning to its ancestral home in Africa.

Five

The eighteenth century was a period of interminable and usually futile wars, both in Europe and Africa. In both continents the profits of the slave trade and its ancillary transactions were always an important factor in the hostilities. England was at war with France and Spain by 1702. The Treaty of Utrecht in 1713 gave an uneasy respite, with the consolidation of power in the Triple Alliance of England, France, and Holland in 1717. In the following year England was again at war with Spain. Peace came in 1729, but in ten years war once again broke out. England fought Spain; then France. The peace of 1748 was merely an overture to global conflict, with Britain and France squabbling over Canada. Not until 1763 was there formal peace among the European powers—a respite before the body blow to England of the American revolution of 1775.

Through all this international unrest the people of half a dozen nations involved in slaving pursued their own campaigns, tardily paying lip service to clauses in peace treaties, half-heartedly recognising allies, and always using the excuse of a state of war to attack and defraud the rival on the coast. Monarchs condoned piracy as privateering. Adventurers prospered in the name of patriotic action by pillaging, firing, and sinking any ship of any other nation, or even of their own if it happened to be operating under some monopoly. News travelled slowly. Peace treaties were signed in Europe, wars were declared—but the information took weeks or months to reach the ships' masters, slave brokers, and company agents operating from Africa to the Indies. Ignorance was always a valid apology for robbery and infringement of treaties. A profitable expedition was justification for almost any illegality.

The madness spread violently behind the African littoral. There were apparently considerable migrations westwards from the interior by tribes grown too large for their ancestral

59

territories, but the majority of the brief and vicious clashes between African peoples were caused by the economic upheaval of trade with Europe and the insatiable demand for slaves. A new source of moral degradation was being exploited—alcohol. The practice of giving the Africans spirits had started innocently enough. All ships carried brandy as a stimulant for the crews and as a medicine to counteract ague and to offset the taste of water from fouled casks. It was natural enough to offer a native chieftain or merchant a tankard of spirits when he came aboard to make his trading agreement. The result was a wave of alcoholism which drove many Africans berserk. Spirits became a highly prized article of trade, and more especially of bribery. "Dash" began always to mean brandy instead of some trinkets or a piece of cloth. The crew of a canoe carrying goods and slaves between ship and shore got a flask every time they crossed the surf. Compound guards got a flask every Sunday. Chiefs expected a keg as a seal on a contract. The Africans' fanatical desire for spirits conveniently provided yet another source of profit. The discovery that the molasses left over from refining sugar was not a waste product but a source of a cheap and highly potent spirit gave the West Indies a new industry. "Barbados water", made by slaves in the distilleries, became one of the basic items in the slave trade, corrupting and maddening their own people to capture still more victims for the plantations.

The situation in the opening years of the eighteenth century fomented ruthless competition in which the Africans were the hapless victims. The various monopolies imposed with varying degrees of success in earlier times had the effect of a reasonable pursuance of trade without undue cramming of the slave ships and the assurance of a working profit on the enterprise. Then the almost total breakdown of any coherent trading policy, national or international, decreased profits unless the very last opportunity was grabbed and exploited.

As regards England, the Declaration of Rights of 1688 had virtually abolished the privileges of the Royal African Company; any English ship could participate in the African trade. Merchants had to pay 10 per cent on exports and imports, the money being used to maintain forts and trading posts. Gold and slaves were explicitly excluded from the export duty. The independent shippers promptly took over 80 per cent of the trade, carrying about 20,000 slaves to English colonies in the Americas every year between 1698 and 1707. This was a triumph for the emergent towns of Bristol and Liverpool over the mercantile interests of the City of London, who were financing the Royal African Company and did their utmost to keep out provincial interlopers.

The City tried to offset this competition by influencing the Government to negotiate with Spain the rights to supply her with slaves. The contract was specifically mentioned in the Treaty of Utrecht, with a stipulation for the supply of 144,000 slaves by 1743. Both the King of Spain and of England were to profit personally, each getting a quarter share of the profits.

This change of attitude by Spain towards a Protestant nation was due to the rapid development of her colonial possessions. The need for slaves was insatiable. Spain had hitherto relied on Portugal to obtain the Negroes in the African market, issuing permits for her to ship the slaves overseas. With the severance of Portugal from Spain in 1640, the latter withdrew trading facilities from the Portuguese.

The result was that Spanish colonists bought slaves from the Dutch in Curaçao and from the English in their Caribbean possessions—an infringement of the regulations banning purchases from foreigners and heretics. Thus began the era of trading in Negroes in the West Indies, where many islands became entrepôt centres. Neither Spain nor England approved. Spain lost the import duties; England was always wary of the colonies taking the law to themselves and earning a potentially dangerous independence.

The royalties and duties payable for the privilege of the Assiento contract with Spain were so heavy that the African Company made considerable losses. By 1739 Spain was demanding £68,000 in overdue payments, war conveniently breaking out so that the contract was cancelled. One major problem had been to try to meet the Spanish standards of slave quality. The Spanish term for a slave was *pieza d'Indie*, and applied to a best-quality Negro. Sometimes it took three Negroes to equal a *pieza d'Indie*, and the usual ratio was three for two. It was by no means unknown for ten or a dozen children, women, and aged males to be counted as one *pieza*. The luckless company might therefore pay duties on three hundred Negroes as shown on the ship's manifest and then receive payment for two hundred or fewer from the Spanish colonial representative.

61

The Royal African Company surrendered its charter in 1750 when the Government took over responsibility for the forts and warehouses, and any merchant could enjoy the privileges of trading under the company's concessions for a fee of £2. With the company's effective activity ended the little imaginative effort to create in Africa a rational system of commerce was weakened. Despite its sorry financial history it had contributed something which was better than the usual exploitation on the coast. The company was among the first to see the possibilities of penetrating deep into the continent for slaves and other commodities in order to cut out the middlemen. A committee report issued in February, 1721, observed that company agents had specific instructions to gather such information.

Enquiries were to be made about the sort of country newly purchased slaves came from; if there was language difficulty, agents were instructed to retain two or three slaves as domestic servants so that in a few months the other servants would be able to talk with them and find out the new slaves' origin.

Details were to be specific. How many days were spent on the march to the coast? Were there large rivers in the native kingdom? What were the laws, customs and method of government? How large were the towns, and of what material were the houses built? How many days' journey were they from neighbouring nations? How great was the population and how many men in the army? What were the manufactures and natural resources? How were slaves obtained?

Slaves providing such information were to be given their liberty, and allowed to return home, taking trade samples and representatives of the company with them.

It was shown by such investigations that profits were great all along the line. Agents penetrated for many hundreds of miles to collection depots where Fante dealers brought the human merchandise obtained by minor chiefs, parents, and villagers. The slaves at these depots, perhaps a dozen or so, were marched to cages set a couple of days' march from the coast, of which Manso on the Kumasi trail was typical. There wholesalers brought the slaves and split them up into groups for sale in the markets in coastal towns close to the European forts or agents' lodgings. These agents took their purchases to slave houses where they could be kept until loaded on to a ship. There were thus at least five stages of trading, with each dealer taking his profit. On the route to the ships the slaves might also be used as beasts of burden: a weight of 60 lb. and a distance of fifteen miles a day being regarded as normal. The time taken on the journey indicated that slaves were being captured at least a thousand miles from the coast.

A French merchant, Ancel, who operated at the mouth of the Sierra Leone river, noted that the number of slaves exported from Africa was estimated to exceed seventy thousand a year, and to meet the demand Negroes arriving on the coast had been marched for sixty, seventy, and eighty days—"we may therefore be convinced that the interior of the Continent is not so desert a space as has long been imagined".

In 1726 the Royal African Company sent William Smith to make a survey of the African coast from Gambia to Nigeria and report on the European settlements, slave markets, and geographical features of the area. Smith described the slaves offered for sale at Accra, which he reported was a very good source of slaves from the interior—and, remarkably enough, from the Far East.

"It is not uncommon," Smith wrote, "to find a Malayan, and sometimes two, among a parcel of other slaves. The Malay people were originally natives of Malacca . . . but being of a rambling nature, have settled upon many other places, particularly Sumatra and Borneo and many of the Spice Islands, all of which are now in the possession of those monopolists the Dutch, who punish with death whomsoever they can find trading with any other nation but themselves; to avoid which oppression many of those people, who have tasted the sweets of trade, go away from thence and settle in remote parts, especially on Cape Guardefer on the African shore [Cape Guardafui, Somalia] at the mouth of the Red Sea, from which they take surprisingly long journeys over the vast continent of Africa into Guinea, where they buy or rather exchange slaves with the Caboceroses; by which means the Malayans are now and then exposed for sale at the European forts. They differ very much from the Guinea Negroes, being right East Indians, of a tawny complexion with long black hair. They all go clad with long trousers and jackets and can write and read."

Enslavement by Asiatic traders penetrating to West Africa is an indication of the extent of the breakdown in the traditional hospitality of Negro kingdoms to peaceful merchants under the temptation of profits from slave trading with Europeans. It is also of interest that the buying agents had no objection to purchasing slaves who were not Negroes, though originally the justification of enslavement had been on the grounds of the inferiority of, and curse on, black-skinned peoples. The blame put by Smith on the Dutch was a view coloured by his employers' dislike of Dutch competition. The Dutch had a good reputation on the coast for supplying goods of better quality and at a cheaper price than the other Europeans. They also had a flair for settling in an alien country and making friends with their African neighbours. They were thus highly successful in obtaining slaves in quantity.

References in eighteenth-century reports are rarely made to sexual liaisons with the Africans, either free or enslaved. The topic was clearly an unmentionable one. Social contacts by Europeans other than the Dutch were non-existent except with tribal chiefs and their elders, invariably described as kings and treated with the courtesies normal for a stranger visiting European courts. Brokers and merchants are mentioned contemptuously—with accounts of the bribes required to finalise a deal and warnings of the duplicity always present in their negotiations.

Afro-European sexual contacts were anathema even to the people in Europe in view of the attitude that the Negroes were merely intelligent animals, but they were inevitably widespread, with European crews on the coast for weeks at a time and buying agents living permanently ashore. Within thirty years of the development of the trade by the Portuguese mulattoes were in responsible positions as interpreters, brokers, and guards. These were the children of liaisons which were voluntary for both partners and semi-permanent. The local Portuguese missionaries did not object to 'marriage between white and black provided, of course, that the African became a Catholic.

Inevitably rape and force were the origins of many of these children. The sadism aroused by the trade could not but direct itself into sexual assault. It is noteworthy how often the contraband slaves smuggled on board by members of the crew were women, even though their value was about half that of male slaves, and still less should they be obviously pregnant when they reached the West Indies.

Almost as quickly as Columbus's sailors spread syphilis in Europe, the crews of the slavers took the disease to Africa. The great and small poxes were soon rampant along the coast. Scarring of smallpox was not regarded as a serious defect; probably half of the Europeans were marked. Indeed, the scars could be a sales asset, proving that no future attack could be suffered by such a Negro. Syphilis was a much greater menace, and the ships' surgeons who checked the slaves in the compounds invariably rejected any Negro with primary sores or proof of long-standing illness with nasal deformation and so on.

Frequently neither of these major diseases nor the various fevers of the coastal area were caught until the slaves had been purchased and put in the holds. A good proportion of the fatalities during the Atlantic passage were due to infection and contagion which would not have been eradicated under even the best conditions. Proportionately the deaths among the crews were in such cases the same as, or even greater than, in the slave holds. Service in a slaver was conventionally described as a nursery for seamanship. For at least a quarter of the men remaining in it, a slave ship became a coffin.

It is of interest to note that when smallpox broke out in the *Africa* in 1762, four hundred of the 630 slaves on board were inoculated; 521 survived. Edward Jenner was then only starting as a boy apprentice to a local doctor, and vaccination as an accepted preventive was forty years away. The method used on the *Africa* is not described, but was presumably direct infection of an incision with matter from a smallpox sore, introduced to England by Lady Mary Wortley Montagu from Istanbul. The brevity of the report about the *Africa* suggests that inoculations of this kind were routine practice. Though the motive was mercenary rather than humanitarian, mass inoculations of slaves gave them protection not available to the people of Europe, where the disease attacked 50 per cent of the population during the normal life span.

The sufferings of Africans—free and enslaved—were slowly stirring misgivings, though not to the extent that a century to be dubbed by history the age of enlightenment should have done. In the influential *Gentleman's Magazine* in July, 1740, an anonymous contributor, writing under the name of Mercator Honestus, made a spirited plea for Negroes. He insisted that men were born with a natural right to liberty and that this was in forfeit only as punishment for attempting to take another's property; he deprecated the enslavement of children whose

65

parents happened to be slaves. In a direct attack on the Guinea traders he charged them with encouraging acts of war between the tribes in order that prisoners could be taken and sold into slavery, and he condemned the West Indian plantation owners for their shocking treatment of slaves.

This challenge was accepted by an anonymous reader who wrote a letter to the editor in defence of the slave trade. The argument followed the lines to become very familiar in later years: that the Africans transported to the American colonies were better off than many of their contemporaries.

"All that can be done . . . is to communicate as much liberty and happiness as such circumstances will admit and the people will consent to: and this is certainly by the New Guinea trade. For, by purchasing or rather ransoming the Negroes from their national tyrants, and transplanting them under the benign influences of the law, and Gospel, they are advanced to much greater degrees of felicity, though not to absolute liberty."

The defence of a system purporting to save the Negroes from themselves is an early specimen of a familiar apologia; its counterpart appears regularly in current literature explaining the general advantages of racial discrimination by religions, education, and class today. What is of significance in the material published in the *Gentleman's Magazine* is that critics of one of the nation's greatest methods of commerce existed, and its protagonists were going on the defensive in trying to justify it as not wholly evil, though admittedly a regrettable necessity.

Whatever blame could be put on victorious African chiefs and the native merchants the ultimate horror of enslavement was wholly caused by conditions in the slave ships and on the plantations.

By the end of the seventeenth century slavers had begun to accept the need for providing better accommodation—not merely to minimise losses through death but from some motives of humanity. James Barbot believed that the under-deck should be built to provide an air space of at least $5\frac{1}{2}$–6 feet, an ideal which hints at the shallow space on most vessels. In any case Barbot conceded that a narrow half-deck could be built round the sides to serve as a bed shelf, thus permitting slaves to lie in two layers.

The Dutch showed initiative in building ships for slave transport, in contrast to other nations who pressed ordinary cargo vessels into the trade, with a minimum of conversion. The Dutch slavers were wider in the beam, had increased space below decks, and apertures, protected by bars, were cut wherever feasible to improve ventilation. The upper deck had gratings at intervals to create a draught, tarpaulins being kept to cover them over in bad weather. In English and French ships ventilation was obtained only through the scuttles, which had to be closed in heavy seas.

Attempts were made to eradicate the worst of the results of several hundred human beings living in such conditions. Members of the crew supervised selected slaves in cleaning out the hold while the Negroes were on deck exercising or feeding. Three times a week, in a well-run ship, all the floors were scraped and scrubbed, disinfected with vinegar, and fumigated with a vapour created by throwing red-hot shot into pails of vinegar. The stench of the slave holds is constantly mentioned in contemporary accounts. It was, of course, inevitable with living beings, many suffering from dysentery, herded together in such conditions, and it was aggravated by the Negroes' custom of anointing the body with palm oil. The heat of a slave hold was so great during transit of the Middle Passage and the air so foul that sick slaves had to be carried to the forecastle so that the ship's surgeon could tend them; he could not examine his patients in the gloomy hold because no candle flame would burn there.

Intensified competition degraded even these conditions. More and more slaves were jammed into holds of cargo ships, with the only conversion being the installation of chain rings and shelves. A brutal attitude was taken that a percentage always died; therefore the more carried the greater the number of eventual sales. Mortality rates varied greatly according to the duration of the passage and the type of sickness breaking out. A fair average figure in the eighteenth century was 12 per cent of deaths between Africa and the West Indies, and 25 per cent within a few months of arrival. The survival rate for more than a year after enslavements was therefore under two out of every three Negroes.

Revolts by the slaves during the ship's passage were an ever-present risk. How many resulted in the total massacre of the crew cannot be known, but may account for some of the losses of the many ships which were never heard of again, even though other vessels a few days' sailing distant experienced no storms. A successful revolt in mid-Atlantic was, of course, tantamount to suicide, for the Negroes were completely unaware of the way to handle a European sailing ship or to navigate outside coastal waters.

The fatalistic outlook of the Negro which enabled a score or so of Europeans to intimidate several hundred slaves during a passage which might take four months was by no means universal. When tribal origins were identifiable by physique or tattoo markings ships' masters developed a useful knowledge of the slaves who would be amenable and those who might be trouble-makers. The latter, though strong and vigorous, were rejected when possible, not merely because of the nuisance of keeping them permanently manacled aboard ship but because the planters in the Americas had also learned about the recalcitrant tribes, and the strong slave was not necessarily the best worker and certainly not the obedient one.

Captain William Snelgrave, a veteran of the trade, tells of a number of mutinies which occurred on ships he commanded. He was fair-minded enough to say that mutinies were usually caused by cruelty: "Wherever therefore I have commanded it has been my principal care to have the Negroes on board my ship kindly used; and I have always strictly charged my white people to treat them with humanity and tenderness."

His first action was to let the Negroes know through an interpreter that the rumours about white men liking to eat black flesh were untrue. He explained that they had been bought for agricultural work in the white man's country. Then followed instructions on how they were to behave, with an assurance that any abuses, when reported to him through the interpreter, would be investigated.

Snelgrave was exceptional in allowing the slaves to come on deck during fair weather at seven in the morning and to stay there all day. Each Monday all received some tobacco, but men were isolated from the women and children.

His determination to avoid the conditions fomenting trouble was the result of his experience on his first slaving voyage in 1704, when he was purser on a London ship, the *Eagle*, commanded by his father. The ship was anchored off Callabar with nearly a full complement of slaves. Through sickness, crew squads on shore, and some earlier deaths, there were only

68

ten white men on board. The slaves were still shackled in twos because the ship was at anchor, but this did not prevent them, when brought on deck for their evening meal, from attacking the chief mate who was supervising the distribution of food. A sentry on the forecastle rushed over and laid about him with the flat of his cutlass, enabling the mate to escape.

Young Snelgrave was in his cabin, suffering from malaria. The noise roused him. He grabbed a couple of pistols and went on deck where he met his father and the mate, to whom he handed the pistols. By then it was impossible to fire because a group of Negroes had got hold of the sentry and were trying to wrest the cutlass from him, any shot being as likely to kill the mate as his assailants. Fortunately for the man his cutlass was attached by a cord to his wrist. The Negroes then tried to throw the sentry overboard, but he hung on to them. The elder Snelgrave fired his pistol in the air and rushed to the rescue. A Negro hit him with a piece of wood, sending him reeling. A second blow was warded off by a young slave to whom the captain had been kind. The mate had by this time run forward and shot the Negro with the piece of wood at point blank range, wounding him severely. The rest of the Negroes fell flat on deck, begging for mercy.

Two Negroes who had been assaulting the sentry leaped overboard, and being in irons, drowned without coming to the surface. The Negro who was shot was treated by the ship's surgeon and recovered in time to be sold before the ship reached Virginia. Snelgrave records no retaliatory punishment of the remaining Negroes, of whom twenty had taken an active part in the assault.

A pleasant detail of this story is that the youth who had saved the elder Snelgrave from the second blow on the head had his broken arm carefully treated, and on arrival in Virginia was given his freedom, a Colonel Carter agreeing to employ him until he "became well enough acquainted in the country to provide for himself".

James Snelgrave disliked the Cormantines, a tribe living on the Gold Coast who had the reputation of being strong and stubborn. In 1721 his ship, the *Henry*, was anchored off Mumford (west of Accra) with five hundred slaves in the hold, three hundred of whom were Cormantines. There were fifty men in the crew, but they failed to keep the slaves quiet. Snelgrave asked through the interpreters what was wrong. The Negroes called him a rogue for buying them and planning to ship them from Africa. The reply was that they had lost their freedom before they had been purchased through committing crimes or being taken prisoner in battle. Snelgrave asked if they had been ill treated or deprived of food, and he alleges that they admitted they had no complaints on that score.

His observation that even if they got away from the ship they would promptly be caught on shore and sold to some other slaver apparently convinced the Negroes that things could be worse, and their spokesmen promised obedience so long as they were not punished.

Trouble broke out again a few days later, some of the Negroes asking the interpreter to find an axe so that they could cut the ship's cables and let her drift ashore. As was usual, the interpreter was a native slaving agent, and he promptly reported to Snelgrave. Once again trouble was averted, and once again there was no extra punishment.

Snelgrave continued trading along the coast for a month, and had some negotiations with a sister ship, the *Elizabeth*, which had 120 slaves on board, but was short of officers, the captain and first mate being dead from disease. That night firing broke out on the *Elizabeth*, and Snelgrave led a boarding party to investigate what the trouble was. On the way from one ship to another they saw a couple of Negroes in the water attacked and killed by sharks. Two more Negroes were in the sea, holding on to the ship's rope. They were taken into the pinnace.

The revolt was over by the time Snelgrave got aboard the *Elizabeth*, with the Negroes secured in the hold, and the crew standing around the body of a sailor who had been acting as sentry, and had been killed with a hatchet. Investigation yielded a confession that one of the Negroes rescued from the sea had killed the sailor after a few others had crept up on deck and found all the crew asleep.

The *Elizabeth's* sailors wanted to execute the Negro then and there, but Snelgrave insisted on taking him to his own ship, where next morning he summoned the masters of eight slavers lying at anchor in the vicinity to attend a sort of court martial. The sentence was that the Negro should be hung from the fore-yard arm and the body left there to serve as an example to the slaves on all the other ships.

An hour glass was set up, and the Negro told that when the sand had run out he was to be executed. Calmly the victim pointed out that his execution would mean the loss of the money paid for him; Snelgrave rejected the plea.

All the slaves on the surrounding ships were paraded on deck, and when the hour was up the killer was hoisted by a rope under his arms high above the deck, where a firing party of ten riddled his body with shot. To intimidate the paraded slaves by denying their hopes in the belief that a man who died unmutilated would return to his homeland, the body was cut down and laid on the deck, whereupon the head was severed and thrown into the sea. As expected, the slaves remained quiet after that, and though they were aboard the ship for four months no further trouble was experienced.

Snelgrave was a firm but just man. His contemporaries did not have his intelligence or his experience, and slave revolts became increasingly common as more and more totally untrained crews entered the trade. Brutality naturally drove the Negro cargo to suicidal action, but undue friendliness could cause trouble too. Snelgrave recounts the story of a captain who used to move around without an armed escort at the slaves' meal time, putting pepper and palm oil in the bowls of rice. In mid-Atlantic the slaves suddenly swarmed around him and beat out his brains with their wooden feeding bowls. The chief mate ordered the crew, who had barricaded themselves on the quarter deck, to fire into the slaves with charges of partridge shot. Eighty Negroes were killed either by the shot or through jumping overboard. On two further occasions they attempted to take over the ship, then they lapsed into a torpor and some starved themselves to death. Plantation buyers offered lower prices for slaves from ships on which there had been trouble. Experience proved that once resistance started it continued. Mass suicide by hanging was not an uncommon occurrence once such slaves were out to work on the plantations.

The more usual policy of a slaver's crew was to intimidate the slaves with bestial cruelty. John Atkins, a surgeon in the Royal Navy, served on board a vessel in an expedition to disperse pirates in 1721, who were battening on ships of the Royal African Company. He went ashore at the mouth of the Sierra Leone river, and made the acquaintance of a private slave trader, John Leadstine, known to the shippers as Old Cracker.

In the buying compound he saw among the mass of dejected Negroes one tall Negro standing defiantly. He was refusing to stretch out his limbs for examination when Leadstine ordered him to do so. For this disobedience he got an unmerciful whipping—"all which the Negro bore with magnanimity, shrinking very little, and shedding a tear or two. which he endeavoured to hide as though ashamed of".

The man was dubbed Captain Tomba because he had been a village leader in an area where the natives resisted the slavers. He had been grabbed one night by a party of men led by Leadstine, but not before he had killed two of his assailants.

Tomba was in due time sold to a Bristol slaver. Once on board he plotted to escape, requesting three or four of his fellow tribesmen to help him. A woman slave, who had freedom to go on deck by night, came down and said there were only five of the crew on guard duty, and they all appeared to be asleep. She had purloined a hammer.

Tomba failed to persuade more than one man to help him. In company with the woman they crept up on deck and immediately killed three men on the forecastle. The other two sentries, at the stern, were awakened by the noise, as was the ship's master. Tomba and his two companions were knocked to the deck and put in irons.

Tomba and the male assailant were magnificent specimens. The captain had no intention of killing them and losing two good sales. They were whipped and scarified. The three Negroes who had originally agreed to take part in the revolt and than had held back were clearly poor specimens. They were sentenced to death, two being forced to eat the liver and heart of the third. The woman was hoisted on a yard arm, whipped, and slashed with knives until she died.

Stories like these were known only to a minority. They appeared in seamen's reports to their employers, in memoirs published much later, and in pamphlets having only a small circulation. The trade was in the hands of men who put profit before everything else; the planters in the Americas were as ready to foment the conspiracy of silence in order to get the labour force they needed. The horror of transatlantic slaving continued, not because of any streak of national cruelty and callousness, but through the blindness of people who preferred not to know what was happening.

Six

The development of slave marketing in the West Indies aggravated the general difficulty of rationalising the trade at government level and augmented the competition among a host of small shippers who preferred that there should be few international agreements, and intended to ignore even those in practice. Companies which had to observe agreements, such as the Royal African and the ill-starred South Sea, were, never able to obtain the fabulous profits which, on paper, seemed certain.

The cut-throat competition, the necessity of evading regulations, and the benefits of taking quick profits, added to the misery of the human merchandise. The charter companies employed skilled sailors and provided seaworthy ships. Some regard was usually paid to maximum loads, and provisions were budgeted on a reasonable scale. The independent shippers had no such preoccupations. Few of the Liverpool and Bristol merchants ran more than three ships, and these were usually bought from firms in other trades. The main consideration was speed. A fast sailing vessel of the day rarely measured more than ninety feet from prow to stern, and was rated at 120–200 tons. It was feasible to get 350 slaves into the hold, and five hundred if a good proportion were children. The ship had a useful life of not more than ten years in the "carrying trade" because of damage to the hull in tropical waters, and this only if it avoided foundering in the Caribbean, a disaster all too common with the unskilled and under-strength crews of these ships.

It was essential that the master of an independent slaver should find the best market. He roamed from island to island, and he did not care about its nationality. Auctioneers and planters in the West Indies were in a far better position to know about the state of the market, and they were therefore

73

prepared to compete with the slaver captains by purchasing job lots of Negroes for transfer elsewhere and re-sale. This semi-illegal trade, which was designed to evade import and export duties, dealt largely in refuse Negroes, the poor quality specimens rejected under the Spanish Assiento scheme or by plantation owners at the port in search of good workers. Such Negroes were good business because of their low price, and worth buying on the gamble that a few months' life remained during which they could be worked to exhaustion.

Such was the avarice of the colonists of Jamaica and Barbados for the profits from re-sale that the planters were constantly short of man-power. The Spanish mining interests of Peru as well as the long-established large-scale plantations in Spanish Central America could offer higher prices than local farmers.

The plantation owners in Jamaica were constantly complaining about the high prices and scarcity of labour. In 1771 the island allegedly imported only 4,183 slaves, yet that year one local merchant sent £50,000 to England as his profits from selling Negroes. The official exports of slaves, obviously incorrect, totalled 671.

Despite the flourishing trade in re-exports the colonists' perpetual calls for still more Negroes were not justified. Sugar production was inefficient and over-manned. French growers were able to sell sugar at 16s. per cwt against the English price at 18s., and legislation to enforce purchases of English sugar in the American colonies was merely a convenient way of disguising the defects of the Barbados and Jamaican operations.

In any event London was worried about the size of the slave population in the Caribbean. A Negro uprising was an obvious possibility; a colonial revolt, with the slaves trained and armed by their owners, was not out of the question. Jamaican intrigues on behalf of the Stuarts under the Commonwealth had not been forgotten; the Jacobites had supporters among the many Scottish settlers.

By any standards the white–Negro ratio was becoming dangerously large. According to a report Burke presented to Parliament in 1755 the West Indian islands had a population of 240,000 slaves and 90,000 whites; in Virginia the figures were 100,000 slaves and 60–70,000 whites.

It was estimated that one in sixteen Negroes died every year, so some 21,000 new slaves were needed as replacements.

In fact, in the next two decades this figure was nearly always exceeded. In 1768 England shipped 60,000 of the 97,000 Negroes exported from Africa. Some 65,000 survived long enough for sale in the Americas, and at most 40,000 of them went to non-British possessions, legally or illegally. There was therefore a build-up in English colonies of at least 4,000 a year over the mid-century totals.

The slave trade created a new class of wealthy Colonial families. The industrialists of the Midlands and Lancashire, the London financiers, and the directors of shipping firms in Glasgow and Liverpool did not create much of a stir beyond their own environment as they enjoyed the fruits of their prosperity from slaving. But the retired and absentee plantation owners soon became envied and admired with their grandiose houses newly built in spacious parks, their lavish parties in rented houses at Bath and Tunbridge Wells, and the success they had in breaking into England's social life despite their lowly ancestry and connection with trade.

Most of these people were descendants of almost penniless emigrants encouraged to settle in the Indies and the American colonies by Cromwell, of servants of royal and ducal families who had considered American lands as their private estates. Before tobacco and sugar developed into major exports life had been appallingly hard. But from that day in 1673 when the Governor of Jamaica proudly despatched the island's first sample of sugar to the home Government prosperity had rarely faltered. It was, averaged over a period of years, a mathematical certainty that every slave purchased for £20–£30 would yield an annual net profit of £10, and there was no activity in the West Indies to which slaves did not contribute.

The comfortable situation of a large income and a retinue of slaves to wait on them was not abandoned when plantation owners came home. The presence of a quaintly dressed Negro footman or carriage flunkey became a fashionable asset of these families, many of whom were only too happy to curry favour with the aristocracy by handing over a Negro who would work without even requiring the servants' usual pittance of the time.

Some 14,000 Negro slaves lived in England at the end of the eighteenth century. A few were brought direct by slave ship captains and officers; the majority had worked for years in the colonies as household and body servants. Negro slaves were therefore quite a familiar sight in England; no one appeared to care.

Or almost no one. A man whose pity was abruptly aroused one day in 1765 was Granville Sharp, son of an archdeacon and grandson of an archbishop. Sharp was a clerk in the Department of Ordnance, with hobbies of theology and English philology. His brother was a doctor in London's eastern suburbs. While Granville Sharp was staying with his brother a Negro crawled to the door and asked for help. The man had a head wound and could hardly stand because of muscular tremors. He said his name was Jonathan Strong (an indication of his physical prowess when purchased), the property of a West Indies planter named David Lisle, who had brought him over from Barbados. For some unexplained reason Jonathan had been belaboured on the head with a pistol at Lisle's lodgings in Wapping, the blows affecting his eyesight. A bout of malaria had then rendered him as weak as a child, whereupon Lisle had thrown him into the street.

Dr. Sharp treated the man and Granville Sharp gave him some money to pay for lodgings and food. Both men kept in touch with the Negro and when he had recovered, found him a job with the apothecary who supplied Dr. Sharp with medicines. For two years all went well for Jonathan. Then Lisle saw him going on an errand for the apothecary. He paid two seamen to kidnap the slave and sold him to a man returning to Jamaica for £30. Jonathan managed to reach Sharp who rushed off to see the Lord Mayor of London, Sir Robert Kite. He took legal advice and ordered Jonathan's release on the grounds that he had been illegally deprived of his liberty. This did not prevent the captain of the ship who had been entrusted with taking the Negro back to Jamaica attempting to waylay Sharp and Jonathan as they left the Guildhall. Sharp formally made a complaint of assault, and the captain took himself off.

Sharp was on tricky ground. He was protected in his action by the opinion of Sir John Holt, Lord Chief Justice of England in 1689 (a man famed for his humane treatment of prisoners and staunch support of liberty) that the Common Law of England and even the ancient principles of villeinage ensured that every person entering England, black or white, slave or free, should enjoy the personal liberties of Englishmen. But later and more effective judgements had contradicted Holt.

Disobedient slaves who caught the scent of England's freedom had been common enough before the Jonathan Strong case. Usually they ran off and only if they were extremely fortunate did they find anyone who would give them work and shelter. More often they were caught and shipped back to the colonies out of harm's way, the local authorities glad enough to be rid of someone who might have to be looked after as an indigent person. The planters, infuriated by knowledge that a few did escape to freedom, applied to the Crown for a ruling. This was in 1729, when from the Crown downwards there were scores of influential persons profiting from the operations of the Royal African Company. The planters, as they no doubt expected, got an opinion from the Law Officers in their favour. The Attorney General and Solicitor General stated that neither baptism in an English church nor residence in England altered a slave's position. He was the property of his owner, and the owner had a legal right to compel him to return to the planta-tions.

The law of England had thus condoned slavery in England. Most of those who were sufficiently interested to heed the legal opinion were deeply content. Only a few cranks had ever bothered about the ancient principles of personal liberty which, in a minor and contrived legal rigmarole, had been sullied. Granville Sharp was such a crank, when judged by the stan-dards of the supporters of slavery; but in reality he was an extremely level-headed and patient man. Whatever anger the Jonathan Strong case aroused in his mind he recognised that to enforce the existing law was his most powerful weapon, rather than to campaign to change the law. That could come later.

To Sharp the law was that embodied in the principles of Magna Carta and pronouncements by a Lord Chief Justice, not the specious opinions of political nominees in the court. He spent two years drawing up an objective survey of the legal position in a treatise called "The Injustice and Dangerous Tendency of Tolerating Slavery in England". He avoided sentiment and relied on an exposition of the Common Law of England.

Then in 1772 he got the chance to challenge the Government to contradict the views he had outlined in his treatise. A Negro named James Summersett (the name suggests that he had originally been sold for work on Somerset in the Bermuda Islands) who was brought over to England. He ran off when his owner, a planter named Stuart, wanted to send him back to the West Indies. Summersett was caught and put on a ship. Then followed the well-known incident when Sharp got a writ of *habeas corpus* and rescued Summersett just as the ship was about to sail.

The melodrama of the last-minute action may have been deliberately contrived by Sharp for maximum publicity. In any event he achieved it. Powerful and wealthy planter interests recognised the danger of the incident. They set up a fund to fight the case through the courts. The best legal brains were engaged and the case took on a political flavour with the engagement of the Whig lawyer Dunning to lead for the defence. The case, heard before Lord Chief Justice Mansfield, lasted for three days. Dunning wisely did not dispute the Holt ruling that a Negro slave was free when he stepped on to English soil, but he argued that this was a privilege peculiar to residence in England, and that there was no law preventing a freed slave's forcible removal and re-enslavement once he was back in the colonies. For good measure Dunning claimed that there was no specific law prohibiting the employment of slaves in England, and anyway the sudden freeing of the thousands of Negro slaves living in the country "would produce great inconvenience".

Lord Mansfield denied that emancipation could be a temporary state and brusquely dismissed the claim as to the lack of laws against slavery. Great a lawyer as he was, he could not conceal that he supported the privileges of wealthy citizens, and he endeavoured to evade the widespread results of an adverse decision by enquiring whether Stuart would be disposed to give Summersett his liberty, thereby enabling him to dismiss the case.

Stuart, foolishly from the point of view of his friends, angrily refused to do so, whereupon Mansfield pompously intoned "fiat justitia, ruat coelum" and gave his decision.

"The question in *this* case," he began, stressing the definitive word, "is whether any dominion, authority, or coercion could be exercised in this country on a slave according to the American laws. The owner says the slave departed and refused to serve, whereupon he was kept to be sold abroad. So high an act of dominion must be recognised by the law of the country where it is used. The state of slavery is of such a nature and so odious that nothing can be suffered to support it but positive law. Whatever inconveniences, therefore, may follow from the decision, I cannot say that this case is allowed or approved by the law of England, and therefore the black must be discharged."

Summersett was free and the law guaranteed that he should remain free while he was on English soil—but it was a unique soil. Though every colony was regarded as much a possession of the Crown as the Isle of Wight, fundamentally subject to its laws and its inhabitants protected by its privileges, even Mansfield had seen fit to refer to "American laws". Plantation owners might in future have problems in intimidating the slaves they brought back to England to continue to serve them; they had no problems about unquestioned ownership of as many human beings as they could afford to buy on the other side of the Atlantic. The date of the verdict in the Summersett case was June 22, 1772. Despite appeals to Parliament by Sharp to take steps to abolish slavery in the colonies nothing whatever was done for four years. Before then the American colonists had shown that they indeed believed they were subject to different laws from the mother country. The American War of Independence had broken out.

A major conflict in the New World created chaos in the slave trade, and was aggravated by the coincidental war in Africa between the Fantis and the Ashantis, which reduced supplies of slaves and sent prices soaring. When a shipper managed to collect a boatload of Negroes—and in many ports he had to pay for them in gold—he then had to face greater problems than those of natural dangers on the high seas. American privateers invaded the Caribbean and captured many slavers. The desperate and ruthless renegade whites and slaves on the run who formed themselves into the Brotherhood of the Coast ranged the shipping routes, looking for loot and revenge. They destroyed for destruction's sake—and gave a glimpse of the latent power in the hands of slaves who were prepared to seek some sort of freedom. French and Dutch shippers, exploiting the relaxation of English control of import regulations, stepped up their attacks on England's supremacy in the trade. Merchants participating in the English franchise of the successor to the Royal African Company were said, in a Parliamentary committee report of 1777, to estimate deliveries of Negroes to the loyal possessions in the New World as only 16,000 in 1775–6. Prices in Barbados and Jamaica had risen to £45–£50 per slave, but even at this figure profits were poor: the Africans were demanding payment in gold—as much as 11 oz. for a male and 9 oz. for a female.

An air of panic, with pleas for official aid to restore the smooth operation of the slave traffic, had the paradoxical result of paving the way for moves to destroy it. The first formal attempt to get Parliament to ban the slave trade was made by the M.P. for Hull, David Hartley. His motives were above criticism, but it is debatable whether he could have made his attack if he had represented a seaport or industrial town dependent on the slave trade. Hull, for long a prosperous centre of trade with Europe, had been eclipsed by the booming prosperity of Liverpool and Bristol. Hartley's motion was that the slave trade was contrary to the laws of God and the rights of man. Members were convinced that however true this might be, the trade was also favoured by the laws of Mammon and of direct benefit to the pursuit of wealth. The motion was dropped.

Moral considerations invariably lost when convenience challenged them. In America Jefferson had been drafting the Declaration of Independence. He prepared a charge against the English Crown of "waging cruel war against human nature itself, violating the most sacred rights of life and liberty in the persons of a distant people who never offended him [the King], capturing and carrying them into slavery in another hemisphere or to incur miserable death in transportation".

This might have aroused an approving word of indignation against England among the peoples of his native Virginia and the other states of the North, where mixed farming, industry and large-scale immigration was gradually easing the need for slave labour, but it would not have pleased the planters of Georgia and South Carolina. Jefferson deleted this clause.

Facile attitudes and attempts to make excuses for the slave trade on the grounds of expediency could not alter the fact that three centuries of frenzied exploitation of one continent to change the face of another were ending. The Negro export and import business was reeling to a major crisis.

The growing campaign against the slave trade resulted in near-panic among the inhabitants of towns which were deeply involved. The City of Liverpool organised a massive petition in 1788 to the House of Commons expressing alarm at the rumours of abolition of the slave trade, pointing out that through Government advice the townsfolk had spent large sums of money on docks to handle the slave ships; there were new canals connecting the port with the manufacturing towns of Lancashire, and that the resultant prosperity of the area, and of the country as a whole, would be put in jeopardy, with ruin for Liverpool merchants.

The mayor and council conferred the freedom of the city on five men selected by the merchants to go to London to lobby M.P.s. A local clergyman, Raymond Harris, who produced a pamphlet, *Scriptural Researches*, which purported to prove the divine approval of enslavement of Negroes, was given £100 by a grateful city.

The town had already experienced the sort of trouble which would arise from a major recession in its principal source of commerce. The slaving ship crews were, in common with sailors in all types of vessel, badly paid. In the autumn of 1775 a mutiny broke out in the *Derby*, anchored in the Mersey, over pay. The men claimed that they were offered £1 per month instead of the promised £1 10s. They managed to unrig the ship before nine were caught and thrown into gaol. That evening three thousand sailors broke into the cells and rescued the strikers. Then they swarmed over the wharves to prevent any ship sailing.

Over the weekend there were meetings between the merchants and sailors which resulted in a promise to pay £1 10s. per month. Simultaneously, however, the merchants quietly recruited three hundred men at 10s. a day to round up the ringleaders. The furious sailors then marched in a mass to the Exchange Building. Shots were fired. Seven sailors were killed, and forty wounded.

Next morning a crowd of sailors, estimated to number a thousand, raided a gunsmiths. They marched on the Exchange and a pitched battle broke out, the rioters using a couple of small cannon. Troops arrived a few hours afterwards and the men dispersed.

This outbreak occurred at a time of severe trade depression in Liverpool. Four years previously, the town had 195 ships busy in the slave trade, and more than 47,000 Negroes had been transported in that year. But by 1775 the American War of Independence had brought a ban on the export of arms and ammunition, thus destroying one of the best lines in trade goods. Ship after ship was laid up. The number of unemployed sailors rose to three thousand, and remained around that figure until the American war ended.

Liverpool, where the Mayor and virtually every leading citizen were directly involved in slaving, was the most assiduous in badgering Parliament to reject abolition. But the most intelligent arguments in favour of non-interference came in the pleas from Bristol. One petition came from the Mayor, burgesses, and inhabitants; another from the Merchant Venturers of Bristol, and a third from the merchants and planters residing in the town and district. The last was the most cogent and factual. It pointed out that abolition would destroy the welfare, prosperity, and possibly actual existence of the West Indian islands, while Bristol itself, one of the most prosperous towns in England, would lose three-fifths of its commerce.

The petition graphically illustrated how completely dependent Britain's international trade and international economy had become on the slave trade. In Bristol itself salting herrings for consumption in the West Indies, ship building, ship repairing, the ancillary industries of ropemaking, sail making, and iron forging would be destroyed. The cessation of new supplies of slaves would cause the termination of sugar cultivation, and the sugar refineries of Somerset, not convertible to any other use, would have to be abandoned. The Newfoundland fisheries, maintained by ships and men originating in Bristol, would lose the bulk of their trade in dried cod for the Americas and the provisioning of the slave ships.

Birmingham manufacturers; the ship owners, manufacturers and tradesmen of London; the manufacturers and dealers in iron, copper, brass and lead of Liverpool; the Manchester makers of African trade goods; the London financiers of the plantations were among the groups who also sent petitions to Parliament. All correctly warned the Government that, apart from the damage to their own interests, tens of thousands of people would be thrown out of work. All stressed that the rest of Europe as well as the newly independent colonies of America were busily developing the slave trade and building new ships in anticipation of the decline of the hitherto leading nation in the carrying trade through needless Government legislation. But very rarely was the old argument that enslavement was somehow beneficial to primitive races put forward.

The movement towards abolition had come too late to have any real effect on the utter ruin of customs and traditions developed over centuries by the indigenous peoples of the countries where Europe's seamen explored and Europe's merchants developed trade. In the New World the Caribs of the West Indian islands had been virtually exterminated when they proved useless for hard labour. Highly civilised and martial empires in Central and South America had been broken up and their peoples driven to hopeless despair by the force of firearms. In the northern continent warrior tribes were already discovering that slave-run farms and plantations meant subjection or refuge farther west.

In Africa the Europeanisation of a narrow coastal belt over thousands of miles was complete. More than 150 fortified trading posts from Cape Verde to the Cuanza river held the economic life of millions of Africans to ransom. Traditional agricultural methods were changed to grow the crops which could be sold to provision slave ships. Native costume and the crafts which supplied it almost halted when tawdry textiles from Manchester and Lyon were available in unlimited quantities—provided, of course, a fellow African could be handed over in exchange. Chiefs and kings, previously ruling according to rigid custom and inspired by tribal patriotism, degenerated into greedy, cunning tradesmen, surrounded by corrupt African officials and advised by unprincipled European and half-caste agents. Tribal wars were interminable and the ultimate cause was invariably the prizes obtainable by collecting slaves. Law and justice were coloured by the slave-dealing economy: instead of a few serious crimes being punished by death and a majority carrying penalties of fines and a period of servitude, every contrived and petty offence meant being sold to a slave dealer. Husbands sold wives; parents sold children; neighbours tried to involve one another in some offence carrying the penalty of slavery. Thousands of villages became derelict because the neighbouring community was strong enough to organise slave raids or because the only security lay in banding together in larger and remoter groups, with their inevitable and insuperable problems of food supplies. Away from the coast the towns which had flourished as market centres for a thousand years and more were half deserted. Only on the coast where ships could safely anchor was there an impression of a prospering Africa. But gold, ivory and skins were but a minor source of that prosperity. The captive Negro was the be-all and end-all of the economy.

Seven

The widespread consternation about possible abolition among those involved in the slave trade resulted from a sense of guilt rather than any practical evidence that Parliament meant to do anything. Hartley had no success whatever in the Commons, and the Quakers, who had for years tried to set an example by disowning all Friends who earned their living directly or indirectly from slaving, were suspect both in the eyes of the State and the Established Church. Much the same attitude existed about John Wesley, who wrote *Thoughts on Slavery* in 1774. But the Society of Friends were able to have a petition accepted in Parliament. Lord North paid a brief and unctuous tribute to the motives of humanity, and dismissed the matter by insisting that the slave trade was necessary to almost every nation in Europe.

An infinitely more formidable and resourceful champion of the Negroes was quietly gathering evidence, acquainting himself with every pamphlet and book for or against slavery, and meeting men like Hartley, Quaker spokesmen, and the Wesleyans. Wilberforce had the gift of making friends easily. He enjoyed the conversation over a lavish dinner, and was equally at home with aristocrat or commoner. Despite a tendency to intolerance, and the impression he gave of having destiny on his side for whatever he did, those he met invariably became his willing allies. He needed every one of them for the campaign he pledged himself to win one summer's day in 1787, when he noted in his diary: "God Almighty has set before me two great objects: the suppression of the slave trade and the reformation of manners."

William Wilberforce was the the son of a Hull business man whose family had for generations thrived on trade with Hanseatic towns and throughout the Baltic. He was born in 1759, the same year as his future friend and colleague, William

Pitt. Both had been at Cambridge, Wilberforce at St. John's and Pitt at Pembroke. They first met in the gallery of the House of Commons during debates on the American Rebellion. They found they enjoyed an identity of views on the mistakes of the Government and a close friendship developed between both young men, while discussing the political careers they hoped to follow.

Wilberforce stood for Hull in 1780, the election coinciding with the birthday celebrations on his coming of age. As a member of a respected and influential Yorkshire family his victory was almost a foregone conclusion. His vote equalled the total of his two opponents. Pitt entered the Commons a few weeks later after receiving the gift of the borough of Appleby. Whatever premonitions of eventual suppression the slave interests may have had at the time, none could have realised that these two young men with precocious political aspirations were launching themselves into a battle which neither would abandon while they lived—nor that within three years one of them would be Prime Minister.

Wilberforce's first move was to form the Committee for the Abolition of the Slave Trade. The original members were Thomas Clarkson, Granville Sharp, and Samuel Hoare. Others who joined soon afterwards included John Wesley, Dr. Paley, and the Bishop of London. For some years their propaganda was devoted to informing the public rather than to attempt legislation.

Revelations of the real nature of the trade abruptly roused the country's conscience without direct action by Wilberforce. They emerged as the result of a lawsuit concerning a voyage of a Liverpool slave ship, the *Zong*.

The ship, with Luke Collingwood as master had sailed from Sao Tomé on September 6, 1781, with a crew of seventeen and 440 (or 442) slaves. She neared Jamaica, her destination, on November 27. For some reason, possibly through a mistaken belief that the ship had made landfall on Hispaniola, she again put out to sea. By then more than sixty slaves and seven members of the crew had died from disease.

In order to make a claim on the insurers for loss of slaves it was necessary to prove that death had occurred from unavoidable causes. Claims had in the past been accepted for slaves thrown overboard in order to save the rest, this being taken as a necessary action. On November 29 a belated check was made on water supplies. Only two hundred gallons remained for the 390 persons on board. The captain called the officers and crew together and explained that every natural death of a slave would be a loss to the owners (and themselves on commissions) while every slave thrown alive into the sea would be a loss to the underwriters.

In the next few days 133 sick Negroes were thrown into the sea. On the last day of this wholesale murder campaign—December 1—forty-two were jettisoned; on that day rain fell in torrents to replenish the water barrels, still by no means depleted. Even with water supplies sufficient for a further eleven days twenty-six slaves were classified as mortally sick, bound and fettered, and thrown overboard. Other slaves on deck for a health check saw this massacre going on. Ten of them leaped overboard to avoid the fetters. They were all drowned. The ship arrived in Jamaica on December 22 with the survivors.

How many such cases occurred can never be known. This one was brought to public notice because the insurers refused to pay. The owners won their case in the King's Bench on their claim of £30 for each slave alive when thrown into the sea. An appeal to the Court of Exchequer resulted in a second trial.

Captain Collingwood had died, so a movement to charge him with murder was not feasible. The very idea angered the counsel acting for the owners who said "so far from the charge of murder lying against these people there is not the least imputation—of cruelty I will not say—of impropriety".

The victims of the *Zong*'s crew were merely a fraction of the tens of thousands who died in the holds, were thrown unconscious into the sea, beaten and mutilated to death, or chose death by drowning to a prolongation of their agony. Most died in vain. Those on the *Zong* were not to be forgotten. The legal action disputing who should bear the cost of murder disgusted even those who were well aware of the evils of the trade; for others, who had lived in deliberate ignorance of what was going on it was a terrible revelation. Wilberforce was ready to unleash his political campaign, and Pitt was ready to co-operate.

Pitt considered that a committee of the Privy Council should report on the whole subject of Anglo-African trade, but before he could propose this in the Commons Wilberforce fell ill. He was not a robust man, and for years had strained his physique with innumerable journeys, meetings and arguments on his favourite subject. Pitt, under contemptuous criticism as "the schoolboy Prime Minister", and bedevilled by a Cabinet which was for the most part composed of members of the Lords, hostile to any kind of change, told Wilberforce that he was ready to risk his career in demanding that the enquiry be held. He presided over the committee in person. When he opened the debate he had two powerful allies, Burke and Fox. Both went further than Pitt with his necessarily cautious approach on the lines of an enquiry before action. His allies were in favour of total abolition.

Pitt's brilliant political acumen had warned him that the battle could never be won by any swift, dramatic attack. Although he privately told Granville Sharp, who was invited to Downing Street to discuss policy, that in his heart he agreed with Wilberforce and the Abolition Committee that nothing but complete abolition was the ideal objective, he wanted to avoid hot-headed and impractical moves which would achieve nothing.

The result was that the slaving interests realised that criticism was not coming from so-called cranks and idealists. Some sort of compromise would be needed if their business was to be saved from annihilation. Unable to contradict the evidence that Negro mortality during transit was anything from 5 to 25 per cent they thrust the blame on a few irresponsible shippers who overloaded their vessels. This, they insisted, could be avoided by regulations on the number of slaves carried.

Pitt told the House that this was Wilberforce's campaign, and he hoped his honourable friend would soon be restored to health and able to handle the debate himself, but he left members in no doubt that if Wilberforce's illness continued he himself would undertake the task.

The slaving interests were intimidated by the tone of the leading speakers, and the resolution was passed. But in the Lords the familiar theories were offered once more: the slave was happy; if he was restless it was because of the talk of emancipation; he was better off than the free English farm labourer; he was, even on the passage from Africa to America, accommodated more spaciously than English troops in their tented camps. Pitt threatened to resign if the Bill was thrown out. The threat worked. By a narrow majority the Lords gave their approval.

This Bill had the support of Pitt because the debates could reveal the tactics of the Opposition and prepare members for the much more acute controversy which would begin when the Privy Council Committee completed its work.

The Prime Minister was making a gesture of encouragement to the ailing Wilberforce who had been convalescing at Bath. Pitt had begun studying the facts for himself, analysing, as was his duty as Prime Minister, the economic factors involved in a cessation of the trade. The statistics were impressive. In the West Indian sugar islands under English control there were 450,000 slaves. Their capital value was £50 per head. The valuation of the farms and plantations on which the slaves laboured was £45 millions. Houses and merchant ships belonging to the islanders were worth £25 millions. The total value of property was therefore £70 millions. It existed because of slavery; it would evaporate after abolition.

With total abolition an impossible dream in the view of some genuinely horrified people, and an economic disaster in the opinion of the majority of politicians and business men, a movement began to regulate the transportation of Negroes across the Atlantic. The campaign was adroitly organised, and undoubtedly many of those who spoke and wrote in favour of regulation as a feasible and speedy remedy of the evils of the Middle Passage were dupes of commercial interests in Liverpool and Bristol.

A powerful argument in favour of maintaining the trade, so long as the mortality rate was reduced, was always possible on patriotic grounds. France, Spain and the Netherlands were enriching themselves by developing their colonies by the use of slave labour; England was lagging behind because of the shortage of slaves. Cessation of English enterprise would not only weaken the nation's imperial power but would destroy the revenue obtained from supplying foreign colonies with slave merchandise. A telling figure, hardly open to any valid criticism, was that upward of £1,800,000 were earned annually by the English slave trade.

The leading advocate of regulation was Sir William Dolben, the ageing M.P. for Oxford University. He was deeply shocked after accepting an invitation to visit a slave ship moored in the

Thames and had seen the available space in the hold. He introduced a Bill to regulate the number of slaves to be carried according to the tonnage of the vessel. The figure was basically one slave per ton.

The Opposition hastily compiled statistics. Small ships of one hundred tons or under were carrying about five slaves per two tons—about 250 slaves as a full shipment. That was the claim, though in fact three hundred appears to have been a more normal figure. On the alleged cargo of 250 slaves it was stated that the net profit per voyage was £763 5s. 6d., 10 per cent on the capital. On the proposed restriction to one slave per ton, in the case of the small vessel of one hundred tons or less there would be a loss on every voyage of £583 6s. od.

Larger ships, of two hundred tons and more, could make a profit of £1,300 per voyage with two slaves per ton, and £1,082 with five slaves per three tons. The former ratio was the usual one. The Bill was ill-conceived with its—probably unintentional —abolition of the small ship as a slave transport. The sloop of one hundred tons or under spent a shorter time on the coast buying slaves than the vessel which had to fill her holds with three to four hundred Negroes. She made a faster passage and the chances of a major mortality rate were fewer because of the decreased risk of mass infection.

The House was told of a cargo of 750 Negroes of whom 250 died, and of an old man-of-war in which 845 out of 1,115 were buried at sea. But in a sloop carrying twenty-five only two died. The percentage of fatalities, as had always been known, varied violently, but the dimensions of death were clearly minimised by carrying small numbers in small ships.

During the course of the debate some vessels berthed at Liverpool were inspected officially. One was the *Brookes*, a vessel of 320 tons. The plans of the Brookes became world-infamous.

The overall length of the lower deck of the vessel was 100 ft., the breadth of the beam at the maximum 25 ft.; the depth of hold 10 ft., height between decks 5 ft. 8 in.; dimensions of male slaves' hold in forepart of lower deck 46 ft. × 25 ft. 4 in.; shelf decks in male slaves' hold 46 ft. × 6 ft.

Amidships was a boy slaves' section 13 ft. 9 in. × 25 ft., with shelves 6 ft. wide. Behind this came the women's hold measuring 28 ft. 6 in. × 23 ft. 6 in. The shelves in this hold measured 28 ft. 6 in. × 6 ft.

Slaves were also stowed in the confines of the half deck, which measured 16 ft. 6 in. in length with shelves 6 ft. wide. The forward half of this half-deck was used as crew's quarters.

The proposed legislation under discussion was designed to permit every male slave a space of 6 ft. × 1 ft. 4 in., a woman 5 ft. 10 in. × 1 ft. 4 in., a boy 5 ft. × 1 ft. 2 in., and a girl 4 ft. 6 in. × 1 ft. Under such regulations the slave complement aboard the *Brookes* would total 451.

Dimensions in figures can have little meaning. A modern single bed is 3 ft. or 3 ft. 6 in. wide. Two such beds side by side provided the space for five men. The boy slaves' room was similar to a rather long double bedroom in a modern house. It was the accommodation for fifty young male slaves. The women's room was not unlike a living room big enough for the usual three-piece suite, dining table for four, a bookcase, TV set and so on. It was the prison for seventy-five female slaves.

Except for those who were shackled in the centre of the hold, who had 5 ft. 8 in. of vertical space, the majority of the captives had only 2 ft. 6 in. below an overhead beam. The only light was from scuttles and a hatch or two, often covered in bad weather. The slaves lay prone in these conditions for sixteen to twenty hours per day for anything up to twenty weeks.

Such were the conditions regarded as sufficiently humane for the transportation of 451 Negroes. A statement was made that the *Brookes* had in the past carried 609 slaves. Allegations were made in Parliament, and not denied, that on some passages slaves had had an average of four square feet of floor area, making it impossible for them to lie down except with their legs and part of their bodies on top of one another.

The Liverpool merchants saw to their chagrin that regulation might well be almost as disastrous as abolition, and was infinitely more likely to become law. They eagerly accepted orders to give evidence at the Bar of the House, but the main result of their statements was to reveal still further the extent of the evils inherent in the trade.

Pitt demonstrated his repulsion in his speech when the evidence was complete. "If the trade cannot be carried on in a manner different from that stated by honourable members opposite me, I will retract what I said on a former day against going into the general question. . . . I will give my vote for the utter abolition of a trade which is shocking to humanity, is abominable to be carried on by any country, and reflects the greatest dishonour on the British senate and British nation. The trade, as the petitioners propose to carry it on, without any regulation, is contrary to every humane, to every Christian principle, to every sentiment that ought to inspire the breast of man."

Regulation was approved by the Commons. The Lords, as expected, fought hard to reject it. Lord Hawkesbury, Liverpool's strongest ally in the Privy Council; Admiral Lord Rodney, Lord Heathfield, the Duke of Chandos, and Thurlow, the Lord Chancellor, sneered at "a five days' fit of philanthropy", insisted that the Negroes were well looked after, and repeated the warning about Negro uprisings if weakness was shown. But Pitt had his way. He would not remain in a Cabinet (consisting mostly of the members of the Upper Chamber) if the Bill was rejected. He got his way—by two votes. On July 11, 1788, the Bill received the Royal sanction.

The Act was a well-meant but complicated piece of legislation, the regulations being all too easily evaded while ships were away from the home country. The cargo ratio eventually decided on was five slaves per three tons' burden for ships not exceeding 201 tons, and one extra slave for each additional ton. Male slaves exceeding 4 ft. 4 in. in height were counted on a scale of one slave per ton in ships up to 201 tons, and on a ratio of 3 : 5 for every additional five tons. Five slaves under 4 ft. 4 in. in height counted as four slaves. This provision unfortunately encouraged slavers to take children without their parents when supplies of slaves were short, in order to make up their cargo. Infringement of these clauses carried a fine of £30 for each slave over the maximum number permitted, half of the fine going to the King and half to the complainant.

Ships had to register as slavers before leaving a United Kingdom port, and the ship's surgeon was required to deposit £100 with the Customs, returnable after he had delivered his report of the voyage. The report had to take the form of a journal, recording the number of slaves taken aboard and the number and cause of deaths, delivered at the first British port reached after leaving Africa.

No person could in future command a slave ship unless he had already acted as master during one voyage or had served as an officer on at least two voyages. This clause appeared to have no motive beyond protecting the existing firms; a similar one, insisting on ships being properly prepared between decks —with no specification of what this involved beyond a warning that spare space was not to be used to store merchandise—was also favourable to the shippers already in the trade.

Insurance of a slaver was prohibited except against the perils of the sea, piracy, insurrection, capture by the King's enemies, barratry of the master and crew, and destruction by fire.

A death ratio of two slaves per hundred was condoned. The master of a ship able to report such a well-managed enterprise was to get £100, and the surgeon £50, from the Receiver-General of Customs. For a death rate limited to three per hundred the officers were to receive £50 and £25.

One regrettable result of the Act was to increase the number of slaves carried to non-British markets. Likelihood of inspection on the African coast or during the Middle Passage was slim. One prominent Liverpool merchant began negotiations to transfer his offices and ships to Rouen; Bristol shippers began using "flags of convenience".

Unbiased evidence of conditions in Africa was difficult to come by. One instance was the report of two Swedish explorers, Wadström and Spaarman who led an African expedition in 1787–8. Sweden had very little interest in the slave trade, her African company being in reality financed and run by Dutch merchants. The report, compiled by Wadström, indicated that there was no doubt that tribal wars occurred simply to obtain slaves—such wars breaking out immediately after the sight of more than the usual number of slave ships on the coast.

Wadström considered the people of Moorish origin living to the north of the Senegal river were the worst predators, partly because the French gave the chiefs an annual retainer, and supplied guns and ammunition free. One chief, called the King of Almammy, prohibited the passage of slaves through his territories with the result that the Moorish merchants could no longer move their captives to the French slavers anchored at the mouth of the Senegal river. Bribes had no effect on the king, and the French thereupon got the Moorish chiefs to go to war, capturing the king's own subjects. Wadström saw these prisoners in the slave compounds. They were chained at the ankles in twos. Several were suffering from wounds received in battle, for which no treatment had been given.

Another useful source of slaves was exploited by some chiefs on their own people. The incitement was in the form of trade goods, particularly spirits. The chief's personal guards attacked his own villages by night.

Individual slaves were obtained by kidnapping. Wadström said that a Negro travelling alone would hardly ever escape such an attack. He observed one fight in the slave hold of a ship when one Negro saw the man who had captured him being brought in himself, having been waylaid just after he had completed his deal.

In May, 1789, the debate in the Commons began, the motion for abolition being proposed by a now completely recovered Wilberforce. He concentrated on the details given to the committee of conditions during transit: of the branding with hot irons on the shoulder or chest, of the stench of masses of Negroes jammed together in the hold of a ship in tropical waters, of the forcible feeding with jaw-openers on a nauseating mess of boiled horse beans, of the grotesque dances the slaves were forced to perform daily while still fettered to one another in order to have exercise, and of the numbers who preferred death by drowning or being eaten by sharks to another day on a slave ship. To stress that cruelty and neglect were not unique to the ships, Wilberforce quoted figures of one-third mortality ashore among the survivors landed in the West Indies. These deaths occurred in what was called the "seasoning period" by the planters, who pretended that the climate in the West Indies was unsuitable whereas it was little different from that in the slaves' homeland.

Wilberforce was supported by Burke and then by Pitt and Fox. The Opposition attempted to scare the House with forecasts of the dire consequences of abolition. The arguments were all too familiar. Other nations would carry on the trade and English possessions in the West Indies would become a hotbed of slave smuggling. The City of London's insurance and banking interests would go bankrupt. Seaports would be ruined. But this time there were not so many claims that the Negroes really enjoyed being enslaved or that serfdom in a Christian land was better for them than liberty in a pagan country.

More intelligent were the delaying tactics of the speakers who well understood how to retrieve an almost lost cause. They made their appeals on the grounds of the rights of property and the privilege of the Commons to examine a problem without dictation from a Privy Council which consisted mainly of members of the Lords. This move effectively postponed action until January, 1790, when evidence was heard all over again. As a result the investigation dragged on till the summer when a general election further delayed progress. But the hopes of the Opposition were dashed: Pitt was returned with a bigger majority, and Wilberforce retained his seat easily. The battle was resumed and continued sporadically for months. In April, 1791, the vote was taken. The Wilberforce motion for abolition was rejected by 163 votes to eighty-eight.

With proof that the representatives of a restricted but powerful section of the prople were in favour of the retention of slave trading, the only thing for Wilberforce and his friends to do was once more to rouse the public direct. The public meetings and petitions which resulted were forerunners of this type of democratic action which reached a zenith in the Reform movement forty years later. The effectiveness of massive pleas to Parliament was first proved during this phase of the abolition campaign. Nearly five hundred petitions were sent from every part of the country, and even M.P.s with safe seats had to consider their future attitude.

Once more Pitt and Wilberforce arranged for a debate. This time their opponents were aided by an ingenious idea—all the more useful because its originator, Henry Dundas (later Viscount Melville), was a close friend of Pitt and a man who had been deeply disgusted by the revelations of the trade's ruthless cruelties. But Dundas was alarmed at the possibility of violence in the West Indies and had the conventional regard for a man to do what he willed with his goods and chattels. He proposed that the import of slaves should be rendered unnecessary by improvement in conditions for existing slaves. They should be encouraged to marry and breed. The children would in a dozen years or so solve the problem of replacement, and in an unspecified time the condition of slavery could be changed to free labour.

The pro-slavery lobby was of course delighted at this idea. Many members who had no definite interest one way or the other grasped at the suggestion as a perfect *media via*.

Fox was no supporter of such subterfuges and told the House that the idea seemed to him, so far from being a method of gradually abolishing slavery by regulation, to be a way of establishing slavery as a permanent institution in the West Indies. He finished with the comment, amid growls of patriotic protest, that if the colonies could not be cultivated without slavery they ought not to be cultivated at all.

Widespread indignation about a ban on stowing cargo in the vacant parts of the slave hold had the unintended result of further revealing the conditions under which slaves were shipped. It was explained that ships took large quantities of gunpowder—as many as three hundred barrels—as trading merchandise. The hold spaces where this was stored were boarded and dry. As the gunpowder was gradually sold, provisions for the slave cargo were purchased. Under the regulation of no dead cargo in any part of the slave hold once two-thirds of the slave complement were aboard, there could be no solution except to store the provisions in the area with the gunpowder, and this area had then to be visited several times a day by the ship's cook, carrying a naked light. This was an objection to the regulations which had some validity.

An indirect result of the investigations into the conditions of Negroes aboard ship was the revelation of the miserable existence of the seamen. The mutiny at the Nore in 1797 gave some hint of the brutality to which sailors were subjected in the name of discipline. In a war in which the Navy was the only effective shield for the United Kingdom no one was greatly bothered about the welfare of the men who manned the ships: Their bravery was all that mattered.

The Royal Navy maintained a rough sort of justice. No such consideration applied to the crews of slave ships, regarded in the seaports as the scum of the profession. The suppression of normal human feelings essential for the running of a successful slaving enterprise meant that the ship's master regarded his crew as of rather less value than the Negroes. Surgeons might pay more attention to a sick slave than a sick British seaman. Malaria and more severe fevers were the almost inevitable result of two or three visits to the African coast; scurvy the normal disease after a few months at sea.

Clarkson spent a long time in Liverpool investigating the recruitment of slaver crews. Youngsters were tempted to sign on by accounts of high wages and of the profits to be made from the capture of their own slaves. If a sailor ignored these blandishments he was given enough liquor to render him insensible; he woke up on board. Debtors had the alternative of joining a slaver crew or going to prison. Wanted men found slaving the only method of evading the law.

Crew rations were one pound of bread and one pound of salt beef per day. Water was allowed at the rate of three pints per day unless the passage took longer than expected. Crews often stole the slaves' food (punishable by flogging) or even begged for some of it.

Desertion on the African coast was common enough—the action of men in hopeless desperation. The life of an unarmed European in Africa was cheap. If he was not killed because he was thought to be looking for the chance to kidnap slaves he was captured and sold to the master of a slave ship. It was wiser to desert in the West Indies, where there might be the chance of joining a buccaneer crew and there was the eventual certainty of being picked up for impressment into the Royal Navy. The Navy did not automatically offer refuge. The health of the Guinea men was so notoriously bad that they rarely could pass even the tolerant standards required for a man o' war's crew. The likelihood of the slaver captain pursuing deserting sailors in the West Indies was remote. In fact he wanted to get rid of all but a minimum number of fit men required to sail the ship back to Liverpool with its cargo of sugar. By leaving men ashore in the West Indies wages were saved and men likely to become helplessly sick were jettisoned.

Clarkson compiled statistics on nine voyages by eight different ships between 1766 and 1780. Out of a total of 2,362 slaves shipped approximately 154 died. Of the 203 sailors employed as crews twenty-two died. The mortality percentage of sailors was therefore nearly double that of the slaves. The crews did, of course, spend almost three times as long at sea as the Negroes, who were in the ship for only one leg of the triangular voyage. The death rates for seamen and slaves are not completely accurate, as they ignore the deaths of slaves within a short time

97

of being landed, and do not take into account the fate of seamen who deserted in Africa, the West Indies, or any port where the ship put in for supplies.

Clarkson estimated that in the late eighteenth century five thousand seamen were employed on slave ships in any one year, and the losses through death, permanent sickness or desertion were 1,950. A further statistical analysis he made showed that out of 910 seamen in the British slave trade about two hundred would die on shipboard.

Possibly the regulations eased the misery in the slave holds. They did little to curb the trade. In the period 1795–1804 authorised departures of slave ships included 155 from London, and 1,099 from Liverpool. The average number of slaves carried was three hundred per vessel.

With traditional care and cautious procedure the Privy Council committee were meantime holding their hearings and preparing their report. The information was collated under five headings—the methods of obtaining slaves in Africa, the means of transportation to the West Indies, their treatment on the plantations, the number of slaves in the West Indies, and extent of slave trading and slavery among other nations.

Pitt, on virtually every other question Fox's implacable adversary, made one of the great speeches of his career, destroying every contention of the Opposition, one by one: the real danger of revolt came from contacts between newly arrived Negroes disturbing those who had become amenable to their work on the plantations; events had indicated that strife broke out where the slave population was greater than the white community and was constantly increased by imports; if the House accepted that the slave trade was a scandal it was offensive to believe that Parliament should vote to continue the scandal even for a stated period.

He turned to Africa. European civilisation had been able to "inject a poison which penetrates to its very centre, corrupting every part to which it reaches . . . How shall we ever hope to obtain, if it be possible, forgiveness from heaven for the enormous ills we have committed if we refuse to make use of those means which the mercy of Providence has still preserved to us for wiping away the shame and guilt with which we are now covered?"

Pitt saw Africa, not as a dark continent full of disease and savage tribes, but in the image which, nearly two centuries later, is becoming a reality.

"If we listen to the voice of reason and duty and pursue this day the line of conduct which they prescribe some of us may live to see the reverse of that picture from which we now turn our eyes with shame and regret. We may live to behold the natives of Africa engaged in the calm occupation of industry, in the pursuit of a just and legitimate commerce. We may behold the beams of science and philosophy breaking in upon their land, which, at some happy period, in still later times, may blaze with full lustre, and joining their influence with that of pure religion may illuminate and invigorate the most distant extremities of that immense continent."

The House, however, was not inclined to accelerate progress towards Pitt's goal. The amendment for gradual abolition gained the day by a majority of 145 votes. The date for abolition was fixed for four years ahead, with control on the number to be imported in the interim.

The Lords prepared to obstruct even more powerfully than on previous occasions. Wilberforce's opponents were indeed formidable: they included the King, at the time enjoying a period of sanity which enabled him to use all his influence in private talks with his Peers to persuade them to oppose the Bill. His most enthusiastic ally was his son, the Duke of Clarence (later William IV), who, despite his youth had already earned a reputation as a naval martinet. Clarence had no worries about the appalling conditions endured by seamen in the Navy; he regarded flogging as a necessary adjunct of discipline. It was not surprising that in his careful assessment of social strata he put slaves well below sailors and, comparing the living conditions and working lives of each class, told the Lords that the slaves he had seen in the West Indies enjoyed a state of what he described as "humble happiness". It was high summer and the session was due to end. There was no need to cause a clash with the Commons by throwing out the Bill. All that was needed was to resolve to hear further evidence later. That meant in the following year. Before the Lords resumed their debate Britain and France were at war.

Eight

Almost immediately the idealism of the abolitionists became suspect. The Convention in Paris announced to the world that France would give help "to all those who wished to recover their freedom". It was partly a call to oppressed nations and partly an appeal to malcontents to stir up internal strife among France's enemies and potential enemies. If the welfare of slaves was considered at all it was of those in French colonies where Royalists still maintained control.

Not even the firebrands in Paris could have at that time envisaged a mass revolt of Negroes in the Caribbean to topple English influence there. But every opponent of abolition immediately pointed out the treason inherent in advocating aid to enslaved inhabitants of English possessions, and a good many others who had hitherto regarded emancipation as eventually desirable believed they had been the dupes of French revolutionaries. In any event England was seething with unrest among the masses in the large towns and among groups who suffered from a sense of injustice, such as the Irish Catholics. No Prime Minister could dare to relax control in this situation.

The abolition of the slave trade had, in fact, become the enemy's tactical move. Paris announced the abolition of slavery in all France and her possessions. The result, whether intended or not, was to cause some unrest among the slaves of all non-French islands in the Caribbean. Pitt could do nothing but indicate his disagreement with Wilberforce's aims for abolition even in the middle of a war, particularly as Wilberforce was also proclaiming anti-war views. The independent M.P. for Hull became an annoying nuisance in the House, opinion being equally divided as to whether his motives were those of hypocrisy or fanaticism.

The forebodings of the average citizen that liberty for slaves would, in the midst of a war, degenerate into anarchy were tragically confirmed by news from the West Indies. What became known as the Black Terror provided an awful lesson on the results of misplaced idealism. Few people troubled to study the horrors in a West Indian island and to see that they were an extension of the revolution in France. The outbreaks of violence occurred in Santo Domingo, the island where Columbus landed on December 12, 1496, and planted a crucifix in the name of his Royal employers "as a sign that your Highnesses possess the land as your own, and principally for a sign of Jesus Christ our Lord and the honour of Christianity". The *Santa Maria* drifted ashore there and was abandoned. Other ships were beached and repaired, and Columbus's sailors constructed living quarters—the first European settlement in the New World.

Soon the Caribs on the island had been driven off or exterminated, and Spain began bringing in African slaves. Over the centuries colonists from England and France arrived in the unsettled areas of the island, and there was a considerable degree of inter-racial breeding. From the French area six members of the wealthy mulatto population sailed for France after receiving news of the Revolution, taking with them a gift of six million gold livres for the National Assembly. In return they hoped that a revolutionary constitution for the island would grant equality of political and civil rights with the white population. This they were at first promised.

But in the National Assembly the white delegates from St. Domingue (the French name for their colony) did their utmost to see that the mulattoes were given no facilities to join in the deliberations. The leader of the mulatto delegation was a wealthy planter named Oge. He immediately took his delegation back to St. Domingue and began preparations for war, arming his slaves and organising the mulattoes into a formidable force. The insurgents struck too soon and were easily defeated by the French military authorities, Oge being executed by being broken on the wheel.

But French troops were no longer to be regarded as reliable. In Port au Prince, at the western end of the island of which St. Domingue formed the eastern half, the garrison troops killed their Royalist commanding officer and challenged the Government. Of the forty thousand white civilians probably about half sided with the mutinous troops. Certainly the forty thousand mulattoes did—and there could be little doubt where the sympathies of the 450,000 slaves would lie should there be a chance of venting their hatred on the whites.

France endeavoured to restore peace by granting equal political status with the whites to all mulattoes born of free parents. The breakdown in social barriers had reached a zenith only a decade or so earlier so that the majority of the most vociferous and youthfully energetic mulattoes were excluded because one parent had been a slave. The die-hard whites had the concession to free-born mulattoes reversed, whereupon large-scale civil war broke out. The forty thousand mulattoes were able to arm one hundred thousand slaves. There were appalling excesses on both sides during the autumn of 1791, but the whites were, of course, hopelessly outnumbered. Some two thousand white men, women and children were killed or tortured to death, virtually all the large plantations were in blackened desolation, and the few surviving white families left penniless and homeless.

Insurrection on such a scale was bound to spread. Slaves and mulattoes rose in other French islands in the Caribbean and there was a quickly suppressed revolt of slaves on the English island of Dominica, far to the south-east. The highly significant fact about the insurrection in French-held St. Domingue was that the leader who emerged was not a mulatto but a Negro. Toussaint L'Ouverture, as he called himself, was the son of a chief in West Africa, sold into slavery as a youth. A highly intelligent man, he was treated with more respect than the rank-and-file Negroes as was the practice when membership of a chieftain's family became known. He was converted to Christianity and learned to read. At the time when the revolt broke out he was approaching fifty years of age and had long been secretly regarded as the Negroes' leader. His personality and family background, added to his literacy, ensured that all the slaves held him in awe. He increased this respect by practising as a witch doctor.

After 1792 Toussaint was regarded as France's military representative in the island. He was invited to send delegates to the French National Assembly, and the end of slavery on the island was announced—or rather confirmed. Both Spain and England began hostilities, the former because of her fears for her own possessions and the latter ostensibly to save the penniless white planters who survived, but mainly as part of the strategy against France in the Caribbean. Toussaint inflicted heavy defeats on both enemies and was able to present France with the whole island. The subsequent events of French treachery and Toussaint's legalised murder by neglect in a bitterly cold prison near the Swiss frontier is typical of the unhappy history of Haiti which ensued.

Intrigue, assassination, and revolution became the almost interminable events in the island's subsequent history, and the pattern has, of course, continued to the present day, turning an earthly paradise into a living hell for most of its inhabitants for most of the time. The preliminary disturbances, occurring during the height of the controversy about slavery, yielded two lessons. For the defenders of the system St. Domingue was a terrifying example of the ruin and misery which resulted from even a slight easing of the slaves' plight; for the few visionaries the menace was contained in the system itself. The island had an inordinately large proportion of slaves and half-slaves to whites. Eventual tragedy was certain. Neither concessions nor force could alter the situation.

Wilberforce had been hurt by Pitt's declining enthusiasm for quick and forceful legislation on the slave trade; like all crusaders he could not see the other person's difficulties. Moreover, Wilberforce was not in favour of pressing the war with France to its limit. With effective action in the Commons almost impossible, he found some outlets for his energy by becoming a director of the Sierra Leone Company.

The Sierra Leone settlement originated in a small piece of land behind Frenchman's Bay, bought by Captain John Taylor of the Royal Naval brig *Miro* from a group of local chiefs. It was an area a trifle optimistically selected by an explorer, Henry Smeathman, as suitable for a Negro settlement. Smeathman was a botanist, and his recommendation to Quaker interests in England looking for a suitable settlement was coloured more by his interest in the rampaging fertility of the place than its suitability for habitation. The Government's experience was that the coast was appallingly unhealthy for white people, and the alacrity of the chiefs in completing the deal suggested that it was of little benefit to Negroes.

This was the minute spot in Africa which was to become an English-sponsored haven for Negroes. The motives of the

Committee for the Black Poor were entirely altruistic. The acceptance of the scheme by the Government arose from a simple solution of a growing social problem. The principle of liberty for any slave brought to England was a fine one; for Negroes who took advantage of it, or had belonged to owners fearful of falling foul of the law, liberty was equated with poverty, cold, and hunger. Frenchman's Bay, re-named St. George's Bay, was described to them as a haven in their homeland. Some 340 indigent Negroes were shipped there in 1787, together with a few skilled white craftsmen and a few score prostitutes. The craftsmen went through motives of idealism mixed with ambitions to start a new and better life. The prostitutes were loaded for much the same reason as the Negroes: it was the simplest solution as to what to do with them.

Once there, the Sierra Leone settlers were on their own, the idea being that they would found a peasant economy easily able to prosper with the aid of a bountiful African climate. The company's terms offered every settler one acre of garden in the area selected for communal living, plus an agricultural holding of twenty acres for himself, ten for a wife, and five for each child. After a year a quit rent of one shilling per acre was payable. Those fortunate enough to have some capital (some of the Negroes had a little money; they were ex-slaves demobilised in Nova Scotia after service with the British in the American war of Independence) could buy additional acreage at the rate of £50 per ten acres, the money being returned in kind as agricultural implements and stores. All settlers were transported free and were given three months' supply of food with a further three months' supply on half rations.

Unfortunately the plans for the peasant economy of this asylum for liberated slaves were not based on African custom so much as the practices in medieval England. The settlement was to be a reflection of the influence of the Church and State as in England, and civil law was to be maintained under the old English system of frankpledge, with householders divided into tens, hundreds and headboroughs, and chiefs representing these groups. The idealists behind the Sierra Leone scheme committed the same sort of error which often confused the campaigns of the American abolitionists fifty years later: while regarding Negroes as second-class human beings in a white community they expected them to show first-class abilities when suddenly given privileges of self-rule in a settlement of their own. In the case of Sierra Leone disease soon decimated the numbers landed under the benign supervision of the Royal Navy which also took the settlers tools, seed, and food. Desertions into the interior soon aggravated the depopulation until not more than half the original immigrants remained. A further disaster occurred as the result of trouble with a neighbouring tribe suspected of slaving activities. A naval party made an example by destroying the native village. In retaliation the chief marched into the settlement and burned many of the buildings.

More practical control was obviously needed. A banker, and M.P., Henry Thompson, agreed to help, and the well-tried system of colonial development of forming a chartered company resulted. The St. George's Bay (Sierra Leone) Company had adequate capital and for a time prospered, more liberated slaves and settlers replacing the dead and deserters. A small community was built and called Freetown. The driving force on the spot was a man who had been nauseated by the evils of slavery while working in Jamaica as the overseer on a plantation, Zachary Macaulay, father of the historian. He managed to survive the diseases which made it almost impossible for white people to remain in the settlement for more than a few months. He adapted English methods of agriculture to suit the African, and with some success persuaded the Negroes to work for themselves—an activity which was difficult for them after years of toil under duress. Then came another disaster. On the excuse that France and Britain were at war, a small French naval force appeared off the coast. Men were landed. Freetown was looted and set in flames. The attack was motivated by hatred of the tiny haven of freedom on the slave coast: the ships had been led to the right place for mounting an attack on Freetown by the American captain of a slave ship. But the final result was a moral victory for Macaulay. Lethargic and refractory Negroes saw during this unprovoked assault by slaving interests the proof that there were white men ready to give their lives to repel the assaults of other white men who were committed to slaving. Morale improved dramatically after the French attack. Freetown was re-built and extended. Crops were not only sown but conscientiously tended through to harvesting. Profits were made from the export of raw materials.

By the end of the century "the asylum for liberated slaves" had justified itself and provided evidence for the abolitionists in Britain to refute the plantation owners' insistence on the Negroes' stupidity and unreliability.

Otherwise, Wilberforce had little progress to encourage him. With his sympathies for the French Republic, he inclined to regard the abolition of slavery in the French colonies as a genuine move towards citizenship for Negroes. It was exasperating that England's enemy should have taken the lead.

Another nation had also displayed that sense of humanity which Wilberforce believed was being suppressed by the influential circles in commerce and government in England. In March, 1792, Denmark issued a royal ordinance abolishing the Danish slave trade from the beginning of the year 1803. The principal Danish islands in the West Indies were St. Thomas and St. Croix in the Lesser Antilles. Despite Wilberforce's belief that this was an idealistic action, abolition of slavery was not intended. King Christian VII believed that the prosperity of the islands would increase if slaves were bred from the existing Negroes and no more were imported. "It would be beneficial and profitable if . . . our islands were, in process of time, cultivated by Negroes born and bred in the islands, accustomed from their youth to the manner of labour, the climate, and the disposition of their masters."

To obtain the necessary breeding stock all nations were to be permitted to transport slaves to the Danish islands until December, 1802. For every Negro imported, sugar could be sold for export to other nations at the rate of 2,000 lb. for every adult Negro, male or female; 1,000 lb. for each adolescent, but nothing for small children. Export of slaves was prohibited. To encourage the import of women, the annual poll tax was abolished on all females and doubled on all males, and females could be imported duty-free. It was, in reality, a cynical attitude to slavery, with all the potential evils exposed by Fox when he criticised a somewhat similar plan offered to the Commons by Dundas.

The latent support for Wilberforce was far greater than he could envisage in this dark, frustrating phase of his campaign. Interest in Africa and the slave question was enormous, even in the middle of a global war. Any first-hand account was eagerly read. One vividly written travel book resulted from an expedition financed by the African Association, a scientific organisation which included the President of the Royal Society, Sir Joseph Banks. The exploration of the Niger river was made by Mungo Park. The account he wrote was called simply *Travels*. It was read avidly in both Britain and America after it was published in 1799.

Park wrote completely objectively. His description of slaving was all the harrowing because of the absence of any bias. Admittedly he had a genuine affection for Africans (when he fell ill he was patiently nursed by a Negro for seven months), but he had no wish to interfere with their customs, good or evil.

When Park was in the vicinity of the source of the Gambia river he met and talked with many slaves, chiefs, and merchants. Slaves increased in value according to their distance from their homeland, the greater the mileage the less likelihood there was of escape. To this end slaves were constantly sold and re-sold in different markets in order to confuse them about the route home. Ideally captives were slaves from birth because they were amenable to discipline and inured to hard labour. There was no possibility of such captives being released, but freemen could be exchanged by their relatives for two slaves if the deal was arranged before the victims reached the coast. Park was impressed by the fear of newly enslaved Negroes about their future. The old rumour about white men eating black flesh was still strong. When Park tried to explain to the Negroes that after a journey across the sea they would be employed tilling the land, one of them put his hand on the ground and asked whether there really was dry earth across the sea on which a man could walk. Park's answer was clearly not really believed.

The captors had to shackle the Negroes to prevent them stampeding into the bush in a frenzied attempt to avoid sale to Europeans. Restraint was effected with a double shackle, pinioning the right leg of one man to the left leg of another. A piece of string enabled the weight of the fetter to be lifted so that they could walk very slowly. In addition to the shackles, a rope was passed round the necks of every four men forming two shackled pairs. At night the hands were fettered. Any sign of resistance resulted in a weight being attached to one foot. It consisted of a log some three feet in length, notched at one end. The log was fixed to the slave by passing an iron staple round the ankle, and fixing the leg into the notch. The man could then only shuffle along, dragging his pinioned leg very slowly so that the weight of the log did not force the staple into the bone of the ankle.

Park remained in one village for nearly three months while slaves were being collected. On the day of departure the leg irons were removed from the thirty-five prisoners. There were thirty-eight other persons—merchants, minor native officials, their wives, their domestic slaves, and six singing men whose job it was to provide the marching rhythm. The slaves were roped together. All had burdens to carry on their heads. After the long period of muscular disuse many found it impossible to walk quickly, and two prisoners had to be removed from the rope leash to stumble along as best they could.

The distance to be covered was estimated by Park to be five hundred miles. The party travelled slowly partly because of the heat in the daytime and also because of the constant danger of attack when in the vicinity of communities known to be rapacious. The slaves, with their heavy burdens, became more and more exhausted. Dropping a load was punished by whipping. One man, who let his load fall twice and was whipped each time, finally sank to the ground completely exhausted. He either died or was killed by his guard that evening. Another slave, gradually becoming more and more weak, was exchanged at a village for a healthy girl who was grabbed without warning while standing with the other village women, watching the column prepare to continue its journey.

Park was, of course, in no position to object to the slaving activities of his African friends. He did, in fact, give gratuitous advice on how to obtain a good market by waiting till more ships arrived, the slave market at the time being in a temporary depression when the column reached the mouth of the Gambia. Park mentions the kindly behaviour of the slaves who "amidst their own infinitely greater sufferings, would commiserate mine, and frequently of their own accord bring water to quench my thirst, and at night collect branches and leaves to prepare me a bed in the wilderness. We parted with reciprocal expressions of regret and benediction. My good wishes and prayers were all I could bestow on them, and it afforded me some consolation to be told that they were sensible I had no more to give."

Park visited an American slaver, the *Charlestown*, buying Negroes for shipment to South Carolina. American vessels were at that time invariably undermanned in comparison with British and French slavers, and shortly after the vessel moved down-river to the vicinity of Dakar to take on provisions, four seamen and the ship's surgeon died of fever, as well as three slaves.

Park volunteered to serve as ship's surgeon (he was infinitely more skilled than the usual doctor on a slaver for he had studied surgery and medicine at Edinburgh) and went among the slaves talking to many of them in their own language. He saw no needless cruelty during the passage, but because of the crew shortage the slaves were kept more severely shackled than might have been normal. Most became ill. Eleven died at sea as well as the original three in the Gambia and six or eight more while anchored in the estuary. The ship was old and in bad condition. After three weeks at sea the fittest Negroes were put on the pumps and worked to the limit. But the leaky hull indirectly eased the slaves' miseries. There was little chance of making the American mainland and the ship headed for the West Indies, arriving at Antigua after thirty-five days at sea.

Literary material of this kind, supported by speeches and meetings up and down the country, almost completely eradicated public apathy on the slave question. Then, political events took place which indirectly paved the way for Wilberforce's final onslaught.

In 1801 the first Parliament of the United Kingdom met as the result of the union of Great Britain and Ireland. Pitt resigned after eighteen exhausting years in office, and with the end of his responsibilities as Prime Minister he was able to heal the breach with Wilberforce. Pitt agreed to serve under the new Prime Minister, Addington, but did not attend the House so frequently. To Wilberforce's joy he took care to be in his place when the usual proposal for leave to introduce an anti-slave trade Bill was made. The motion was defeated by only four votes in a thin House, but on the next occasion the Anti-abolitionists rallied their forces, and the vote was eighty-four to fifty-four. Pitt was able to comfort his old friend a little at this setback by having a little known Order in Council rescinded. Although Britain was officially at war with Spain continuance of trade between the colonies of the two countries had been authorised by the Order, and a flourishing business in slaves was going on.

Pitt resumed the premiership in 1804, and he gave at least tacit approval for Wilberforce to intensify his campaign in the House. He had unexpected allies in the presence of members for Ireland. The Irish were not involved in the slave trade but they were anxious to contribute to the business of Parliament. They materially helped Wilberforce to enjoy a majority of seventy-five in favour of his motion. As Wilberforce expected, the Lords once more organised delaying tactics to prevent any law being passed in that session.

Eighteen hundred and five came and with it more interminable debates. Pitt was weary. Once more he stood aside from controversy. He died in January, 1806. The loss Wilberforce felt in the death of a friend and powerful ally was eased by knowledge that Pitt's successor, Grenville, was strongly in favour of abolition, as were several members of his Ministry, notably Fox. Practical results were almost immediate. British ships were banned from shipping slaves into ex-enemy colonies taken from the enemy by British forces. No ship, British or foreign, could be fitted out for slaving in a British port.

On June 10, 1806, a resolution to approve a motion for total abolition was passed in both the Commons and the Lords. In order to prevent a last-minute increase in slaving to beat the ban no ship not previously engaged in the trade was allowed to leave a British port.

In January, 1807, Grenville rose to propose a Bill for the abolition of the slave trade. This was, of course, in the House of Lords and the manoeuvre meant that if the first hurdle was passed the task in the Commons would be comparatively easy. The Bill provided for complete abolition of trading in slaves after May 1, 1807; the banning of their transport from Africa to the West Indies or any other territory; forfeiture of any British ship engaged in slaving; penalties for insuring slave trading, and payment of rewards to officers and crews of Royal Navy vessels for all slaves liberated. The slaves taken off captured ships were to be offered service in the armed forces or supervised apprenticeships in private employment.

The Opposition in the Lords knew they faced defeat. Their attempts to minimise the effect of abolition included an employment tax on slaves, the rate rising gradually until it became prohibitive. Several speakers repeated the old theories of Negro revolt, financial ruin, and weakening of Britain's imperial power. It was all futile. The Lords approved by a majority of sixty-four.

In the Commons Lord Horwick (later Earl Grey), as Foreign Secretary, opened the debate. The House was packed, but the opponents were soon showing that they expected defeat by their half-hearted opposition. In the rolling periods of the rhetorical style of the time the Solicitor-General, Romilly, wound up for the Government. His praise of the private member for Hull roused the House as it has rarely been roused before or since. More than three hundred M.P.s were soon on their feet, cheering and waving. The noise was intensified when the result of the division was announced. Only sixteen Noes, and 283 in favour. The man who had battled for more than a quarter of a century for human beings in far-off lands he had never visited sat immovable in his seat, his head close to his knees and his hands covering his face. The tears ran between his fingers.

The King assented to the Bill on March 25, 1807. Britain was bringing to an end one of its staple trades which had been a mainstay of its overseas prosperity for 250 years. This historic Act abolishing the British slave trade from May 1, 1807, was a remarkably clear and effective piece of legislation, considering the complications of the subject and the resourcefulness of those who would do their best to discover loopholes. Anyone trafficking in slaves was liable to a fine of £100 per slave. Any ship involved would be seized. Every ship owner, part-owner, agent, captain, mate, and ship's surgeon participating in slave trading was liable to be individually fined £100 per slave. Insurance of a slave ship was prohibited, with a fine of £100 for each insurance policy issued, plus three times the amount of the premium.

Enemy ships seized or detained as prizes, and proving to have slaves on board, presented a major problem. The solution provided in the Act was that, along with the ship, they became the property of the Crown. The slaves were to be offered enlistment in the armed services or apprenticed to approved employers under indentures not exceeding fourteen years.

The desire to get Negroes into the Army or Navy was understandable at a time when Napoleon had declared

England to be in a state of blockade and it was obvious that the war would spread and be prolonged. Man-power was a major problem, and it was known that, as seamen, Negroes could be valuable. Both Portugal and France employed African and half-caste crews, sometimes on slave ships. Negro soldiers and sailors were to be treated as if they had enlisted voluntarily so that from the outset no colour bar existed during their service. The black serving man enjoyed the privileges, such as they were, of his white comrades. However, it was specifically stated that pensions or allowances paid to British men after discharge would not apply to Negroes. So far as the provisions of the Act were concerned there was apparently no reason why slaves released from enemy ships taken as prizes should not be apprenticed in England.

In view of the appalling treatment of underprivileged women and juveniles in the mills and mines of the United Kingdom it was probably fortunate that the implied object was to use them as indentured workers on the plantations.

The problem of what was to happen to such apprentices when their apprenticeships expired was evaded. The Crown would issue orders for the disposal and support of such Negroes at a later date. The thought at the back of the minds of the lawmakers was that some Negroes could be returned to Africa to work as free men and British subjects in the Crown's colonies. The Cape of Good Hope had been occupied; Sierra Leone and Gambia became colonies soon after the Abolition Act became law.

Nine

The abolition of the slave trade by Great Britain automatically introduced a tremendous task for British diplomacy. If abolition was to achieve the main objective of ending the misery of the people of Africa other slave trading nations would have to co-operate. The possibility of success appeared remote in the midst of a major war involving most of the powers participating in slaving. Nevertheless Canning, secretary for foreign affairs under the Duke of Portland, immediately issued instructions to all ambassadors to begin negotiations.

The first discussions were with Portugal. She was the nation most deeply involved in the marketing of slaves on the African coast. Lisbon did her best to delay the negotiations, and Britain was obliged to temporise, after twelve months of wrangling, by proposing that the agreement should be for the "gradual disuse, and the ultimate and not distant abolition of the slave trade". Britain expected, however, that Portugal would immediately abstain from selling Negroes to the shippers of other nations.

The Peninsular War not inconveniently created an opportunity to force the issue. In a treaty of alliance signed between Britain and Portugal at Rio de Janeiro in February, 1810, one article bound Portugal, in the cause of humanity and justice, to adopt the most efficacious means for bringing about a gradual abolition of the trade throughout the Portuguese dominions. Further, Portuguese subjects should not be permitted to carry on slave trading on any part of the coast of Africa not actually belonging to Portugal, and in which the trade had been discontinued and abandoned by the powers which formerly traded there.

The Portuguese idea of gradual abolition was different from Britain's. In the ensuing two or three years British patrols captured many Portuguese slavers, to the violent annoyance of Lisbon. The best that Britain could do was to get an agreement on minimum standards of treatment of slaves in transit. The maximum loading was fixed at five slaves for every two tons deadweight, a doctor or medical attendant was to be employed on every ship, and adequate rations loaded for the passage.

The practical results of Portugal's delaying tactics were that she regained her original place as the premier slave trading nation. Between 1810 and 1815 her estimated traffic averaged thirty thousand Negroes a year. But she had greater difficulty in ignoring the declaration signed at the Congress of Vienna by eight nations, which included Portugal. The declaration was typically well meaning but vague, stating that the trade was repugnant to the principles of humanity and of universal morality, and that the powers assembled in Vienna voiced "the wish of their sovereigns to put an end to a scourge which desolates Africa, degrades Europe, and afflicts humanity".

However deeply the sovereign of Portugal may have wished to end this scourge nothing much changed on the African coast. Accordingly, the major powers meeting at Aix la Chapelle in 1818 sent a pointed note to Portugal, urging her to state a definite date for abolition.

To encourage the Prince Regent of Portugal to take some practical action about his purported misgivings about his country's flourishing trade, Britain offered £300,000 as indemnity for the slave ships which had been captured by the Royal Navy. In return, Portugal signed a treaty declaring slave trading in Africa north of the Equator to be illegal, and agreed that slaves should only be bought for Portuguese possessions in the Americas. Portugal could well feel satisfied with this façade of humanitarian progress. It left her free to tap the newest and cheapest sources of slaves in the area of the Congo and in Angola. The market in which she was almost exclusively interested was the slave labour force in her own colonies. In the event, Portugal did little to observe even these tolerant regulations. Maximum numbers of slaves on the five slaves per two tons agreement were regularly exceeded. Negroes were bought and loaded in areas just north of the Equator, or loaded after assembly at Sao Tomé, which was right on the Equator. Sailing instructions were made out to Portuguese possessions, but the captains dropped off slaves wherever the market was open. Apart from this illicit trading, an estimated 56,000 Negroes were landed in Brazil in 1822.

Canning's patience was exhausted by the flagrant infringements of the agreement, and in 1823 he issued a strongly termed reproof, expressing the disgust and indignation which was growing up in England at the apparent determination of Portugal not only to foster the unprotected slave trade but to connive at every infraction of the treaties by her seamen. There was no reply, whereupon Canning withdrew the right of compensation payable for the detention of Portuguese slavers by Royal Navy patrols.

By this time Brazil had proclaimed her independence, and Portugal could no longer hide behind the permit to service her own possessions with Negro labour. But Brazil's separation merely aggravated the situation. Portugal obstinately resisted abolition not only because of her need to earn revenue from the trade, but because admission of the illegality in taking slaves to Brazil would confirm her acceptance of Brazil's severance from the mother country. Not until 1826, by which time Brazilian independence was recognised, did Portugal acknowledge her duty to observe the treaties and abolish her slave trade. This she was then able to do without much damage to Portuguese business interests. Brazil professed to be bound by the international treaties signed by Portugal prior to the former's independence, but in practice she ignored those concerned with slave trading. While Portugal loftily proclaimed her support of abolition of a trade in which her main market had revolted against her, Brazil played for time. She signed a convention with Britain on November 23, 1826, promising to abolish slave trading in three years. This, of course, enabled Portuguese slavers to change to Brazilian colours and continue as before. When the three years' respite was drawing to a close Brazil applied for an extension, but Lord Aberdeen, who was appointed Foreign Secretary after Canning became Prime Minister, rejected the proposal. Obstinately Brazil tried again in the following year to persuade Britain to agree to a postponement. Influential London financial interests which were acting as private bankers to the Emperor of Brazil helped to exert this pressure. But Aberdeen was adamant. He again refused to approve an extension.

The real culprits remained the slave shippers financed by Lisbon business men who used Brazil as a screen for their operations. Internal political upheaval in Portugal made it impossible for Britain to organise any agreement which had any chance of being observed. But in 1832 Palmerston reminded the Cortes that with the independence of Portugal the country's arguments on the vital need to maintain slaving had disappeared. For a year Portugal managed to avoid a written reply, though she gave suitable verbal assurances. In the autumn of 1834 Britain once again forcibly reminded Portugal that it was high time that the agreement of 1815 was put into force. For eighteen months the negotiations dragged on; then Palmerston summoned the Portuguese ambassador to the Foreign Office and handed him a note which recorded evidence of the blatant connivance of the Portuguese government and the governors in her African colonies in slaving. It was a degrading experience for Baron de Moncorvo, the ambassador, to have to admit that the charges were correct, and he had to apologise. The interminable negotiations were resumed, and as interminably interrupted as one government after another fell. Finally, in December, 1836, Portugal announced the final and entire abolition of the slave trade.

The fine-sounding words were, in fact, intended to apply only to traffic in slaves between Africa and America. There was no restriction on the transportation of slaves between the African mainland and Portuguese islands on the coast. As Portugal had for centuries built up an efficient system of collecting Negroes at assembly compounds on off-shore islands the basic system remained in operation. Transit from the islands to the Americas was the problem of the slave runners. The practice of sailing along the African coast for thousands of miles, and always having the defence, if boarded by a Royal Navy investigating party, that the Negroes on board were merely being shipped from one Portuguese African settlement to another was immediately adopted by shippers of half a dozen countries. The flag of Portugal became a flag of convenience. Ship's papers confirming Portuguese hire or ownership were readily sold in Lisbon to any applicant. None of the slave traders in the Portuguese colonies had any qualms about selling Negroes to French, American, or British brokers on these ships, whether they had the correct papers or not. The colonists regarded the agreements with Britain as an aberration of a government in Lisbon which would soon fall like all the others. The contempt for the central government was such that the

Governor of Mozambique refused to make the order banning slavery public.

The decree of 1836 had in theory been a voluntary action by Portugal. No formal treaty had been signed. A draft was drawn up in July, 1838, which Portugal refused to sign. Britain at long last lost her patience. In August, 1839 a Bill passed both Houses authorising British naval ships to detain and search suspected Portuguese slavers, and authorising an Admiralty Court to have them broken up if suspicions proved correct.

By this time the daughter nation of Brazil had in effect become the kingdom of the Portuguese monarchy and Don Pedro, who had proclaimed himself Pedro I, was happy enough to indicate the progressive character of his rule by issuing a decreee that all slaves brought into Brazil should be free, all slave traders fined and physically punished, and all slave ships confiscated. Pedro abdicated shortly afterwards, but even if he had remained in power it would have been impossible to enforce his emancipation decree. Slaves were simply landed on any deserted part of the coast which offered an anchorage instead of the slave ships entering Rio de Janeiro, though even in that port the search regulations were openly ignored. As late as 1839 more than sixty slave ships openly discharged slave cargoes in Rio. In no other port in the Americas was the trade so blatantly carried on, and the result was an intensification of British patrols. In 1840 the known landings at Rio did not exceed ten ships. Within the country some slaves were given their liberty and then offered the same jobs as they had had before. A widespread scheme was launched to make the ex-slaves self-employed. Agricultural and cattle workers were loaned money to buy tools, saddles, animal feed, seeds and so on; miners were sold tools on credit. The figure was invariably fixed so that with interest the Negro got steadily deeper into debt. The misery of life when even food was beyond the means of the free slave was an effective example for other slaves; they feared emancipation. Their owners were happy enough to agree that they should not have it. The edict of Pedro I was soon forgotten. Not until 1888 was slavery officially abolished within the borders of Brazil.

The second greatest market for slaves—the Spanish colonies —proved as obdurate as Portugal. The Marquis Wellesley was the British ambassador in Madrid when the first attempt was made to obtain Spain's signature to a treaty in 1809. Perhaps understandably, with the Napoleonic wars sweeping through the Iberian Peninsula, the Spanish Government did nothing. Not until July, 1814, with Napoleon presumed permanently out of harm's way on Elba, were negotiations resumed. Britain dangled an attractive loan of £800,000 in return for restriction of slave purchase to the same area as Portugal, south of the Equator, with cessation of all trading by 1819. The money and the agreement were rejected, the Crown confining itself to a pious statement of a distaste for the traffic, and a half-hearted hope that in future Spain would confine her trading supplies to her own possessions.

Spain was compelled to go along with the major powers at the Congress of Vienna and sign the anti-slave trade declaration. It had no effect, and Britain continued to exert pressure on Spain. In 1817 Spain agreed to abolish the trade in all her possessions after May 30, 1820, to stop trading north of the Equator immediately, and to grant Royal Navy patrols the right to search and detain Spanish ships if they had slaves on board and if it could be proved they had been shipped from a port north of the Equator. Spain got £400,000 as compensation for past and future losses of slave ships and trading profits.

Slave ships continued to sail under the Spanish flag, but most were ostensibly based on Cuba. With some justification Madrid protested that she could not control the planters and local officials in Cuba. England had had experience of ruling Cuba for one unhappy year in 1762, and had been glad to return the island to Spain in exchange for Florida. Britain accepted this half-hearted apology but warned Spain that unless more forceful control was imposed on Cuban slavers Spain would look to Britain in vain for help in suppressing any Cuban effort to obtain her independence. Obligingly Madrid issued a royal decree ordering the Governor-General of Cuba to check every vessel entering Cuba from Africa and to prosecute all persons involved if it contained slaves. The order had no effect.

Between June, 1830 and June, 1835 ten formal approaches were made to Spain to enforce suppression of her slave trade. Usually Spain made verbal assurances but omitted to put anything in writing. She finally gave way and on June 28, 1835, signed an abolition treaty. It was stringently drawn up, but there was one loophole. Both British and Spanish naval vessels were given the right of search of suspected slavers, and the mixed courts set up in Cuba and elsewhere were to deliver released Negroes to the government of the capturing naval vessel. Thus it was merely necessary for Spanish patrols based on Cuba to increase the efficiency of their search, or to "capture" a slaver with the connivance of the merchants, for the slaves to be sold in Cuba as usual. In theory such slaves were supposed to get their liberty. In practice they were given apprenticeship papers which they could not, of course, read. Their employers then treated them as slaves. By 1840 at least eight thousand Negroes were existing in Cuba under this form of apprenticeship, and Palmerston tried to persuade Spain to order them to be taken before the mixed court of justice at Havana to check on the degree of freedom they enjoyed, and to ask them if they would prefer to be transferred to a British colony. Spain refused to consent to this interference with her internal affairs.

But the treaty did have some benefit. After it came into operation in 1836 slave ships putting into Havana, after landing their Negroes along the Cuban coast, decreased to three in 1837 and two in 1839, an understandable drop when Spanish ships were liable to search and breaking up for sale as lumber. But the traders were busily financing expeditions by other nations. Portuguese slavers entering Havana rose from eight in the pre-treaty year of 1835 to forty-eight in 1837. Brazilian and American ships were frequently seen, and even one flying the Russian flag.

Cuba was in the midst of an economic boom and at that time needed slaves probably more urgently than any other country in the New World. Sugar plantations were being extended every year, and her sugar exports exceeded those of any other country, or combination of countries. News of the Congress of Vienna agreement on abolition of slave trading sent the planters into panic, and between 1817 and 1820 the number of Negroes imported averaged 39,000 a year. Even after the treaty of 1835 the intake decreased only slowly, and five years afterwards nearly fifteen thousand a year were still coming in—plus an unknown number landed secretly and hurried off to the plantations by night.

Cuba's dependence on a massive slave population produced a classic proof of the basic economic defects of the slave system.

The local authorities and the wealthy merchants advocated slavery because of the profits from import duties and slave sales. The planters who had been long established in the island were turning against it; some had noted the greater efficiency resulting from free labour, however badly paid and tied with long-term contracts. Many acutely feared the competition of new planters who could start plantations with little capital provided they could get credit to buy a few score slaves. The Madrid Government feared the consequences in a colony of a powerful, restless community with a potential slave army at its disposal. It also wanted to solve problems at home by settling Spanish peasants in Cuba on smallholdings, and some six hundred Catalonian people were sent to Cuba in 1840.

They had little chance of making a living in a slave-dominated agricultural economy. But the most formidable resistance came from the Creole population. Large-scale slave immigration had begun about a century earlier, and by the 1830s first and second generation families of mixed ancestry had become numerous. With the Catholic tolerance of such unions, provided the Negro was converted and the marriage properly celebrated, there was no great barrier to their integration. As a result the population of just over 1,100,000 in Cuba consisted of 660,000 coloureds and 440,000 whites. More than 160,000 of the coloured population were free. While a minority of the coloureds exploited Negro slaves with greater viciousness than the whites, the overwhelming number had the intelligence to realise that rigid discrimination by colour for standards of freedom could react to their disadvantage. These people were therefore strongly against slavery. The result was that nearly 50 per cent of the Cuban population was unenthusiastic about maintaining a slave economy.

The third pioneer slaving trading nation, the Netherlands, co-operated with Britain from the outset. At Britain's request an order was issued on January 15, 1814, banning slaving by subjects of the Netherlands on any part of the African coast, and a proposal that, if the Dutch colonies were restored after the war, the trade should also be abolished in those territories. The agreement was confirmed by treaty in May, 1818. Holland was the most conscientious of all the countries with whom Britain concluded anti-slave trading treaties at this period, though one peculiar point of controversy arose in 1840 over

Dutch Negro mercenaries. Holland was one of the first European colonial powers to form native units in her army. They were required to serve in any Dutch possession and were not normally maintained in the locality of their origin. The simplest way to obtain these recruits was to purchase slaves. Recruiting officers were supposed to satisfy themselves that the slaves knew why they had been purchased and to agree to service in the army. The Dutch Government considered that the system was merely a form of conscription, though obviously the majority of the Negroes came from territories which were not in Dutch possession and they could not opt out since they were already enslaved. After protest Holland agreed to abandon the scheme in December, 1841.

Negotiations with France were inevitably difficult on account of her status as an enemy at the outset of the diplomatic campaign and the changes in the regime which followed the wars. During Napoleon's temporary eclipse Britain persuaded Louis XVIII to order an end to the French slaving trade by 1819, with restriction on the trade before that year on her own colonies. The Prince Regent personally entreated Louis to hasten the complete cessation of trading. Wellington was British ambassador in Paris at this time, and he persuaded France to agree in principle to an early instance of economic sanctions as a weapon in international disputes. The proposal was for an alliance of powers to reject imports from any colonial country refusing to combat the illicit importation of slaves. To help persuade France to abolish slaving in her colonies Wellington repeated an idea of the Prince Regent: a sum of money or a West Indian island in compensation. Louis eventually rejected both offers. The best that he was prepared to do was to restrict the purchase of slaves to the coastal belt south of Cape Formosa (near Port Harcourt, Nigeria)—an idea which meant the highly organised Portuguese market was still open to her.

Napoleon's immediate and total abolition of all French activity in the slave trade on March 29, 1815, nine days after he had entered Paris, was, perhaps to the surprise of Castlereagh, confirmed by Talleyrand on July 27, 1815, under the restored monarchy. In effect France was proclaiming lofty views but doing little about taking any action. As a defeated nation she was understandably sensitive to any move which further eroded her independence, and she refused to brand slave trading as piracy or to prohibit imports from the slave-trading colonies of any European power. However, in 1827 a law was passed making French nationals liable to fine, imprisonment, and banishment for participation in the slave trade. Few attempts were made to enforce the law, and providing the slavers, based on Nantes and the ports of Brittany, provisioned with slave supplies outside France they ran little risk of investigation on the high seas.

This lack of maritime supervision of France's slave ships was the principal reason why Britain persisted in requesting rights of search for the Royal Navy. This was grudgingly agreed to in March, 1833, with severe restrictions. Search rights were granted along the African coast from fifteen degrees north of the Equator to ten degrees south (roughly from Cape Verde to Luanda) and out to sea as far as thirty degrees of longitude. Other search zones covered the waters round Madagascar (Malagasy), Cuba, Puerto Rico, and along the Brazilian coast. The areas were later extended to cover virtually the whole o the Atlantic.

The only remaining large-scale slaving nation, the United States, had prohibited the importation of slaves in March, 1807. It was largely a formal gesture to confirm one of the articles in a treaty between the two countries signed in 1806 but never ratified. American shippers rapidly became among the most numerous running the gauntlet of the British patrols. The new American vessels, forerunners of the famous clippers which became supreme on the Atlantic in the middle of the century, were very fast, sailed by highly paid crews and navigated by well-trained masters. They were commodious and built of light weight timber, and consequently could carry a large cargo. Slaves were carried both to the States of the Union, principally the Carolinas and Louisiana, and to Spanish America. These American slavers constantly out-sailed British patrols, and reduced the Royal Navy to a state of impotent fury. But in December, 1809, a patrol overhauled a vessel named the *Amedee* and took her to Tortola, a British colony in the Virgin Islands, where the ship was condemned for destruction. The American owners sued for compensation in the British courts, and appeals eventually left the Privy Council to decide. The decision went against the claimant on the grounds that both

Above, a fragment from *Histoire de Barbarie*, 1637, by Dan, depicting various tortures inflicted on Christian slaves; *below*, H.M.S. *Gorgon*, a British steam frigate attached to the East Coast Slaving Squadron

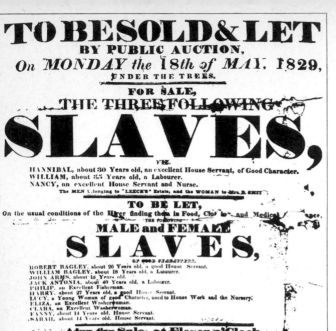

TO BE SOLD & LET
BY PUBLIC AUCTION,
On MONDAY the 18th of MAY, 1829,
UNDER THE TREES.
FOR SALE,
THE THREE FOLLOWING
SLAVES,
VIZ.

HANNIBAL, about 30 Years old, an excellent House Servant, of Good Character.
WILLIAM, about 35 Years old, a Labourer.
NANCY, an excellent House Servant and Nurse.
The MEN belonging to "LEECH'S" Estate, and the WOMAN to Mrs. B. SMIT

TO BE LET,
On the usual conditions of the Hirer finding them in Food, Clothes and Medical ance,
THE FOLLOWING
MALE and FEMALE
SLAVES,
OF GOOD CHARACTERS.

ROBERT BAGLEY, about 20 Years old, a good House Servant.
WILLIAM BAGLEY, about 18 Years old, a Labourer.
JOHN ARMS, about 18 Years old.
JACK ANTONIA, about 40 Years old, a Labourer.
PHILIP, an Excellent Fisherman.
HARRY, about 27 Years old, a good House Servant.
LUCY, a Young Woman of good Character, used to House Work and the Nursery.
ELIZA, an Excellent Washerwoman.
CLARA, an Excellent Washerwoman.
FANNY, about 14 Years old, House Servant.
SARAH, about 14 Years old, House Servant.

Also for Sale, at Eleven o'Clock,
Fine Rice, Gram, Paddy, Books, Muslins, Needles, Pins, Ribbons, &c. &c.
AT ONE O'CLOCK, THAT CELEBRATED ENGLISH HORSE,
BLUCHER,

Left, a slave-sale bill, 1829 posted in the West Indie to advertise a public auc tion; *below,* the Anti-Slavery Convention held in London 1840

Right, slave chains brought from Africa by Dr. Livingstone; *below*, a captured negro wearing a slave yoke

Above, a section of an embarkation canoe; *below*, cross-sections of a nineteenth-century slave ship illustrating how the slaves were stowed for the voyage to the United States

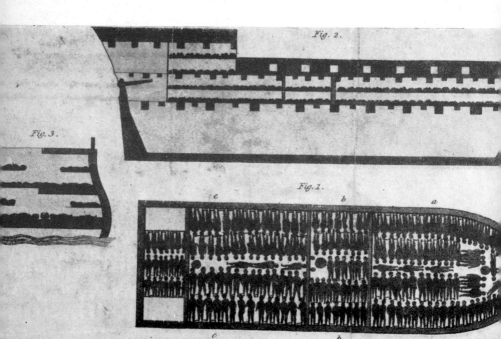

Above, a typical slave-market scene in Cairo in the 1840s; *below*, H.M.S. *Brisk*, under the command of Rear-Admiral Sir Henry Keppel, engaging with the slave ship *The Sunny South*

Above, a slave auction in Virginia, 1861; *below*, a slave-dhow run ashore to avoid capture by a patrol ship

Right, some of the slave traders captured by the British in the 1880s; *below,* a slave chain-gang under the guard of a native soldier

Left, the Nazir of Messeria, a former slave trader who fought in the Battle of Omdurman; *below*, slaves under armed guard clearing a road through the bush in South-West Africa

the USA and Britain had condemned the slave trade as illegal. The delicate matter of the rights of search of a ship under the flag of a friendly nation was diplomatically ignored. Expensive lawsuits satisfied neither country, and the tensions of both the USA and Britain increased.

More effective was legislation passed by the USA in May, 1820, branding the transportation of "any coloured person not being already a slave by the United States' law, in order to make such a person a slave" as piracy and punishable by death. Britain's attempts to confirm her rights of search, forcible seizure, and trial by an international tribunal, were rejected by the USA as an infringement of national security and individual liberties.

Instead the President proposed closer co-operation between the two navies so that a patrol of the suspect's own country could be summoned to investigate after being stopped by a foreign warship. This was ostensibly a reasonable enough idea, but American patrols outside North American coastal waters and the Caribbean were very few. Communication was, of course, impossible unless ships of both navies were in visual contact. The Royal Navy, overwhelmingly the most numerous and powerful, could and did patrol the known sea lanes on both sides of the Atlantic and kept the Middle Passage fairly well covered. The commanders had to watch helplessly while a ship, purporting to be Portuguese or Spanish, but from her lines American built, sailed west from Africa. When an American warship could be spared for patrol off the African coast she soon learned that slavers flourished. The USS *Cyane* on a patrol towards the end of 1820 reported that he had found the coast of Africa "lined with vessels engaged in the slave trade". Five of them he considered were in fact American-owned, and they were sailed back to America for adjudication. Some time later the captain of the USS *Alligator*, on a similar African patrol, boarded four ships believed to be American (though equipped with French papers) and sent them to the United States under guard. Three of them managed to escape to the shelter of French colonies.

The months' long wrangle which developed was not motivated by evasiveness on the part of the USA. She wanted slave trading to be classified as piracy, and she proposed this to every nation with which she had diplomatic relations. Britain was unwilling to endorse a move which could make slave trading a capital charge, with all its attendant problems of who and how many of those involved were to be executed. The USA repeated its dislike of rights of search on American ships being given to foreign nations or of investigation and trial being conducted by an international tribunal, though in fact the House of Representatives was not so sensitive on these points as the President. Compromise was reached by August, 1823, with Presidential approval for negotiations to begin on the basis of international rights of search on condition that the captured master and crew be handed over for trial in their own country.

Britain thereupon rushed through a Bill making British slaving an act of piracy, but this proof of goodwill did not impress the US Senate. It objected to British patrols on the coast of North America, and to British proposals for the trial of suspects sailing under spurious papers or in ships which were neither British nor American. Britain was prepared to give way on the second objection, but not on restrictions on her patrols along the American coast. In 1825 the negotiations completely collapsed.

More pressure was exerted on the United States in 1831 and 1833. Delays in replying were inevitable because of political considerations. Government spokesmen unofficially explained that the President was wary about aggravating the "excited feelings in the Southern States". Britain was therefore not surprised when in October, 1834, the USA formally refused to be party to any international agreement, the explanation being that its own methods were best suited for its own people and for meeting US obligations to the civilised world.

A natural Anglophobia among those US representatives who had personally experienced the cost and pain of gaining independence was natural enough. Liberty was not to be lightly surrendered to an ex-enemy pre-eminent in sea power at a time when a steamship had successfully crossed the Atlantic and had heralded a new era of maritime supremacy. This objection was at least as valid politically as the practical demands of the Southern States for slave labour.

There were numerous examples of the genuine efforts of the USA to enforce its own anti-slave trading laws. The courts did not hesitate to condemn ships arrested while carrying slaves when there was no doubt of their nationality. But judges found these cases of growing complexity where the letter of the law was observed. No court, British or American, could have taken action. One famous instance was the *Butterfly*, boarded and captured on her way from America to Africa. There was no doubt that the ship had been chartered, fitted out, and provisioned for a slaving expedition by United States citizens. However, just prior to her departure a contract was drawn up to deliver her for sale to a Spaniard living in Africa. Thus the ship was American while outward bound and so free from search by British patrols. On the homeward trip her Spanish papers would effectively eradicate any risk of the charge of piracy applying to a US slaver. The ship was boarded and captured by a US patrol shortly after she left the States. The court's decision was that the ship had in law been sold when the contract was signed for transfer prior to her voyage; she was therefore Spanish when captured. The judge said that the *Butterfly* must therefore be delivered to the American claimant so that he could honour his contract with the Spanish purchaser. The Appelate Court reversed this decision, stating that the sale could not be regarded as completed until delivery at the specified port in Africa. Therefore at the time of capture she was American. The ship was condemned for destruction.

When a ship with this kind of complicated ownership was stopped by a Royal Navy patrol the investigation became much more of a delicate matter, with the USA watching for any trespass on national privileges. The case of the *Mendon*, a ship of about 140 tons built at Weymouth, Mass., is typical. She was commandeered off Havana in March, 1807, and taken to Dominica by the English privateer *Elizabeth*, whose captain, George Cunningham, made formal application for the ship to be classed as a prize at the Admiralty Court in Barbados.

The *Mendon* had first been observed by a British Navy squadron which was blockading the La Plata river. The squadron commander, Sir Home Popham, finding she was carrying slaves, warned her not to attempt to enter any port except the English-held one of Maldonado. The *Mendon*'s captain, Jonathan Fitch, went to Montevideo instead, but was refused landing permission by the Spanish authorities. He then went to Rio de Janeiro for provisions and repairs. He was captured when en route from that port to Cuba.

Fitch, a United States subject, said the ship was sailing under

American colours and had no papers of any other nationality on board. He had been given the command of the ship by John Mackay of Boston, had travelled to Buenos Aires where the ship was berthed, and a Richard Curtis there handed over command to him. Curtis held a United States clearance from the port of Portsmouth, Virginia, issued in 1801, for a voyage by the *Mendon* to the Cape of Good Hope.

Under Fitch's command the ship (which had just finished a round voyage Rio–London–Mozambique–Rio) was loaded with tallow and sailed for London. With an assorted cargo of trade goods she then sailed for the mouth of the Congo, where she bought slaves. These Negroes were on board when she was captured.

On the face of it a clear case of wholly American ownership, with easily identified persons involved. But subsequent evidence showed how complicated promoters of a slaving enterprise could make discovery of the real ownership of such a ship. The actual owner appeared to be Mungo Mackay of Boston. He obtained the ship by a bill of sale made out in Buenos Aires by the previous owner, Philip Riley, to Mungo's brother, John Mackay. However, all cargo was the property of Jonathan Fitch who had been living in London for twelve months and therefore claimed that he was a temporary subject of Britain. Still further complications arose with the information that Fitch had chartered the ship for the voyage from London through a British shipping agent, William Todd, and documents proved that Fitch had indeed paid £500 to Todd for the charter. In return Todd had effected insurance with London underwriters and obtained all necessary British authorisation for the voyage.

The case went to the Lords. The ship and cargo were restored to Fitch and John Mackay. Under the letter of the law it was the inevitable finding. The slaves had been taken in the Congo, an area not subject to restrictions. The ship was stopped when genuinely en route for Havana. The master's defence, when stopped in the La Plata estuary, that water and provisions were urgently needed, could not be contradicted. And the ship was almost certainly American owned, despite the cargo owner's residence in London and the direct interest of London shipping agents.

Subterfuges of this kind became numerous, and neither

country was anxious to get involved in costly and futile lawsuits, so that the temptation was to turn a blind eye to fraudulent papers, and to accept the claims of legal trading instead. This was wise because, as time went on, the legal niceties were carefully covered by documents bearing every indication of authenticity. Frequently US consuls in countries still permitting slaving gladly arranged for American ships to be furnished with appropriate papers of nationality. Particularly notorious in this regard was Nicholas Trist, the US consul in Havana. Trist had been secretary to Andrew Jackson. He was an honourable and responsible career diplomat, and his activities on behalf of American slave traders, however infuriating to the Royal Navy, were undoubtedly inspired by patriotism and not by bribes. He was only one of the numerous American officials who believed British activities to suppress slave trading were an example of England's characteristic hypocrisy. The belief was not only that Britain was consolidating her world-wide mastery of the seas but cunningly creating a new colonial empire for herself. By making it impossible for other countries to participate in Africa's staple trade Britain was paving the way to take every kind of African trade and future industrial development.

Such sensitiveness about British ambitions neatly played into the hands of shippers and southerners who had selfish reasons to maintain the slave trade. Movements to maintain or renew African imports of Negroes continued sporadically in the USA well into the 1850s.

If negotiations with the major slave trading nations were difficult and prolonged, there were also other complications in Britain's international campaigns because numerous countries might be tempted to enter the slave trade should the large maritime powers abandon it. Some presented no problem because of their willing co-operation. Sweden, Denmark, Austria, Russia, and Prussia all promised support for the slaving restrictions discussed at the Congress of Vienna. As none was at that time engaged in any large-scale slaving, or ever had been, agreement was neither costly nor did it necessitate internal legislation—a fact which merchants looking for flags of convenience later remembered. The unfamiliar colours of Russia were later seen on a slave ship off Africa bearing the equally unfamiliar name of *Goloubtchic*. At about the same period Greek ships appeared off Africa, and in 1840 Greece was belatedly approached to ban the trade. This was a rather embarrassing matter for Greece; while the ships off Africa were in fact chartered by non-Greeks, there were Greek sloops in the Mediterranean carrying slaves from North Africa to Istanbul, a traffic she shared wtih the independent Italian state of Tuscany. Both states were persuaded to abolish this traffic, though Turkey still got her slaves overland.

The break-up of the Spanish Empire in Central and South America presented almost insoluble complications in an area where slaves could be counted in millions and replacements were constantly required. Not the least of the difficulties were the revolutions and counter-revolutions, break-ups and confederations which continued right through the century. But with patience and persistence Britain approached every country where she had diplomatic representation or could make contact through trading agents. Strong leanings towards liberty after colonial oppression aided these efforts even if signatures on agreements were the only positive action many of these nations took. Usually treaties similar to those made with Spain were most acceptable to these nations. Generally speaking states with borders on the Atlantic approved of, or at least agreed not to resist, search by British patrols.

This prolonged and wearisome campaign of legal negotiation to destroy the Afro-American slave trade took close on thirty years before every nation in Europe and America with any pretensions to a merchant navy had agreed to brand slave trading as criminal. In most of these nations of the New World slavery still existed, and the effects were not noticeable on the economy nor of much benefit to the slaves who worked for it.

But the dimensions of the benefits to the African races were to be seen along that sorry African coastline which for nearly four centuries had been the source of immense fortunes for the white races and untold tragedy for the black.

For the first time since the adventurers of Europe had sailed into the river estuaries and harbours of West Africa the sight of a great sailing ship created a sense of security instead of terror. British naval ships were anchored at the mouth of every large river and at every point where slave compounds had been built. Tribes on the coast understood dimly that the British were there to prevent slave loading. For some the news was well-nigh disastrous and they disappeared into the interior in the face of financial ruin and the possibility of vengeance. For the ordinary Negroes, especially after slavery and transportation were not the inevitable punishment for a petty crime, the result of defeat in a minor war, or sudden kidnapping, the change restored their tribal pride and enabled them to re-build their traditional way of life almost forgotten for generations.

Many of the Negroes living in areas exploited by Portugal, Spain and France, who had been converted to Christianity, knew that their Holy Father had endorsed their right to freedom. A Papal Bull issued in December 3, 1839, called "the carrying of human beings into bondage an act disgraceful to humanity", and earnestly admonished all Christians to abandon the trade. This Bull was distributed by Protestant Britain throughout the world to augment the normal information channels of the Roman Church.

Naval landing parties went ashore and destroyed the slave compounds where niceties of colonial control permitted; elsewhere native chiefs themselves organised the destruction, with the European agents not daring to interfere. Native slave traders were compelled to keep their slaves farther from the coast, waiting for messages about some zone of clandestine trade or hoping that the watching British sloop would weigh anchor and depart. For scores of these men the cost of feeding the slaves while they waited weeks and months for a trading opportunity proved too high. The slaves were abandoned.

Domestic slaves in African communities revolted and took their freedom without suffering retaliation. During 1841 a series of agreements was made with chiefs on the coast of the Gulf of Guinea to abolish slave trading. Favours in trading of goods were offered in exchange, with the warning that infringement of the agreement would result in a cessation of supplies. Inevitably the agreements were frequently broken because of the soaring prices offered by slave runners when supplies of Negroes became short. But such infringements were due more to the inability of the chiefs to prevent the passage of small groups of slaves through their territories rather than their connivance in the traffic. The lesson that trading in merchandise could be more profitable than in human beings was learned by experience.

Ten

The propaganda to end the slave trade had been concentrated on the methods of capturing Negroes in Africa and the horrors of the Middle Passage. Surprisingly little was known about the slaves' lives once they arrived in the New World. The general attitude of the time was that all work was exhausting and prolonged. It was "the curse of Adam", and the bulk of humanity had to live with it, in contrast to the minority who were privileged by birth to enjoy a life of leisure.

Revelations of long hours of toil in excessive heat would have brought little reaction. The labouring classes of Britain were accustomed to work for almost every waking hour of their days from childhood to death, and then to earn only just enough for survival. Work was the alternative to starvation; however miserable it made life, it was the only desirable activity. "Honest labour" was a virtue, too; as the leisured classes constantly reminded their employees. No doubt the most humane abolitionist saw nothing wrong in having his life made easy for him by household servants who worked every hour of their lives from dawn to bedtime. Most who were wealthy enough to finance the campaign drew their incomes from commerce run by overworked and underpaid staffs.

Consequently, the reaction of the West Indian planters to the impossibility of abandoning slave labour, the revelations of the enormous fortunes which had been made for decades, and the natural curiosity about the fate of those thousands of Negroes who survived transportation, all aroused interest in this distant part of the world where Britain had annexed, conquered, or negotiated a mass of islands.

Quickly the propagandists supplied the information the public wanted; as quickly the defendants of the slave system issued their versions of what happened—often with a result contrary to their intentions. The lives of the Negroes when they were brought on deck for the last time began to fascinate, and often horrify, a nation which had deliberately blinded itself to a situation which had made their own existence, West Indian nabob or Birmingham blacksmith, more comfortable and pleasant.

The first activity was, of course, the sale of the Negroes. A West Indian slave market was the great social and mercantile event of the islands. The traditional method was to spend a day or so fattening up the slaves, making them massage their bodies with oil, and then parading them round the town with drums beating and bagpipes or flutes playing. The slaves were then grouped in the market place (often on a Sunday when the usual market holders were absent and planters could leave their holdings) where an expert factor negotiated the sales.

These public auctions were of prime slaves. The refuse Negroes were sold at candle auctions in the yard of a wharfside tavern. Bids were accepted until an inch of a lighted candle had burned away. The Negroes at these candle auctions were in sorry shape and the buyers had to gauge how much work could be forced out of them before they died. Disgusting methods were used to conceal their defects. The scabs and sores of smallpox and syphilis were covered with iron rust and grease. A case was reported of a group of slaves suffering from dysentery having the rectum sealed with wads of oakum used for caulking ships' decks. Refuse Negroes were ignored by most planters. They were bought by small traders and mulattoes. Some of these Negroes were in such ill-health that even bargain hunters ignored them. They were then abandoned to die where they lay, their bodies later being thrown off the wharf.

There remained one further chance of a bargain when supplies were plentiful through several ships arriving simultaneously. This was the scramble sale. The slave factor, in co-operation with the slaver captain, drew up details of available healthy slaves, giving the prices for men, women, boys and girls. Sales were completed on shore, each purchaser getting a receipt for the number he agreed to take. At a given signal, usually made by firing a gun, the purchasers were allowed on board. The first-comers had the pick of the cargo, the crew merely checking that they had the number and type they had paid for when they left. The sight of a horde of men rushing towards the ship, anchored a hundred yards or so off-shore, the shouts as they fought one another to clamber aboard, and the jostling as they grabbed the best "bargains" terrified the slaves, among whom the rumours about being captured to be eaten had never completely died.

The larger plantation owners selected their "parcels" of new slaves with great care. Those from the Slave Coast known as Whydahs and Nagoes were regarded as obedient and strong workers. The Gold Coast Negroes were preferred for house-work, so the females were selected from these deliveries. Those from the Congo and Angola were strong but of low intelligence. The Senegalese were intelligent and quickly learned crafts. The Ibos were bought cheaply because they were prone to suicide, often in hysterial outbreaks which resulted in mass deaths. Apart from these ethnic characteristics, slaves were selected by tribe and language so they could be taught by existing slaves on the plantation.

Life on a plantation was described very fully, if rather subjectively by Bryan Edwards, a wealthy Jamaican plantation owner. He wrote: "The first gang is summoned to the labours in the field either by a bell or the blowing of a conch shell just before sunrise. They bring with them, besides their hoes or bills, provisions for breakfast; and are attended by a white person, and a black superintendent called a driver. The list being called over and the names of all the absentees noted, they proceed with their work until eight or nine o'clock, when they sit down to breakfast which is prepared in the meantime by a number of women, whose sole employment it is to act as cooks for the rest. This meal commonly consists of boiled yams, eddoes, ocra, calalue, and plantains, or as many of these vegetables as they can procure; seasoned with salt and cayenne pepper; and in truth it is an exceedingly palatable and wholesome mess. By this time most of the absentees make their appearance, and are sometimes punished for their sluggishness by a few stripes of the driver's whip.

"At breakfast they are seldom indulged with more than half or three-quarters of an hour, and having resumed their work, continue in the field till noon, when the bell calls them from labour. They are now allowed two hours of rest and refreshment, one of which is commonly spent in sleep. Their dinner is provided with the addition of salted or pickled fish, of which each Negro receives a weekly allowance.

132

"At two o'clock they are again summoned to the field. At sunset, or very soon after, they are released for the night. If the day has been wet or their labour harder than usual they are sometimes indulged with an allowance of rum."

The average hours of work daily, according to Edwards, totalled ten, though in the cutting season the slaves in the crushing mill and boiling house might work all night, the group being divided into watches. The field workers also toiled the maximum possible hours during cane harvesting. Normally every Sunday was free, as well as alternate Saturdays. There was at least one day off for the three Christian festivals of the year.

The heavy field work as described above applied to the so-called first gang, which consisted of the strongest men and women. The second gang was composed of juveniles, pregnant women, and those suffering from some ailment or disability; they hoed, weeded, and fetched and carried. The third gang consisted of small children, supervised by an ageing Negro woman, who collected fodder, pulled weeds, and took drinking water to their labouring parents; they were there as much to be kept out of mischief and within sight of their mothers as for any work.

Edwards claimed that one English agricultural labourer could do the work of three slaves, and this was possibly true if the comparison is ignored between working in the enervating heat of a sugar cane plantation and labouring in the English countryside. But it must be admitted that when a planter was as wealthy and humane as Edwards, the physical conditions of slavery were not bad. The diet he describes is rich in vitamins and the fish provided protein. Certainly farm workers all over Britain worked ten hours a day and longer in harvest time. Few got any Saturdays off, and those tending animals had only part of Sunday.

In addition to the work rations, Edwards' slaves got regular issues of an unspecified kind of meat, salt and molasses. Their huts, built from twigs interwoven between upright posts and thatched with palm leaves, stood in, or adjacent to, waste land where they were allowed to keep pigs and chickens and to grow food, including bananas and coconuts. That these slave gardens produced a surplus is shown from the fact that on Sundays the Negroes went into the towns and displayed their fruit and vegetables in a market, buying clothes and household goods with the money they took. The sight of these established slaves did have the effect of reassuring newly landed Negroes as they were paraded around the market place prior to the usual Sunday auction.

If the majority of the West Indian plantation slaves lived in conditions comparable to those described by Bryan Edwards, there were thousands who existed in perpetual fear of cruelty as a method of enforcing obedience or of punishing mistakes. Case after case of brutality was revealed during the campaign for abolition. They helped to indicate the basic evil of slavery— its annihilation of human decency and respect.

An incident on the small British island of Nevis illustrated the impossibility of obtaining justice for Negroes even to the extent grudgingly allowed by local legislation. Ten male Negroes and ten female Negroes had been ordered to work at night. This was an infringement of a local work code. The slaves had been driven into the fields by their employer, Edward Huggins, and had then scattered under cover of darkness. At dawn they had been easily rounded up and were then marched by Huggings and his two sons into the market place of Charlestown. There, two expert whippers flogged them. The number of lashes ranged from forty-seven to 365, including 291 on a woman.

Some of the men were permanently injured and one woman subsequently died. Five magistrates watched the flogging, which was legally permitted except for a vagary that whipping must not be cruel. Not through any action by the magistrates, but after moves by some members of the assembly, Huggins was accused of inflicting barbarous and illegal punishment. Members of the jury included Huggins' or his relatives' employees. He was acquitted. Almost immediately after the trial began the death of the flogged woman occurred. The jury absolved Huggins of responsibility.

The Huggins family, one must hope, was exceptionally sadistic. Two years later a son of Huggins shot a Negro boy alleged to be about to commit a theft. The court refused a charge of murder but settled for a fine of £250 for manslaughter. Five years after that Huggins senior was again involved in a whipping incident. He had five Negroes flogged for alleged theft. Put on trial, he was again acquitted.

The worst excesses occurred on the smaller islands or in

remote plantations where public opinion was not strong enough to curb planters with sadistic aberrations. The Nevis case aroused universal anger when the abolitionists published details, with the result that the Governor of the Leeward Islands made a personal investigation. While collecting evidence on the treatment of slaves on Nevis he was told of a wealthy planter in Tortola, a tiny island in the Virgin Islands group, which lay in the extreme north-west of the governor's area of control and was hardly ever visited except by coastal skippers and the occasional customs official. Despite Tortola's distance from Nevis, the notoriety of its most prominent planter, a man named Arthur Hodge, had spread.

Enquiries revealed such a ghastly series of crimes, and such resentment against any interference with a slave owner's rights to do what he willed with his Negroes, that the island was put under martial law. Hodge would clearly be regarded as insane by modern psychiatric opinion, but his mania festered because the law, or absence of law, made his excesses possible.

Hodge hated Negroes, but not to the extent that he refrained from seducing the Negro women. His own mulatto daughter he had kicked so hard on the head that her skull was fractured. He had then booted her body into the air. She was eight years old. Slaves' children had been picked up by Hodge and lowered into tubs of water till they nearly drowned. He then suspended them by their wrists and horsewhipped them. One ten year old boy had been dipped into a cauldron of boiling water. The motive was purely sadistic; no offences by the children were known.

Real or imagined offences by adult slaves were punished with appalling cruelty. Two Negroes who had annoyed Hodge were pinioned to the ground face downwards and flogged for more than an hour; both died. A privileged slave, sent out to locate some runaway slaves, was whipped to death for failing to find them. A slave freed from another plantation, and employed by Hodge as a cooper, was clubbed to death when he grumbled about having to do unskilled field work. A household slave had a hot iron rammed into his mouth; he died from the injuries. Two women slaves, accused by Hodge of putting poison in his food, were held motionless while boiling water was poured down their throats. They died in agony. Altogether

135

Hodge had been responsible for the murders of nearly a hundred Negro men, women, and children.

Despite the notoriety of Hodge's murderous activities, he was accepted as a respectable member of the island's society and was a member of the council. Charged personally by the Governor of the Leeward Islands with the murder of a Negro in a case where Hodge's plantation manager gave irrefutable evidence of the crime, the jury could not possibly find the defendant innocent. Instead a majority put in a plea of mercy. Both the judge and the Governor rejected this plea, and Hodge was executed.

Maniacal crimes of this kind were not, of course, unknown in free societies of the eighteenth and nineteenth centuries. The Marquis de Sade was their contemporary, and even if his writings were unpublished his crimes were well known. And this was a generation which had lived through the excesses of the French Terror. The Hodge case with all its sensational bestiality was, however, a means of dramatically indicating what could— and occasionally did—occur in those "fair jewels of the Crown" in the Caribbean.

Examples of outrageous cruelty were not horrifying on account of their number, but because of the conditions which made brutality possible and the moral state of a white society which condoned it. When a planter ordered a little Negro girl thirty lashes for weeping after she had seen two slave boys given a hundred lashes each for pilfering, the authorities attempted to charge the owner with common assault. The jury considered there was no case.

In another case a clergyman named Rawlins who supervised slaves on a plantation in St. Kitts ordered a slave who had attempted to run away to be flogged till he was unconscious. Next day, chained to another slave, he was made to work in the fields. When he fell to the ground he was beaten until he got to his feet. Before the day was over he was a corpse still attached to the other slave. Despite the jury's verdict that the slave had died "by a visitation of God", on this occasion the culprit was put on trial. The murder charge was altered to manslaughter and Rawlins went to prison for three months and was fined £200. The verdict and punishment caused a local sensation on the grounds of its severity. The whites disapproved of the con-

136

cept that laws applying to the assault and killing of white people could possibly apply to Negroes.

To the white population the Negro slave was an animal—and not a very pleasant animal. Their attitude was summed up concisely by one of their spokesmen in the Parliamentary debates.

The inhabitants of the eastern and western coasts of Africa were stupid and unenlightened, "immersed in the most impenetrable gloom of barbarism, dark in mind as well as body, prodigiously populous, impatient of all control, unteachably lazy, ferocious as their own congenial tigers [*sic*] nor in any respect superior to these rapacious beasts in intellectual advancement but distinguished only by a rude and imperfect organ of speech, which is abusively employed in the utterance of dissonant and inarticulate jargon".

This sort of observation summed up the psychological inability of the West Indian planters, their families, and their white employees to regard a slave as a human being. Very few could agree to any control by an outside body on what they did to their slaves. They could punish in any way they wished, work their labourers to the uttermost limit of their strength, maim or kill in temper or in cold intention.

The courts were rarely able to impose any sort of penalty, for there were few laws against any sort of excess. Lord Seaforth, who was Governor of Barbados during the period when the home Government was framing the anti-slave trading legislation, was one of the few colonial officials who was disgusted at the indifference to the Negroes' sufferings. He was, of course, free from the taint of being reared from childhood in conditions which hardened normal feelings of humanity. Seaforth compiled a report on the number of slaves who had been murdered in Barbados, and cited a typical case to indicate the impotence of the law to do anything about it.

A white soldier, for motives which Seaforth could not discover, shouted at some Negroes returning from cutting sugar cane that he would kill them. Either because they did not understand what he said or believed him to be drunk, they took no notice and continued to walk past him. The soldier, whose name was Hall, thereupon stuck his bayonet into a pregnant woman slave, killing her instantly.

A white man named Harding who had come up at that moment told Hall that he should be hanged for his crime.

Hall laughed. "Why? for killing a Negro?"

Harding determined that something should be done and reported the incident to a local magistrate, who explained that he could do nothing under the law, but he would consult his superiors. From this it appeared that under a technicality, involved with the loss of revenue accruing to the Crown when a slave was exported and duty paid, there might be a penalty of £11 4s. od. for the wanton destruction of a slave. Hall was held in custody for this debt. By the standards of conduct prevailing in Barbados he was extremely unfortunate to have a bill for £11 4s. to pay for a human life. His misfortune was that he had killed wantonly and had been seen by someone with feelings of humanity. Normally a white man killing in temper or from sadistic motives could discover some excuse, the most convenient one being that the death of the victim was an accident.

Seaforth's subsequent attempts to make the murder of a slave a felony was violently resisted by the Assembly in Barbados. They considered it should be a misdemeanour with a fine payable to the Crown. These were the people who had earlier demanded execution for treason for Wilberforce should the slaves in Barbados cause trouble through hearing rumours that they were to be liberated.

But the West Indians holding these obtuse views were for the most part affectionate and kindly according to their own standards. They were prepared, within limits, to be fond of their black, hard-working animals. On the average plantation the Negroes were treated as well as the donkeys and draught horses, though not usually so kindly as the favourite dog or riding horse. The commendatory pat on the head was perhaps the best that the average household slave could expect; those in the fields were for the most part anonymous work animals, known only to the slave master, who might be a mulatto or degenerate white, retaining his job by methods of getting work out of the slaves in ways which the plantation owner preferred not to investigate too closely.

The animal idea was genuine enough. The wives of planters who observed all the rigid conventions of the time as regards exposure of any part of the body or limbs would sometimes have no objection to being waited on in bedroom or bathroom by a male slave. Responsible and intelligent men, called away from their homes on personal or public duties, would order a male slave to sleep on the floor in the wife's bedroom like a guard dog.

Yet the sexual hunger and the virility of the Negro had long been recognised. The Negroes were primitive people with strong passions. Those who managed to survive the passage and subsequent "conditioning period" were in the first flush of adult life and physically very fit. Their hard physical labour, as today's medical knowledge proves, enhanced potency and fertility. In non-Catholic countries, where the animal attitude was strongest, little or nothing was done to institute permanent monogamous unions between a male and female slave, nor was there close supervision of the sleeping quarters which were normally divided into groups of huts for men and women, but built adjacent to one another. All the permissive customs and prohibitive taboos of native Africa were in abeyance. By Christian standards therefore the slaves were sexually immoral and very actively promiscuous. It has been said with some truth that the only pleasures which existed for them were sex and singing. Both were virtually irrepressible.

The contempt for the "pigsty morals" of the slaves did not alter the fact that Negro women were regarded as sexually attractive. A black woman was socially acceptable as a white man's sexual companion by all but the most censorious members of West Indian society. Governor Rickets of Barbados openly maintained a Negro girl at Government House and only at the most formal of functions was she absent. Many of the children of such unions were sent to England for an expensive education, and there were constant attempts to find a compromise on laws designed to prevent Negroes or half-Negroes from inheriting property and the rights of British citizenship. The slaves were not slow to see the advantages of a sexual liaison with their employers. It meant all the difference between working to exhaustion on the land and living in comparative luxury. Even a cast-off mistress of a white man enjoyed great prestige, while a slave woman could consider nothing more desirable than that her daughter should attract a white man. Indeed it was the only chance for the child to evade physical labour as a slave.

By the time of abolition the social classification in the West Indies was based on shades of body colour. At the top were the pure whites; the musteefino, the hybrid of a white man and a mustee; the mustee was the offspring of a white man and a quadroon; a quadroon that of a white man and a mulatto; the mulatto the original racial admixture of a white man and a Negro. The first three stages of descent ranked as white. They were, of course, always free. A mulatto might or might not be free; it depended largely on the attitude of the father. The normal etiquette was to give the child its freedom on reaching adolescence. But as many of these children were the result of chance and temporary liaisons they as often remained slaves. Equally a retrograde union—between a mulatto and a Negro—condemned the offspring to slavery; they were known as Sambos.

The need to breed slaves instead of importing them confronted the planters with a complete reversal of their established policy. So fearful were the planters at any social progress among the slaves that even religious instruction was discouraged. The Anglican Church heeded the planters' claims that Christianity could be a dangerous cult, likely to arouse a reaction of discontent among the slaves. The most active missionaries in Jamaica were at the outset Moravians and Wesleyans, working in the face of the strong opposition that dissenters also experienced in Britain and America.

Deprived of their native religious customs and prevented from embracing those of their white masters, the slaves' spiritual and moral health inevitably deteriorated. An adult Negro, male or female, sold into slavery in Africa was almost certainly married. Only the greatest of good fortune and a series of kindly and considerate traders, slave captains and auctioneers ever resulted in a man and a wife ending up on the same plantation.

Any form of marriage ceremony on the plantation was a rarity, at least until large-scale missionary enterprises got under way as a result of the abolition legislation. Consequently promiscuous sex relations were normal. These were inevitable with the disproportion of the sexes. Six male slaves to one female were a typical ratio on the average plantation. Immorality was increased by the drivers and stronger Negroes keeping half a dozen women for themselves.

Yet breeding slaves proved a formidable task until freedom became a certainty. African women had considerable knowledge of contraception, based largely on the rhythm method but also including herbal pessaries; they knew still more about abortifacients. Pregnancy meant misery while being forced to work when heavy with child, and reduced rations when it was impossible to work. Stillbirths were common because of the prevalence of yaws (a form of syphilis) and the breakdown of native customs at the birth resulted in an abnormally high death rate of new-born babies (and of the mothers) through septicaemia or puerperal fever.

Bonuses and gifts to Negro women were offered to increase the birth rate. Two dollars when the child survived to one year of age or a length of cotton material for swaddling clothes were typical of these bribes. More beneficial to the slave owner was a tax rebate of £1 allowed by Jamaica for every live child born to a slave which maintained or augmented the total number of slaves on the plantation. The short-sighted planter, who could not visualise the situation ten years or so in the future when new slave imports were just a memory, did not consider such a rebate compensated him for the trouble of providing food for a slave child who could not be put to work for at least six years. The rebate was then increased to £3 and any owner of a female slave who had given birth to six children was absolved from paying a poll tax on her.

The breeding policy aided the rich planter and hurt the small farmer. The latter might be glad enough to get rid of a pregnant slave who would be useless for field work for two or three months and buy an ageing man cheaply with a couple of years' work in him. The wealthier man was ready enough to purchase the expectant mother as a long-term investment. He was also prepared to pay a good price for a notoriously virile young male, known as a stud or buck Negro. The reputation of these breeding males is the origin of the belief in Negro virility and sexuality which is widespread today among white men, emerging as a righteous disapproval of miscegenation but based on sex jealousy, and the equally prevalent myth among white women about the Negro's sexual prowess. The generalisation is, of course, a fallacy. There are no physiological or psychological differences to justify such views.

Eventual emancipation or not, the encouragement of Negro increase was slowly recognised as of great ultimate benefit to the West Indies. The locally born creole black, who grew up to accept that he was an inferior in a white society, was amenable to discipline and more intelligent than the imported adult slave, thanks to his knowledge of English and his familiarity with the white man's implements and methods of working. The creole slaves could obtain craft work, and though their servility was as complete as that of the unskilled labourer, their work was less fatiguing. Because of their value they could expect rather better treatment. Many slave owners in the towns had no other source of income beyond that of hiring out craftsman-slaves on contract. Some allowed their slaves to seek work for themselves, taking a specified sum in return. This could leave the craftsman-slave a tiny surplus for his own use. Thus a status one degree above slavery was slowly emerging.

A handful of planters were enlightened enough to experiment with alternatives to slave labour. An Irishman named Josiah Steele with a plantation in Barbados had founded an organisation as early as 1781, which was modelled on the Society of Arts in London. The object was to develop a mixed economy with cottage industries, smallholdings, and small factories. On Steele's own estate physical punishment of employees was abolished, works courts were conducted by Negroes, and all work was paid for. Like so many reformers of his era, Steele considered the Negro was in a stage of civilisation comparable with that of Europe five centuries earlier. He inaugurated a manorial system in 1789, with his ex-slaves bound to the land, and liable to cultivate the manorial lands for specified periods. Steele died before his system could really be tested.

Another progressive planter also failed through his untimely death. He was a novelist, Mathew Lewis, who inherited a plantation from a relative who had been an absentee owner. Lewis visited his inheritance, and was appalled by what he saw, putting down most of the misery to the ignorance of owners, who were humane themselves, but preferred to evade their responsibilities by never visiting the West Indies. His efforts were really constructive—investing in better tools and such machinery as was available, shortening hours of work, and giving holidays. The changes were made in 1816; Lewis died two years later, and his innovations were abandoned.

The almost complete cessation of Negro imports presented an opportunity, never to return, to reach some kind of economic and social integration. The majority of the Negroes were becoming Westernised; they could speak a form of English and readily understood it; they were eager to emulate the white man's ways. More particularly they were hungry for the white man's religion.

For far too long they had been deprived of this spiritual privilege. To the average planter, conscientiously visiting his church several times on a Sunday and holding family prayers morning and evening, the creed of universal love among men did not apply to black men. Too many of the Anglican clergy succumbed to the conventional attitude to slaves. Too many were tempted to augment their stipends with secular activities, so that they were plantation managers six days a week and priests on only one. Only in Jamaica was an official and genuine effort made to give the slaves some religious teaching. In 1816 the appointment of twenty-one curates, and the construction of hutments (so the white worshippers' churches need not be used), were authorised. The stipend offered was so small that no applicants came forward. An increase in pay and a relaxation of the qualifications brought in part-time clergy who rarely had any sense of vocation and did not intend to devote more than a minimum amount of time to their religious duties. Army and navy officers retired on half-pay after the Napoleonic Wars found the curacy of the souls of the slaves a delightful sinecure. One calmly explained that it was impossible for him to officiate in the hut more frequently than every other Sunday because of his business activities.

The Baptists, Methodists, and Moravians remained the most active and conscientious, though hampered by lack of money. Contributors to missions both in Britain and the USA were more interested in the conversion of Negroes in Africa than among the slaves in European colonies.

Few planters had the vision to see that Christianity could help in the transition to emancipation. Yet they could see for themselves that the converted Negro was more moral, more cheerful, and more willing to work conscientiously under decent treatment—these benefits apart from the spiritual rewards which they purported to believe accrued to themselves from membership of the Church. But they raved about the menace of the dissenters, branding the Methodists, for example, as "meddling, fanatical, hypocritical, canting knaves", attacking the missionaries and in some places committing acts of vandalism on their gimcrack little houses of worship.

The Established Church inaugurated two colonial dioceses in 1824—Jamaica, and Barbados and Leeward Islands. The two bishops, William Coleridge and Christopher Liscomb, were given salaries of £4,000 and their duties were clearly to provide adequate religious instruction for the slaves and to investigate the attitude of the white congregations and clergy.

The hostility of both local priests and slave owners was such that the bishops and their assistants were regarded as spies. The few clergy who spoke out against the abuse of the Negroes were branded as troublemakers. Any priest actually condemning slavery went in risk of being hounded out of the islands. He had little support from the local religious organisations which accepted the principle of slavery. Even the Codrington estate on Barbados, run by the Society for the Propagation of the Gospel as a training centre, employed three hundred slaves.

Some of the clergy were active propagandists for the retention of slavery. The Rev. George Bridges of Jamaica was well paid by the planters for the stream of pamphlets and letters he produced. This attitude by many priests of the Established Church resulted in outright suppression of the Non-Conformists. Local legislatures prosecuted Wesleyan missionaries for failure to report for military service. Slaves were forbidden to attend services. Planters' white employees broke up meetings. When slave unrest occurred in Demerara in 1823 John Smith of the London Missionary Society was arrested on a charge of inciting the slaves to revolt and put in prison. He was already dying from tuberculosis and was able to cheat the gallows before the sentence of death could be carried out.

A few weeks later, on Barbados, William Shrewsbury was attacked, his home and chapel destroyed, and he and his wife were forced to flee to a ship at St. Vincent about to sail for England.

A pamphlet distributed the next day described this incident as the action of "a party of respectable Gentlemen [who] formed the resolution of closing the Methodist concern altogether. With this view, they commenced their labours on Sunday evening, and they have the greatest satisfaction in announcing that by twelve o'clock last night they effected the total destruction of the Chapel."

The Governor's offer of a reward for information on the identity of the vandals had no result. Posters appeared warning informants that there would be retaliation and "punishment which their crime will justly deserve".

The violent temper of the West Indies indicated by this sort of incident was the result of the decline in trade since supplies of new slaves had been terminated and the realisation that events were moving inexorably to total abolition. For years the planters had been living through an economic storm, with violent changes from boom to depression. First there had been chaos as the result of the American Rebellion. Then actual war swept through the islands in the clash between England and France. More significant changes, as regards the economic results of any end to the slavery situation, came with the Negro revolt in St. Domingo. The island had been by far the biggest exporter in the Caribbean of tropical products such as sugar, cotton and coffee. The revolt of the mulattoes and slaves in that island resulted in an almost total cessation of supplies, with consequent increased demand for the produce of other islands. Between 1792 and 1800 the price of sugar and coffee from English islands at least doubled, largely because the planters were unable to increase production to meet the demand. Price controls imposed by Parliament made it unprofitable for the planters to go in for expansion, costly because of the lack of slaves.

The potential boom which could have been maintained by the planters if they could have increased the acreage of cultivation turned into a depression. Sugar began to arrive from India, where the East India Company was encouraging production in Bengal. The success of this competitor once more illustrated the economic advantages of free labour over slave labour. In India the workers were adequately paid and could earn more by extra effort. To make their work profitable they were given good tools. In turn Bengal became a market of vast potential for British manufactures required by workers with money to spend. On every count the Indian paid labourer had advantages over the West Indian slave. Despite energetic activity by planter interests in Parliament Bengal sugar, hampered by preferential import duties for the West Indian produce, began to arrive in quantity, and was soon cheaper. The records of a London firm, John Travers and Sons, show East Indian sugar quoted at 48s.–66s. per cwt and West Indian sugar at 60s.–86s.

This deleterious situation was aggravated after slave trading was prohibited. Plantations in Cuba, Brazil and other American possessions of the European powers which had refused to abolish the slave trade or were blatantly ignoring the treaties, grew apace. Cuba alone increased her slave labour force by 320,000 Negroes in the first twenty-five years of the nineteenth century. The Cuban planters had to pay from £25 to £40 for a slave brought despite the difficulties involved in evading the naval patrols, but this was infinitely cheaper than breeding a Negro worker, estimated in Jamaica to cost £120 before the child reached the age of fourteen and was ready to work like a man. The result was that Cuban sugar was landed in Europe for 30s. per cwt; the best that Jamaica could manage was 53s.

There seemed to be no end to the planters' troubles. From July, 1824, movement of slaves from one British West Indian island to another was prohibited except in the case of personal servants. There were, inevitably, instances of planters moving to another island with a hundred or so "personal servants", but on the whole the law was obeyed. It had further serious economic effects. Many of the plantations in Barbados and Jamaica had been cultivated for a dozen generations, and the soil was exhausted, while by contrast Trinidad had not been fully developed by the Spanish, and virgin soil was readily available. But migration from the dying Jamaican and Barbados plantations to new land in Trinidad with an adequate labour force was impossible.

The shortage of slave labour soon became acute in the islands. The planters then approached the East India Company and arranged for the delivery of Chinese labourers, together with implements and supplies of rice, with the object of helping out on the sugar plantations and starting rice production. The Chinese numbered 192 and they were put to work under government supervision of wages and working conditions. The conditions of labour were undoubtedly far better than those in China, but the coolies had been transferred without their women. Most asked to be sent back home. Those who remained used their characteristic flair for trade and became shop-keepers.

The idea of engaging indentured foreign labour was suspected by abolitionists to be a method of reviving the slave trade in another guise. But there was no compulsion to migrate, and labour contracts were fair and reasonable. Large numbers of Indians gladly accepted the offer of work, and proved more stable than the Chinese. Intakes of Indians into the larger islands, such as Trinidad and Jamaica, and into Guyana continued into the twentieth century. The racial mixture of Indian-Sino-Afro-Anglo hybrids in the Caribbean today are the most remarkable and interesting examples of *homo sapiens* as he might be—and as he will be eventually through evolution, according to some anthropologists and geneticists, when the entire population of the world will be coffee-coloured.

Expensive importations of Asiatics, programmes of breeding slaves, illicit purchases of contraband slaves, were no more than palliatives. Many planters believed that London was encompassing their complete ruin. Feeling ran so high that the British Government feared there would be revolution. In March, 1831, a conference was held in Barbados attended by delegates from eleven British islands—easily the most comprehensive meeting of representatives of island legislatures held until that time. The object was to complain about the hopelessness of trying to compete with the slave-importing islands belonging to other European powers and to protest against the emancipation of the inadequate number of slaves the planters still owned.

Despite demands for representation in Parliament, and even for independence or union with the United States, the islands were informed in November, 1831, through their Governors, of regulations they must observe. These included standards for slave housing, rations, and clothing, restriction of punishments, and, most important of all, the institution of a nine-hour working day. This last stipulation caused the greatest resentment. It was, of course, a radical change. Most workers in the United Kingdom would have been delighted if a law existed enforcing a nine-hour working day. If it had been promulgated no doubt the farmers and manufacturers at home would have reacted as violently as did the West Indian planters.

Mass meetings were held, and enforcement of the order described as the road to ruin. In St. Lucia all merchants closed down their business for nine days in protest. Many planters promised to shut their sugar mills and to withhold tax payments. Parliament thereupon conceded that a twelve-hour day might be worked during harvesting.

Inevitably, the slaves learned of the major changes in their lives which the masters of their masters were planning. They were kept under stricter control by planters who could never forget the massacres of St. Domingo. But outbreaks of trouble were surprisingly few.

The worst incident was that in St. James, Jamaica, during the slaves' feasting and singing over Christmas, 1831. The Negroes went on the rampage, believing that the planters were disobeying their Royal master's order to free them. They allegedly caused more than £1 million worth of damage before the rising was ruthlessly suppressed by troops firing into the bands of rioting slaves. Later more than a hundred Negroes were hanged and large numbers flogged.

The outbreak was said to have been caused by the sermons of Baptist preachers on the subject of the Nativity. Five of them were arrested. Local newspapers demanded that they be hanged, as shooting was too good for them, and pointed hints about mob rule were made with details of suitable trees for hangings. The Colonial Church Union, ostensibly an organisation to further the slaves' spiritual welfare, became the most vociferous persecuter of the Non-Conformists. The Union was instrumental in encouraging mobs to destroy a score of chapels and missionaries' homes. All attempts to obtain proof of the preachers' complicity failed, and they had to be released, some of them wisely retiring to England. A year later the Colonial Church Union was declared by a Royal edict to be an illegal organisation.

Thereafter militant action declined in favour of various suggestions, some genuinely constructive and some merely sarcastic, on methods to achieve emancipation without economic disaster or civil upheaval.

Money was, of course, the dominant factor. One idea was for the Negroes' sympathisers to contribute to a liberation fund; £16½ millions at compound interest for fifteen years would produce enough to buy the freedom of every slave in the Caribbean. Another was a special United Kindom tax to produce £3 millions annually for fifteen years. An alternative was a tax of ½d. per lb. on all sugar sold in the United Kingdom, the money purchasing slaves as it came in.

More thoughtfully conceived were schemes for the Home Government to buy the slaves and then hire them to planters as Government employees at a rate to cover the outlay by

1868; for all plantations to be nationalised, the owners getting 4 per cent bonds in return; for slaves to do additional work for wages twenty-five hours per week so they could buy their freedom from compulsory saving of the money they earned.

The Government was already decided. Lord Stanley, the Colonial Secretary, prepared a scheme for emancipation in the West Indies which was a humanitarian plan far in advance of anything his Ministerial colleagues envisaged in the way of domestic legislation on child labour, the Poor Law, or hours of work in mine and factory. It was proof of how deep was the public feeling about slavery in British territory.

The Emancipation Law came into effect on August 1, 1834. All slaves became apprentices for six years in the case of field workers, and four years for all others. At the end of the apprenticeship they were completely free, and they had the right to buy their freedom earlier if they had the money. All Sunday work was prohibited, and the working week was to be forty-five hours.

The small colony of Antigua was the first to end slavery. Low rainfall and intensive cultivation for a very long period (English colonists arrived in 1632) had reduced production, and few planters amassed very much wealth. They personally worked on their plantations and had developed comradeship with the Negroes toiling alongside them. As soon as news reached them of the new Act, they decided on immediate emancipation rather than any sort of gradual liberation. The Bermudas adopted the same policy shortly afterwards.

This abrupt yet entirely peaceful change-over from a slave-run to a free social economy was a heartening example for the worried Ministers in London. The lapse of a year between the passing of the Act and its operation was a difficult one. The Negroes were aware of the legislation and not unnaturally they became restless as the weeks passed slowly by. The Governors were carefully briefed by London, and a policy of keeping the slaves informed and explaining exactly what was to be done worked admirably. For the first time, perhaps, a white nation treated the Negro slave as an intelligent human being, capable of recognising justice and of facing realities, pleasant or unpleasant. The official proclamations effectively succeeded in suppressing wild rumours.

A great contribution came from the Non-Conformist

preachers, those despised and persecuted men who were the only really accepted friends of the slaves. They calmed the excitement of the Negroes at their services, visited them in their huts and taught them self-restraint.

Emancipation Day, August 1, 1834, came and passed without untoward incident. Slavery in the British possessions of the Caribbean had ended. Almost three centuries of a system of commerce which had put untold millions into the economy of the United Kingdom were terminated. The compensation paid to the planters was £20 millions. Compensation worked out at £37 10s. per slave. Claims for about £18½ millions were accepted, indicating that the British West Indian slave population at the time of Emancipation totalled half a million.

The apprenticeship arrangements covering a maximum of six years simply withered away. Within four years all slaves in the Brtish West Indies were entirely free. All the pessimistic forecasts about uncultivated plantations and prohibitive production' costs were disproved. The free Negroes were often unwilling to work for their ex-owners, but there was considerable competition for available jobs, and the good employer found no difficulty in engaging labour.

Eleven

The still inviolate stronghold of a slave-maintained economy in the West, and the potentially greatest customer for slave imports, remained the United States. Progressives in England who had admired the American colonists' fight against British domination had been placated, so far as their hatred of slavery was concerned, by the declaration of the Revolutionary Congress in 1775 that none of the thirteen colonies should import slaves. It was in fact a gesture of defiance rather than a declaration of intent.

Prohibition of slave imports by individual States followed— Delaware in 1776, Virginia in 1778, Maryland in 1783, South Carolina in 1787, North Carolina in 1794, and Georgia in 1798. These were more genuinely motivated actions, inspired either by the idealism of Quakers or the fears of white workers. But the laws did not affect the rights of the States' citizens to participate in the slave trade in slave-holding States; the latter were soon claiming with some reason that the abolition States were the most energetic in promoting the slave traffic.

The principle of slave labour had become deeply embedded in the social and economic systems of the original colonies. The agricultural prosperity of one-crop farms had been built on it ever since the first batch of twenty Negroes had been landed in Virginia in 1619. The purchase of Africans for farm work seemed far less objectionable, and was much cheaper, than the purchase of white workers. Many migrants from England signed away their freedom to obtain a passage across the Atlantic, agreeing in return to work for a stated period without wages. The agents negotiating these arrangements usually had no direct interest in any American farmholding, and they sold their interest in these migrants' indentures for profitable sums to the colonists.

Apart from privileges of justice and some rights as citizens these indentured workers for a good many years of their working lives did not enjoy many more benefits than the black slaves on the next farmstead, and the work of both groups might well be identical. And Negroes and indentured whites were better treated than the "gaol dregs"—the thirty thousand prisoners transported from England after 1717, mostly to Maryland and Virginia.

The descendants of these underprivileged English, as well as those of the Huguenots who settled in South Carolina, and the Scots-Irish peasants in Virginia, Maryland, and Pennsylvania, were extremely wary of the slave system encroaching any further and jeopardising their own jobs. In the Northern States the employers were, on this point, in agreement with them. The steady influx of reasonably skilled, intelligent, and racially similar people hungry for work provided a far better pool of labour than shiploads of frightened, semi-savage Negroes. At least until the British Government suspended emigration on the outbreak of war in 1775 there was no hostility to unlimited white immigration, but for practical reasons as well as on moral principles objection to the importation of Negroes was already growing.

After the Revolutionary War migration from Europe increased enormously until by the late 1830s it was approaching half a million a year. Most of the immigrants arrived possessing only the ragged clothes they wore. The pre-Revolution Americans, easily forgetting their own background, showed considerable hostility to this competition. The newcomers were ready to work for low pay in the mills of Massachusetts and the mines of Pennsylvania. They provided a tough, hard-working army of navvies for building canals, and, later, railroads. Employers in the North and on the Atlantic seaboard had no reason to require slaves; they had all the cheap labour they could absorb.

Thus a complex situation arose where pro- and anti-slavery interests were inextricably mixed. Down South the poor whites refused "nigger work" but ascribed the lack of jobs to the presence of slaves. The Southern planters, imbued with the colonial outlook and committed to an agricultural system necessitating the use of large-scale human labour, were determined to maintain their social patterns and did not want hordes of poor Europeans from a dozen nations for employees. In the fast industrialising North there were the established workers suspicious of the immigrants' cut-throat competition, and the immigrants themselves were fearful that their jobs might be taken over by slave labour. Silent but not inactive were the business men and industrialists: they did not require Negroes for their own enterprises but they found that the existence of the slave trade in the South could be a source of profit.

New England mills were able to compete with Britain in the production of cheap textiles, and the bales of cloth formed the basis for trading for slaves and ivory on the east coast of Africa. A growing industry was more directly based on the slave trade. Both before and after the Rebellion New England had a flourishing reciprocal trade with the British West Indies. New England ships caught fish on the Newfoundland Banks. A quarter of the catch was sold as "Jamaica fish", the salted food which provided the chief protein in the slaves' diet. This fish, with timber, was exchanged for sugar and molasses. British sugar was considered of very high quality, but molasses was both good and cheap in the Spanish islands. Part of the return cargo was therefore bought from the Spanish, and to correct the trade deficit with the British traders they would take a handful of slaves as "deck cargo". After the prohibition of slave trading there was little risk of the contraband being discovered. Large numbers of free Negroes were to be found on New England vessels. In the Atlantic seaboard trade the ratio was as high as one Negro to six white deckhands.

The trickle of slaves smuggled into the United States by these means was, of course, a trivial source of profit. The real business came from distilling the molasses. European slave buyers had accomplished the moral degradation of the chiefs on the coast with the result that the most avidly desired trade goods (apart from gold) were firearms, tobacco, and alcohol. European countries had gained almost a monopoly on supplying the sort of firearms the Africans liked. But America was well to the fore in supplying tobacco and spirits. The distilleries were most numerous in Connecticut, a State which was, incidentally, among the most conscientious in enforcing its law against the import of slaves. Ninety-four gallons of rum in a hogshead would purchase a prime slave. Lesser quantities served as bribes for minor officials, and a generous tot reduced a refractory slave into an acquiescent captive. Thus molasses, produced by slaves in the West Indies and distilled by anti-slavery citizens of the USA, became essential merchandise for obtaining more slaves.

A more pressing consideration necessitating the maintenance of the US slave system was the demand of England's textile mills for raw cotton. The manufacturing processes which heralded the Industrial Revolution were developed at the time of the campaign for abolition of slave trading by Britain. For industrialists and financiers faced with the probability of the cessation of a network of trades and industries woven into the massive transportation of Negroes, the series of inventions in the textile industry was a godsend. Richard Arkwright's spinning machine, James Hargreaves' spinning jenny, Samuel Crompton's spinning mule, and Edmund Cartwright's power loom, made mass production possible provided there were unlimited supplies of cheap raw cotton.

Slave labour kept the cultivation costs at a minimum. The invention by Eli Whitney in Georgia of the cotton gin slashed costs still further. Lancashire industrialists, setting up their factories in towns where few welfare bye-laws or restrictive practices existed, vied with the American plantation owners in keeping labour expenses low. Their workers cost them as little as, and perhaps less than, slaves. Large numbers of pauper children were put into the mills as soon as they reached the age of seven and worked fourteen to fifteen hours per day, six days a week, for wages as low as 3s. 7½d. per week. In 1811 adult mill workers were being paid between 9s. and 15s. a week, and this at a time when the quartern loaf cost 1s. 2d. The cotton industry was basically run on two slave systems in two continents.

Planters in the Cotton States expanded their output just at the time the British Abolition Law came into force. To some extent they were able to use the existing slaves by transferring them from worked-out land to new plantations, but by the early 1830s a large number of new workers were needed for land clearance and cultivation as far west as Texas.

Man-power had to be found. A small number of slaves were obtained from the Northern States and from the British West Indies. They hardly affected the shortage, and the most feasible source was to tap the supplies of freshly captured Negroes arriving in Brazil and Cuba at an estimated rate of one hundred thousand a year.

Large slave markets existed in the Bay Islands (off the coast of Honduras). These were a type of wholesalers, replacing the compounds on the African coast. Here Negroes were sorted, fattened, and had their blemishes concealed. They were sold to dealers from Cuba and the South American states, and to US importers from the ports in the Gulf of Mexico. So far as Negroes for the USA were concerned, they were taken for re-sale individually or in small batches at two principal markets, in Memphis and New Orleans. According to the report of the American Anti-Slavery Society as late as 1858, over 15,000 slaves had been imported into the USA in that year.

Another important smuggling route prior to 1819 was through Spanish Florida. Pensacola Bay was the transhipment area. Here slaves from Cuba or direct from Africa were sold by Spanish and other slave runners to American agents. The slaves were moved by night up the rivers into American territory. Once landed, they were mixed with existing slaves and marched for hundreds of miles deep into Georgia, Alabama, and Mississippi. The Governor of Georgia, David Mitchell, who was himself deeply involved in slave smuggling, estimated that in 1817 some twenty thousand newly arrived slaves moved from Florida to Georgia.

Pirates and adventurers infested the Gulf of Mexico to hijack the illicit cargoes run across the Atlantic and the Caribbean in defiance of the British patrols. Partly because of the Royal Navy's inability to police the maritime area effectively, and partly because of the defiant spirit of patriotic activities against the British in the war of 1812, these ruthless men were able to ply their trade without much interference.

They had no lack of customers. Colonel James Bowie, inventor of the double-edged hunting knife, was, for example, able to buy Negroes at $1 per lb., which suggests that his sellers had obtained their slaves at no cost to themselves a few miles out at sea. Bowie marched his merchandise to the best markets in the cotton-growing States, and reckoned on getting $4–7 per lb., or about $500–1,000 per adult male slave.

The Bowie transaction was not an unusual one. He was operating at a time when the British ban had sent prices of newly arrived slaves in the Southern States to fantastic figures. Just prior to the British Abolition Law the rise had begun. In South Carolina a prime Negro fetched $500 at that time.

Twenty years later the price was $1,500. By then the risks of collecting slaves and marshalling them on the African coast were such that African brokers were only too happy to sell as fast as they could get rid of their captives. The shippers' purchase price dropped to $25–50. So eager were buyers in America to obtain any kind of slave that the price-per-lb. arrangment used by Bowie developed. In the *Anderson Gazette* (South Carolina) in 1853 Negro boys were reported as fetching $5 per lb.

Enmity with Britain, and a young but splendid maritime tradition had created a vigorous and efficient US mercantile marine. American shippers had for long been engaged in the profitable Atlantic slave-carrying trade. For commercial and patriotic motives the New England business houses had no intention of being intimidated by British laws. Nor were the complex regulations of the individual States of great moment.

Dozens of firms on the eastern seaboard, especially those of New York, Rhode Island, Baltimore and Portland (Maine) were deeply involved in slave smuggling, usually sailing under Spanish colours. The captain of the *Cyane*, one of the four United States patrol vessels attempting to stop American slavers on the African coast in 1820, estimated that three hundred such ships were engaged in the trade. Each had two or three sets of papers and flags. They sailed outward-bound as American-owned in order to avoid interference from the Royal Navy, changed to the most convenient European flag on the coast to prevent both British and American investigation, reverted to American ownership during the return passage, and became Spanish when they reached American coastal waters.

The tragedy of the situation was that often the slaves endured even worse conditions than in the years prior to abolition. Speed was the essential to evade capture. Ships' hulls became narrower and the spread of sail greater. Once in the Trades these ships could outsail the best of the Royal Navy's ships, even those under steam. With every square foot of canvas in use the ship had one side awash most of the time, and green sea continually swept over her. The pummelling was tremendous, straining the comparatively light and thin timbers so that the pumps had to be in constant operation. Because of the need to suppress the suspicions of interfering authorities in the USA and to help the appearance of innocence if halted on the high seas, the owners did not fit up the hold with slave benches. The Negroes were simply pushed on top of ballast, water casks, and ordinary merchandise. When running before a moderate wind the hatches had to be closed, and ventilation ceased. In bad weather the hatches might be closed for days on end, the master reckoning that a quick passage would compensate for slave mortality. Ships were seen with the steam from the slave-packed holds rising from every crevice.

Profits from slave smuggling were so great that captains were prepared to jettison a cargo of Negroes to evade arrest, estimating that the value of a ship which might be condemned to destruction was greater than the easily replaced human cargo.

Admiralty reports confirm that this destruction of slaves was carried out quite frequently on the West African coast, including one case of a slaver named the *Regulo*, lying in the mouth of the Bonny river, which threw overboard 238 Negroes when a patrol hove in sight. But it is only fair to say that some of the stories were exaggerated by anti-slavery organisations and sensation-seeking journalists.

A notorious one, widely used by anti-slavery campaigners in the USA at the time, alleged that the master of a clipper, becalmed in an area where British patrols were known to be in operation, draped his anchor chain round the sides of his ship and tied 500–600 slaves to it. When, as the master feared, the Royal Navy approached at twilight, the anchor was dropped and the slaves drowned. The vagueness of details of where this occurred, or what ships were involved, makes it suspect.

The temptation to murder the living evidence of slaving was minimised when an amendment to British anti-slaving legislation in 1839 authorised capture of a ship if there was clear evidence of her use as a slaver. More than the usual number of ventilation gratings, the existence of shackles, chains, and cooking cauldrons and similar articles of slaving equipment were regarded as sufficient proof. Staining of the hold with urine and excrement was evidence for the conscientious officer boarding a suspected ship—or even the characteristic smell of palm oil and sweat which everyone in the trade knew well.

Measures brought counter-measures. The slavers began to arm themselves and did not hesitate to fight it out when cornered. In any event, armaments were almost essential when the ship reached the Caribbean and the buccaneers started to take interest in the booty. The terror of the slaves, battened below deck, as the ship's guns fired, and the answering fire tore into the decks, may be imagined.

The regular skirmishes between Royal Navy vessels and slavers, in fact if not ostensibly American-owned, created severe tension between the two countries. British boarding of suspected ships, even if they were later allowed to go, infuriated American opinion, even among those sections in the North actively attempting to abolish slavery. The right of search became a matter of patriotic principle. Rather smugly President Tyler, in his annual message to Congress in 1841, insisted that American subjects "prosecuting a lawful commerce in the African seas under the flag of their country are not responsible for the abuses or unlawful use of that flag by others". The President knew from his Minister in London that the British believed that war was inevitable, but he refused to give ground.

The general dislike in the USA of British power politics on the high seas was aggravated by a dramatic case involving one slave and a small American coaster, the *Creole*. The slave, who had run away from a plantation in Virginia and lived free in the North eventually returned in order to find his wife and bring her to freedom. He was caught by one of the many slave hunting parties roaming the State borders and sold among a batch of slaves to be shipped for work in a Southern sugar plantation.

The *Creole* carried about 130 slaves. The runaway slave, named Washington, organised a revolt when the ship was well clear of Hampton Roads, and succeeded in getting control of the vessel. He then had the intimidated white crew sail the ship to Nassau in the Bahamas where, as he knew, he and his fellow slaves would be free the moment they stepped ashore.

One white man had been killed during the mutiny, but the British Government refused to hand over either Washington or the Negroes. After angry exchanges Britain won a moral victory. The USA was not prepared to break off diplomatic relations in what the world would have regarded as a defence of slavery rather than the upholding of punishment of mutineers. A semblance of amity was achieved by agreement for joint patrols off Africa, with personnel from ships of the US Navy boarding vessels showing the American flag and Royal Navy personnel investigating all others.

It sounded like a notable advance in Anglo-US co-operation to suppress the slave trade. In fact the USA wanted to show the flag in the face of the British. Little effort was made to provide effective US patrols. Only two ships were sent at first, and they were based on Cape Verde, a week or ten days' sailing from the main slaving zones. In ten years the US African squadron captured only nine slave ships.

In order to evade capture the New England slavers shifted their trade to the Congo estuary and the east coast of Africa. Some of the vessels were very large. One which was observed by the British agent in Zanzibar in 1858 was carrying 1,200 slaves. A similar number were on board an American-built ship in the following year. On each occasion the ownership was ostensibly Spanish and the destination given as Cuba.

Behind the commercial campaign to maintain the slave trade and the slavery system in the States there was, of course, the infinitely greater war between pro-slave and abolition interests. Some States were committed, not merely to a ban on slave trading, but to the abolition of slavery itself. Vermont had opted for gradual abolition as early as 1777; Massachusetts (including Maine) made a gesture towards abolition in 1780 and in the same year Pennsylvania announced gradual abolition. New Hampshire, Rhode Island, Connecticut, New York, and New Jersey made similar decisions between 1783 and 1804.

Consequently in the Convention of 1787 drafting the Federal Constitution, the prohibition of slave imports could be favourably discussed. Due to pressure from Georgia and South Carolina, which had had second thoughts on the wisdom of cutting out the principal source of man-power, the abolition of the slave trade to the United States was set for the comfortably distant date of 1808. In the meantime an Ordinance abolished slavery north of the Ohio and east of the Mississippi rivers.

The abolitionists in the North imitated, and often excelled, their friends in Britain. The slave-holders in the plantation areas were not merely alarmed; they were becoming angry about a campaign which they believed was hypocritical. Fear was increased after the St. Domingo revolt in 1791. More than fifteen thousand French colonists on the island managed to get away. They took refuge in the towns along the Atlantic seaboard.

Their horrifying stories of carnage and destruction of property aroused two kinds of reaction. One was that a large slave population was a potential menace; the other was the need to keep Negroes under stringent discipline.

All sorts of excuses and subterfuges were offered to justify slavery. South Carolina slave owners believed the trade should be maintained for the benefit of the natives of Africa; there should be contracts of apprenticeship for life; Negroes were desirable immigrants just to counteract the Europeans migrating to the Northern states.

But the North became more insistent and intolerant. The aim was immediate abolition of slavery; the most the South was prepared to concede was gradual emancipation, and the South was in the majority. By 1831 only four of the original thirteen states of the Union had constitutionally abolished slavery. The bitter controversy over slaves had resulted in States being admitted in pairs—one slave-owning and one slave-prohibiting. But Louisiana, an enormous territory, with an economy based on slave labour, purchased from France in 1803, broke the "one of each" policy. The application for admission of Missouri as yet another slave-owning state aroused resistance, eventually settled by the Missouri Compromise, with the Mason-Dixon line along 36.30 latitude as the division between slavery and emancipation.

Compromises rarely work. In 1854 the Missouri arrangement was abandoned in favour of squatter sovereignty. Nine years earlier both sides had found little satisfaction when Texas was admitted as a semi-slave State. This vagueness was now increased with Kansas and Nebraska left to decide for or against slavery as they wished despite their situation north of the line.

The locality of Negro slaves at the time of the Missouri Compromise provides an accurate forecast to the sides which the States would take some forty years later when civil war became inevitable. The census for 1820, published in Washington in 1821, indicated that the slave population of the United States then totalled about 1,556,000. In round figures the state totals were, in numerical order, Virginia 425,000; South Carolina 258,000; North Carolina 205,000; Georgia 150,000; Kentucky 127,000; Maryland 107,000; Tennessee 80,000; Louisiana 69,000; Alabama 42,000; Mississippi 33,000; Missouri 10,000; New York 10,000; New Jersey 7,000; District of Columbia 6,000; Delaware 4,000; Arkansas Territory 2,000; Illinois 1,000. Connecticut, Indiana, Pennsylvania, and Rhode Island had a further five hundred between them.

Yet there was a diversity of opinion even in the States heavily dependent on slave labour. Virginia, for example, was quite strongly hostile to any continuance of the traffic in slaves from Africa. The reason was not an idealistic one. As the State with more Negroes than any other it had an adequate labour force. The majority of her four hundred thousand slaves were thoroughly acclimatised, and many were Virginian-born. In fact the State was the leading slave-breeding area in the country, the birth rate not merely supplying her own needs but providing a steady surplus for sale in the South and Deep South.

But many Virginians not in direct need of large-scale Negro labour were worried by the huge slave population—English speaking, energetic, and ready listeners to any talk about human rights. Thousands of Negroes were free, through manumission, or in such positions of trust that they lived better than the poor whites. The long past St. Domingo revolt was not forgotten. The white population of Virginia was 620,000—a significantly similar proportion to the St. Domingo figures.

All such forebodings seemed to be justified in 1831 when a brief but savage revolt occurred. The leader was a Negro named Nat Turner, a religious fanatic who believed God had chosen him to free the slaves. He roused some sixty Negroes in Southampton County to a frenzy. White men, women, and children were killed without reason or mercy. Predictably the reaction of the inhabitants in nearby Jerusalem was to retaliate with still greater ruthlessness. Aided by the militia they exterminated virtually every slave involved in the uprising.

From that time Virginia was in principle in favour of obliterating slavery by any possible means if the practical problems of work could be solved. There was a serious study of a scheme to send all Negroes, free or enslaved, to Africa. The scheme was abandoned on the grounds of expense, and because of second thoughts regarding the slaves' usefulness if kept under strict control.

Virginia failed to abolish slavery even though the slaves were hated and feared. The State's attitude set the future example for the South's policy. Any anti-slavery idealism which existed in the South changed to an anti-Negro neurosis. Missouri banned any ship from entering her ports or rivers with free Negroes in the crew. South Carolina held Negro sailors in custody while their ships were in port; Louisiana passed a similar law. Mississippi issued warnings that free Negroes crossing the border would be whipped.

Secret societies flourished, all born of fears of minorities and underprivileged groups. Suspicions about the flood of Irish immigrants created anti-Catholic organisations. The Order of the Star-spangled Banner advocated "nativism", which meant citizenship rights only for persons born or resident in America for twenty-one years. Pledged to secrecy, its members denied all knowledge of the society's activities and so were called the Know Nothings.

Even more extreme was the Society of the Knights of the Golden Circle, formed in the Cotton States. This was not merely a bigoted group jealously guarding its own interests, but an expansionist force envisaging additional American States southwards, based on a permanent slave system.

The inspiration came from the writing of an amateur economist, Edward Pollard. He appealed direct to the poor whites by advocating a slave for every white person. This would in some magical manner banish poverty and provide the capital for the economic development and eventual annexation of Central America and the nearest islands in the Caribbean. The idea was almost certainly the motive for attempts to seize Cuba, typified by the Ostend Manifesto of 1854 in which England, Spain, and France learned (by a contrived leak) that the USA was prepared to pay Spain generously for Cuba, and if Spain refused, the USA would be justified in seizing the island by force. Cuba was the key to the projected empire of the Golden Circle, with its vast slave population. Its Negroes would be the slave labour force opening up the new territories; thereafter independence would enable Negroes to be imported in quantity direct from Africa.

The imperial concept was, of course, the dream of extremists. But it aroused interest among the planters who feared what they saw to the North.

There, the Negro, regarded by the South as a criminal, was being treated as a hero. A slave had only to escape over a State border to be cosseted by the Northern abolitionists. As a result of the slave-owning States' pressure, and the regard paid by both North and South to the rights of property, the Fugitive Slave Law had been passed in 1793, and still gave the South powers over the efforts in the North to protect runaway Negroes.

Southerners regarded those who aided fugitive slaves to escape along the famous Underground Railroad as no better than thieves. A white man caught helping a fugitive to escape might be branded with the letters SS (slave stealer).

The Underground Railroad was particularly well organised on the borders of Maryland and Delaware, which were slave States in the North. It brought out many thousands of Negroes. The originator of the idea is generally accepted as Charles Torrey, a clergyman. Torrey thought of the Railroad while in prison at Annapolis in 1842 after his arrest at a slaveholders' meeting. In the following two years he helped four hundred slaves to escape. He was then caught and died in prison.

The differences between North and South over the slave question remorselessly moved towards the point of no return. Slave hunters from the South used bloodhounds to trace their quarry over the borders of emancipated States. Informers flourished everywhere, earning a few dollars for testifying that such-and-such a Negro was in fact A.B., the property of C.D., of Georgia. The supporters of the Underground Railroad with scores of routes starting all along the borders of the slave-owning States from Kansas and Nebraska to the Atlantic coast of Delaware, were as ready to ignore the law and use force. The slave hunters' dogs were poisoned or shot; the hunters were kidnapped. By the late 1840s these partisans of North and South were at undeclared war.

Probably the fugitive Negroes were better served by people of their own colour, who took no interest in States' politics but concentrated on the safety of their clients. Easily the most successful of the coloured Underground Railroad organisers was "General" Harriet Tubman, an American-born Negress from Maryland. As a child she had been severely injured when a slave overseer hit her on the head with a 2 lb. weight. She was an immensely strong woman, and before her escape was said to be capable of replacing a horse in hauling a loaded river boat. At the age of twenty-nine she escaped to Pennsylvania. In Philadelphia she was befriended by a Negro, who was a clerk in the offices of the local anti-slavery organisation and an agent for the Underground Railroad. She then organised an escape route which ran from Maryland through New York and Schenectady across the border to Canada. She devised an intricate system of passwords, coded messages, signals, and hide-outs which defeated the slave hunters. On scores of occasions she personally went to Maryland to escort the fugitives. The number of Negroes she brought out is unknown. It certainly reached many thousands. Only a small handful were ever caught.

For the South the Underground Railroad was a treasonable enterprise gnawing at the very heart of State law. For the North activities of people like Harriet Tubman were romantic exploits completely in line with US principles of liberty.

This romantic theme was exploited by Harriet Beecher Stowe in *Uncle Tom's Cabin*, published in 1852. The author had little direct knowledge of slavery beyond that after a brief visit to a Kentucky plantation. The book was a sentimental work, with escaped slave George as pale a Negro as the author dared make him. The Negroes were quaint, simple, and (when devout adherents to Christianity) quite likeable. But Mrs. Stowe had the typical New Englander's attitude to Negroes, enslaved or free: their future lay in Africa, not in America.

The book had a fantastic influence on the slave controversy. The South regarded it as an attack on their constitutional rights; the North hailed it as an exposure of a cancer in the body of the United States.

And perhaps President Lincoln was not entirely exaggerating when in 1862 he hailed the author as "the little woman who made this great war".

But Lincoln was no advocate of abolition, no matter what the cost. He did not condemn the Southern pro-slave citizens out of hand. "They are just what we would be in their situation."

In a letter in 1862 to Horace Greeley, reformer and founder of the New York *Tribune*, Lincoln wrote: "My paramount object is to save the Union, and not either to save or destroy slavery. If I could save the Union without freeing any slave I would do it; if I could save it by freeing all slaves I would do it, and if I could do it by freeing some and leaving others alone I would also do that."

Lincoln respected the Union and wanted to save it. But there were lesser men whose ambitions and fanaticism fed the passions of the pro- and anti-slavery groups.

The most notorious of American abolitionists, John Brown, had not in the early years of his adult life interested himself greatly in the slave question. He had been too busy in trying to earn a living in a variety of business and farming enterprises, most of which were unsuccessful. At one period he was in England and may have there first caught some of the crusading enthusiasm for emancipation. By 1855 he was in Kansas. From unknown motives, though it was said a child of his was mentally ill through ill-treatment by pro-slavery people, he became active in organising a group to aid Negroes. His gallant deed on their behalf was in reality a brutal and futile attack on pro-slavery partisans at Pottawatomie in May, 1856, in which five men were murdered. An objective view would have branded him a villain, or at least a man barely responsible for his impetuous actions. But the North wanted a hero, and John Brown was their man.

He spoke at meetings and appealed for funds. He carried out badly planned rescue sorties of captured fugitives and had no compunction in shooting his way out. As the result of the death of a slaveholder in Missouri he was branded as an outlaw. The hospitality and adulation he received all over the North fertilised his ambitions, and soon he was planning insurrection far into the Deep South, with slave rescues almost an incidental factor in his schemes.

His ambitions rapidly became grandiose. In May, 1858, he was in Canada, presiding over a conference of free Negroes and white volunteers for which Brown drew up a constitution and a provisional government with everyone enjoying an important post in it.

On Sunday, October 16, 1859, John Brown, as C-in-C, ordered his "army" to take up their arms. They marched from the Maryland farmhouse where they had been living for more than three months and marched to Harper's Ferry. The force consisted of sixteen white volunteers and five Negroes. Brown's object was to occupy the local US arsenal, whereupon he believed the Maryland Negroes would rise in revolt. He captured a few of the arsenal staff without difficulty. The only man who did not surrender quickly enough and was killed was a Negro.

Brown was so convinced of the rectitude of his action that he made little attempt to ensure secrecy even in the preliminary stages. A train stopped, the crew and passengers were informed of the coup, and it was allowed to continue its journey. The result was the arrival of militia and government troops. Brown had plenty of time to escape with his prisoners or at least to improve his defences. He did neither. After he had been wounded during the assault by the troops he was interviewed by several officials, including Henry Wise, Governor of Virginia. Perhaps unwillingly in view of the evidence of the poor defences and the absence of any sensible plans, Wise decided that Brown was sane. On a charge of rebellion and treason the punishment could be death (even though Brown was not a citizen of Virginia). Brown was executed on December 2, 1859.

The Negroes had not revolted on hearing the news of the capture of Harper's Ferry. But they were subjected to violent repressive measures as a result of the alarm in the Southern States. In the North voices were raised in deprecation of Brown's violent methods. Abraham Lincoln's was one of them. But there were more eager to make Brown a martyr. Prominent and wealthy Republicans could not completely repudiate him because evidence was easily obtainable of their friendship for and support of Brown at some stage of his anti-slavery career.

South Carolina, believing Lincoln to be the arch leader of the abolitionists, and jealous of State rights, passed the ordinance to secede from the Union six weeks after Lincoln was elected President on November 6, 1860. By the spring ten more States had joined South Carolina. The war which had been looming for so long broke out, and four years were spent in welding the USA into a real Union—and a nation without slaves.

Lincoln issued a proclamation declaring all slaves free on January 1, 1863. It proclaimed that slaves were free in districts not under the control of Federal troops, which in effect imposed emancipation in the revolting States. If they returned to allegiance there would be no immediate freedom for the slaves. No revolting State heeded the proclamation, which was technically illegal.

The legal enforcement of emancipation resulted from a resolution passed by Congress on January 31, 1865—the historic Thirteenth Amendment. On April 9 the South surrendered. All America's slaves were free after 246 years of serfdom.

During the American Civil War the blockade of the Southern States had been instrumental in curbing slaving activity, while the demands of war itself lessened the need for slaves on the derelict plantations. A few ships, however, managed to land their Negroes after hostilities broke out. The ship with the dubious claim as the last American slaver was the *Erie*, under Nathaniel Gordon, a native of Portland, Maine. The *Erie* was a small, fast vessel of 476 tons, but Gordon managed to cram 890 slaves from the Congo into her. More than six hundred were children. Almost immediately after he began the westward passage the Union warship *Mohican* caught him. After the Negroes had been landed in Liberia, the ship, captain, and crew were taken to New York. Gordon was tried for piracy and found guilty.

He was condemned to death, despite frantic efforts by influential persons, probably financially involved in the enterprise, to save him. Friends did manage to smuggle some strychnine to him, but his cries after taking the poison alerted the guards, and his life was saved for the few hours left before he was due to be hanged. Nathaniel Gordon was executed at midday on February 21, 1862, the only man involved in the American slave trade ever to suffer the extreme penalty under the piracy law of 1820.

Though there were stories of successful runs to Cuba by American-owned ships as late as 1864, the death of Gordon marked the death of the slave trade to the USA.

Twelve

The formidable difficulties of evading the Atlantic naval patrols and the eventual abolition of slavery in the majority of the colonies and countries in the New World produced a situation full of potential danger for Africa itself. Few of the supporters of emancipation saw this risk at the outset. Yet it was inherent in an almost inevitable solution of the plantation owners' problems. If it became impossible to buy Negro labour for the West Indian plantations or even to keep those slaves already purchased then obviously there would be great possibilities by transferring the holdings to Africa.

From the Gambia southwards rainfall was adequate for most crops. Temperature was at sub-tropical and tropical levels. The Portuguese had for centuries farmed the off-shore African islands with considerable success. Indeed, the slave-maintained plantation system could be said to have been devised in Sao Tomé and transferred to the Americas.

Generalisations of this kind ignored the many problems of soil, seasonal extremes, and the climatic differences between the African land mass and the islands of the Caribbean. Sheer ignorance of the geography of Africa a few miles inland from the coast perhaps engendered optimism. But the political facts of the time indicated that on the west coast European control did not extend far inland from seaport settlements, forts, and trading posts. Beyond them were kingdoms ruled by chiefs who had been as unwilling to abandon the slave trade as were their white customers. Plantations in those areas would have a limitless supply of slaves, with no problems of middlemen, maritime transport, or any of the restrictions of international law.

The British Government eventually recognised the danger of slave trading disappearing so far as transatlantic traffic was concerned, only to be replaced by a growth of white-organised trade within the continent of Africa. Naturally enough, the African masses had learned of the cessation of European slaving with joy. As understandably the chiefs and their officials were both bewildered and angered. For at least three centuries they had been cajoled, bribed and intimidated into regarding the capture and sale of Negroes as the staple form of legitimate commerce with Europeans. The entire economy of some kingdoms in West Africa was based on slave trade profits. There was no other product but the Negro available in sufficiently large quantity to pay for imports. Now, suddenly, for seemingly highly impractical reasons, slaving became a forbidden trade.

Moreover, the forms of trade which the British hoped would be substituted for slaving appeared to involve interference with tribal independence. The slaving agents had been content to remain in the forts and trading posts or in their ships. They rarely went inland to organise supplies, being satisfied with the African system of capture, purchase and collection. But with the plans to buy timber, palm oil, gum, and to organise cropping of cotton, coffee, and nuts, white men insisted on supervising production and delivery.

British policy was two-fold. It was both to develop trade and to continue the anti-slavery campaign. The many treaties made with the African chiefs after 1840 were really in the nature of bribes. Chiefs got a small annual payment in return for agreement to the suppression of slave trading by agents working for the illicit European buyers on the coast, the protection of fugitive slaves, and the recognition of the rights of slaves to enjoy sanctuary in British forts and trading posts. At first little was done about demanding that chiefs abolished domestic slavery because of the impossibility of enforcing such conditions. In the space of a dozen years after 1840 sixty-five chiefs in West Africa signed agreements to end the slave trade in their territories.

The standard agreement with the chiefs provided the following terms:

No white Christian persons should be made slaves; any such persons already slaves or brought in as slaves should be instantly freed.

No persons of any colour, wherever born, should be taken out of the country as slaves, and no persons should engage in the trade for the export of slaves.

Ships and boats in the coastal waters or rivers of the African territory concerned could be seized, tried, and condemned.

British subjects could enter, live in, and leave the country in freedom.

Trade would be encouraged with English merchants; trade routes to other native kingdoms should be kept open.

British subjects should be able to buy, sell or rent land and houses.

British residents would observe the local laws and could be punished after trial by the nearest English military commander according to English law.

The British Crown could appoint an agent to visit or reside in the country.

In special cases additional terms included the abolition of human sacrifice; the sale of defined areas to the British Crown in perpetuity; and guarantees of protection against attack resulting from the chief's measures to end the slave trade.

The pressure group in London which encouraged the Government to pursue this policy of individual agreements with African tribes was the Society for the Extinction of the Slave Trade and the Civilisation of Africa, formed in 1840. The society rightly argued that the development of steam navigation would provide faster and more regular services between Africa and Britain, allowing perishable cargoes to be carried, and a much more generalised commerce to be developed. Further, they believed that the exploration of the areas behind the coast, and particularly the opening up of the river basins, such as the Niger, would enable the Africans to increase their agricultural exports.

The society was moving dangerously near to the plantation concept, and it was perhaps only the cynical disbelief of the financiers that any business but that in slaves could succeed which prevented the general promotion of agricultural enterprises on lines the Civilisation Society proposed, to be worked by Africans who would in reality have been slaves. Model farms were actually planned for the Niger area, and an expedition organised. It managed to complete agreements against slaving with two chiefs near Lokoja where the Niger and Benue rivers joined. Land was bought for a model plantation. But disease, and damage to the small steam launches, forced withdrawal of the main party for recuperation on the island of Fernando Poo. The farm was an utter failure, and the whole scheme was abandoned in 1842.

Agreements with tribal chiefs—Lord Palmerston was realistic enough to forbid the arrangements to be called treaties— created a host of problems. Chiefs expected military aid in their wars with neighbouring tribes; they required compensation for the loss of revenue when they observed the anti-slave clauses; they wanted inordinately favourable terms in the new kinds of trade. Where it was of advantage to Britain to grant such concessions the territories concerned became British protectorates in everything but name. A sort of involuntary colonial empire was steadily growing on Africa's west coast, a fact noted by rival powers which had always suspected Britain's motives in the anti-slavery campaign.

Another problem was the status of liberated slaves when they left British controlled zones such as Sierra Leone. While they were under British care British law protected them, and they enjoyed the privileges of British citizenship in most matters, though perhaps it would be fairer to describe them as second-class subjects. But when they left, as they were regularly encouraged to do, to return to their own tribes it was impossible to give them the protection which a British subject had a right to expect unless an agreement existed with the chief of the liberated slave's tribe.

In practice, in the first sixty years of the nineteenth century British judicial power did not extend far beyond the West African forts and settlements. Within the grounds of a building where British whites resided slavery did not exist. A hundred yards away, in the warehouse of an African merchant, domestic slaves were at work.

The number of Negroes who had to be cared for was not inconsiderable. Their future, after being liberated from captured slave ships was principally decided by four main tribunals. In the Americas one was at Rio de Janeiro, concerned with Portuguese and Brazilian ships; that at Havana with Spanish vessels, and a third at Surinam (Netherlands Guiana) with Dutch vessels. The fourth, in Africa, worked in Freetown, Sierra Leone, and handled cases involving British, Portuguese, Spanish and Dutch ships. This was by far the busiest tribunal. In the first twenty years it condemned 403 ships and liberated more than 59,000 slaves. In Havana forty-three ships were ordered to be broken up, and more than ten thousand slaves liberated. At Rio, possibly because illicit slave ships took good care to land their cargoes at hidden coves along the Brazilian coast, only sixteen ships were condemned and 2,700 Negroes given their freedom. Most of the ships involved were Portuguese or working on behalf of Portuguese slavers. These were the greatest problem and the Royal Navy ranged the whole of the South Atlantic in search for Portuguese ships.

There were also naval courts at St. Helena, Cape Colony, and one handling inter-island offences in British Caribbean possessions. They were responsible for condemning sixty-five ships and releasing three thousand Negroes in the first two years of their existence.

The obvious method of easing the problem of supervising the welfare of liberated Negroes thousands of miles from their homes was to increase the patrols to ensure they never left Africa, and to make the importation of slaves uneconomic.

In 1850 a select committee of the Lords issued a report on the situation. It indicated that abolition was succeeding thanks only to the Royal Navy patrols off the African coast. By the same token removal of the patrols would instantly result in the entire coastline swarming with illegal slave runners.

After deprecating the way that Brazil and Spain were disregarding their treaty obligations, the committee criticised the importation of slave-grown sugar into Britain, hinting that trade sanctions might prove extremely effective in influencing the planters in Brazil and Cuba to change to paid labour. Nothing was done in this regard except for same voluntary campaigns by retailers and consumers against "slave sugar".

On the African coast the committee recommended an extension of the forts and settlements (both of whites and freed slaves), and the establishment of consular agents wherever slave trading centres had been abolished so as to replace them with normal trading enterprises.

Development of the supervised settlements was an urgent need as the situation in Sierra Leone indicated. By the time of the Lords' report the population increase in the settlement was such that emigration had become necessary. Many freed slaves had no desire to return to the areas where they were born, advisedly so because of the possibility of re-enslavement. Several thousands moved voluntarily to other coastal areas and islands. These could not absorb many more, and arrangements began for emigration to the West Indies. The persuasion was decidedly forceful, and a bounty was payable to the shipping agent on each Negro he persuaded to emigrate, and chiefs were given gratuities based on the number of subjects they cajoled or ordered to leave. Liberated slaves were fed and housed while the advantages of emigration were considered. It was official policy to prevent known opponents of work in the West Indies from speaking to the Negroes. Many of those who decided to go before rations and shelter were withdrawn were mere boys. The normal contract for Negroes over fifteen years of age was for eight years. The prevalence of juveniles resulted in special apprenticeships for boys under fifteen to work till they were eighteen.

By 1863 at least eight thousand freed slaves had crossed the Atlantic to work as labourers on the plantations in the British West Indies. In addition some thirteen thousand Africans, both from Sierra Leone and other settlements, emigrated to British Guiana (Guyana).

Both the Africans and Asiatics who were simultaneously imported were, of course, voluntary emigrants and had the right to a return passage. But they were illiterate and only a minority of the Negroes had ever lived in the West Indies. They could have no real knowledge of the sort of life they were choosing. Abolitionists in England had misgivings about this massive importation of coloured humanity into the once notorious West Indian plantations. There was little supervision of their conditions on board the ships that carried them beyond requirements of twelve superficial feet of passenger deck space per adult. Doubts about the conditions of employment, particularly in Guyana, were made, Further, the numbers allegedly volunteering of their free will to work in the West Indies were suspiciously large.

In fact, as time went by, emigration was virtually forced on the Negroes. In Sierra Leone grants of rations were abolished. Compulsory residence was reduced to one week from the day of arrival. Those who were unable to maintain themselves were told to leave. Thus for many liberated slaves after 1860 arrival in Sierra Leone meant a sojourn of a week or so, after which he had to decide whether to wander off into territory where slaving still continued or to agree to go to the continent from which they had been saved. The basic absurdity of capturing a slave cargo on the high seas, shipping the slaves to Sierra Leone, and then carrying them across the Atlantic resulted in the West India Committee suggesting that slaves from captured ships should be taken direct to the West Indies. Earl Grey agreed. How many liberated slaves were thus taken to the destination originally intended for them is unknown. It is probable that the system applied only to slave ships boarded in the Caribbean.

As the result of public misgivings, supervision of the volunteer emigrant ships became a Government responsibility. The ships were provided by private firms under charter. They compared favourably with the emigrant ships plying between Europe and the USA, which was not saying much for them. The same ships were used for emigrants who wanted to return, a free passage being guaranteed after five years' work. This facility was later dropped, largely because the migration in either direction had dwindled away to nothing. Better economic conditions in Africa eased the unemployment problem for the liberated Negroes, and the decline in the number of slave ships captured caused the inflow of released Negroes to drop to a dozen or so every few months.

Controversy continued over Sierra Leone. It was centred on the degree of political freedom the liberated Negroes enjoyed; they were freed from serfdom but regulated for labour. The alternative to accepting this benign discipline was for the African to seek a living with some tribe which might or might not welcome him.

In the view of the critics of Sierra Leone Liberia was the example to emulate. This free African territory originated in a refuge on Cape Montsenado on the old Grain Coast. The land was purchased by the American Colonisation Society in 1821 as a refuge for freed American slaves. Soon there were two miniature republics, Maryland and Liberia. These were combined in 1857. Conditions were extremely difficult, and aggravated not only by the natural conditions of dense forests, unnavigable rivers, and disease-ridden swamps, but also because of the diversity of the tribes living in the area. Right up to the present century Negroes in Liberia were being forced to labour within the country and sent to adjacent areas, notably the Spanish island of Fernando Poo, where conditions of semi-slavery on the cocoa plantations were revealed by an International Commission of Enquiry as late as 1931. It was a sorry example of the tendency of Africans in a position of power to institute directed labour schemes hardly distinguishable from slavery, with recruitment for both public works and private commercial enterprises which was tantamount to slave trading.

Of far greater political moment than the social and economic changes in West Africa caused by abolition was the clash of European interests in the south of the continent. In Cape Colony, which the British had occupied during the Napoleonic Wars, there were about forty thousand slaves at the time of notice of emancipation by 1838. The orders to liberate these workers, with compensation which the farmers considered inadequate infuriated Dutch sentiment, still resentful at the action of the four thousand strong force which Britain had landed on the pretext of forestalling a French coup. Stronger than the Boers' exasperation at the attack on their livelihood was their genuine religious belief that God had ordained that there should be no equality between black and white. The beliefs inspired the Great Trek of 1835 across the Orange river and the founding of the Transvaal and Orange Free State Republics.

When Britain's "last imperialist war" of 1899–1902 resulted in the annexation of the two countries the British High Commissioner, Lord Milner, had to find supplies of labour to replace the exploited Africans. He brought in many thousands of coolies, the action producing the charge of "Chinese slavery" from the Liberals in the General Election of 1905. But the Chinese, like the Malays and Indians first imported by the Old East India Company and later arriving voluntarily, were certainly not enslaved, even if exploited. The number of Indians increased enormously due to the labour needs on the sugar plantations. For once, the traditional European agricultrial enterprise involving Negro workers had to be built up without their aid. The Zulus were a uniquely proud and martial African nation, preferring massacre to enslavement.

Abolition and emancipation created a major crisis in the British colonies of the Caribbean; in the United States it was a motive for Civil War; in the south of Africa the obstinacy of two European points of view, aggravated by the immigrant and exploited labour force which was substituted for slavery, sowed the seeds of disharmony which, unfortunately, still grow.

When those reasons for resentment and the desire for revenge burst out the result was shown by the excesses accompanying independence in the Congo. The tragedies of Africa, there as almost always, originated in well-meaning and genuinely honourable activities of men attempting to erase the evils of the past.

Leopold II of Belgium has become a symbol of all that was most vicious and ruthless in the European colonisation of Africa. It is a harsh and over-generalised assessment of a man who originally interested himself in Africa for the loftiest of motives. As a youth he had been one of those forward-looking moderns who felt impatient with the narrow outlook of a generation born at the start of the nineteenth century before Napoleon and the revolutionary movements of the 1840s had transformed world politics. On ascending the throne Leopold found himself bound by narrow concepts of a minor nation and he sought avenues of expansion.

Stanley's famous despatches to the *Daily Telegraph* and New York *Herald* describing his expedition across Africa from east to west were avidly read by Leopold. He saw a chance for his kingdom to contribute something to progress in Africa in a way which was impossible in Europe, because of the numerous treaties of the powers designed to keep Belgium neutral and uninfluential.

The King's conference in Brussels in September 1876 was the first truly international meeting summoned for the purpose of bringing enlightened civilisation to Africa. Explorers, missionaries, and humanitarians were welcomed as warmly as politicians, financiers, and merchants. Leopold insisted that the conference was scientific and cultural, with no political implications. He asked the distinguished Ministers of seven nations attending to speak and act as private individuals. He himself stressed that he was speaking as a geographer and not as a Head of State. The International African Association which was formed as a result of the conference made suppression of slavery one of the main objectives of the exploring programme that was drawn up.

It was hardly Leopold's fault that the lofty objects of the association gradually gave way to political manoeuvre so that in effect the IAA became the front behind which the European powers divided Africa among themselves. National offshoots of the main body acted independently, and the IAA itself lapsed into what was virtually the Belgian branch.

Leopold slowly succumbed to the prevailing lust for colonisation, and his founding of the Comité des Etudes du Haut Congo did not conceal the fact that this was a commercial and colonising project. However, Leopold genuinely believed, as Livingstone and Stanley had taught him, that the development of communications and trade was the most practical way of helping the Africans. Stanley, as Leopold's representative, moved into the Congo with a porter carrying a flag which did not symbolise Belgium, but was the gold star on a blue field of the IAA. This emblem did not stifle the alarm of the other nations, notably Portugal, clinging to her centuries' old rights to the area, or France, busily exploring the north bank of the Congo river.

Britain, anxious to counter French imperialism, backed Portugal. The cynical view that the European powers were penetrating deep into Africa and using the pretext of suppression of slavery and slave trading in order to colonise the continent now appeared to have some validity.

The resulting exploitation of the natives in what became the Belgian Congo was not real enslavement. In fact, Leopold II's original object was to arm the Africans so they could resist Arab slave traders. The appalling revelations of the brutality which had grown steadily were not known until 1897 when a Swedish missionary, E. N. Sydblom, sent a report to the Anti-Slavery Society in London. Investigations by an international tribunal in 1904–5 at length revealed that the King and his colleagues had run the Congo as a private estate of nine hundred thousand square miles and had made £3 millions personal profit by pillaging everything of value in the country and reducing the population by 12 millions in the process.

The conditions in which the Africans existed had been worse than those of slaves. If they had been serfs they could have expected to be fed and to have bodies of some monetary value. As it was, a human life had been equated at the price of a rifle cartridge, and troops were expected to hand in a severed hand as proof that a bullet had not been wasted. Control of the Congo passed in 1908 to the Belgian Parliament, and a regime, enlightened by the standards of the period, was inaugurated and another chapter of the Negroes' tragedy ended. The

Belgian Congo scandal provided a bitter lesson on the need for constant precautions against the emergence of some form of slavery in areas where racial minorities or conquered races existed even when the occupying power seemed above suspicion.

Leopold was the patron of the most important and effective anti-slavery measures in the closing years of the nineteenth century. He was a leading figure at the Berlin Congo Conference of 1885 at which seventeen nations pledged themselves to suppress slavery in the whole region of the Congo basin. He convened the Brussels Conference of 1890 which produced what has been called the Africans' Magna Carta. This man of complicated personality perhaps deserves to be remembered for his good actions, even if they do not balance his greed.

The first article of the Brussels Convention dealt with combating the slave trade within Africa. Improvements in communications and transport and restriction on the availability of firearms to Africans were reasonable and innocuous proposals. Organisation of civil and military services, the setting up of military stations in the interior, and mobile columns to intercept slave caravans, were dangerous precedents permitting a signatory power to administer a region by military force and treat any tribe or community as candidates for a civilising process enforced by bullet and bayonet.

The subsequent articles required signatories to repress the slave trade in every way they could, including the introduction of legislation imposing penalties on the organisers and abettors of slave hunting, on those mutilating male adults and children, and on all persons taking part in the capture of slaves by violence. The vagueness of required evidence of complicity in any inter-tribal clash involving prisoners which might be enslaved made virtually every African male a potential victim of a white coloniser looking for an excuse for repression. The ban on the sale of firearms to Africans in any area where slaving existed ensured that they would have no weapons with which to defend themselves.

The section dealing with measures against slave ships was less suspect because any naval vessel of seventeen nations had the right of search of vessels under five hundred tons in defined maritime zones. Britain, incidentally, still recognises this right of search, despite the general view of international jurists that the Brussels Treaty lapsed on the outbreak of the First World War. In November, 1956, the Parliamentary Under-secretary of State for Foreign Affairs confirmed in the House of Commons that there was an obligation to observe the policy of securing the complete suppression of the slave trade by land and sea as set out in the 1890 treaty.

Despite the loopholes, the Brussels Convention was important because it was the first international agreement of its kind in which high-sounding proposals were backed by schemes to see that they were carried out. A bureau at Brussels, run by the Belgian Foreign Office, circulated information, compiled statistics, and handled legal problems. It went into such details as returns of the amount of alcohol sent to Africa, and the amount of ammunition expended.

The Brussels Act, despite the flagrant though technical breaches like that of the Congo victimisation and a few others, notably excesses by a British-registered rubber concern in Peru, was the final and effective weapon against international slave trading. Because it had been an agreement freely entered into by all the major powers of the world, the resentment and suspicion of power politics which were felt when Britain took upon herself to tackle the Atlantic slave trade, were absent.

In 1867, three centuries after Elizabeth I bade God-speed to Hawkins as he set out to capture slaves, Victoria authorised the withdrawal of the Royal Navy's Atlantic Slaving Squadron. It was no longer needed. Two years later, the courts organised to investigate slave ships were wound up.

Victorian England rejoiced in the triumphant end of a great crusade. Wilberforce slept in Westminster Abbey near Pitt. In the West Indies nearly a million slaves and children of slaves lived in freedom. Yet the satisfaction in one of the noblest campaigns in British political history had the blemish of refusal to look too widely for vestiges of slavery: there were still untold thousands of African-born people facing enslavement.

Thirteen

Throughout the campaign for abolition the attacks had been concentrated on "The Trade", which meant the purchase of slaves on the west coast of Africa and their transportation to the American continent. Little attention was paid to an older, and possibly even more ruthless, traffic in Africans which was centred in markets on the eastern seaboard. Its ramifications extended into areas which were still completely unknown to Europeans at the time of abolition, and the extent of the trade in the centuries before then was—and remains—unknown.

Negroes were being shipped across the Red Sea and the Indian Ocean at least from the first century AD. The trade was never interrupted until recent times, and though the market was not as insatiable as that created by the West in America, the total toll of Arabia and Asia over a period of 1,800 years may well have been greater than the formidable millions quoted for the Atlantic traffic.

Kilwa in Tanzania thrived as one of the biggest of the slave exporting ports for centuries. Arab sailors had probably penetrated thus far south before the beginning of the Christian era. The Arabs exchanged iron implements and wine for spices, ivory, and slaves. The supply of Negroes gradually declined through this prolongd trading until by the early nineteenth century an enormous area behind Kilwa had been depopulated, and the Arab traders were pushing inland as far as Lake Malawi in search of slaves, dhows being built on the eastern shore of the lake in order to transport captives taken in Malawi and Zambia. The Arab merchants bought slaves on the coast to carry trading goods to the interior. They, and a proportion of the new slaves purchased as part of the general exchange of goods, were worked to exhaustion, the profits of the expeditions being so good that heavy casualties among the porters were counteracted by the value of the ivory, rhinoceros horn, and animal skins they managed to carry to the coast.

By the middle of the seventeenth century the slave collectors for the trade conducted by Europeans were working on the east coast of Africa. The Royal African Company was sufficiently worried about the competition from supplies of Negroes picked up in South-East Africa and Madagascar (Malagasy) to approach the East India Company, within whose trading territory the eastern market lay, to check slaving operations by independent English ships. In 1677 the East India Company was disturbed by information that vessels had been sent direct from East Africa to the West Indies. Counter-measures included the idea of prohibiting ships from watering at St. Helena.

Restrictions could not, of course, be effectively enforced, and Madagascar Negroes were delivered direct to the West Indies in considerable numbers, while a regular slave trade existed between New York and the East African markets, the ships being owned by colonists in America. That such voyages took place when Negroes were plentiful in Guinea indicates the enormous demand for slaves. Not only was the distance almost double that to the West African coast, but it was virtually impossible to sail through the Mozambique Channel without inviting an attack by pirates. The Arab merchants who sold the slaves were not above recapturing the Negroes later because they were anxious to prevent European infringements of supplies for their own Asiatic markets, although eager enough to make a business deal to their own great profit.

The Madagascar market was sufficiently far south to avoid a direct clash with the Arabs on what was a monopoly for supplying the Middle East and some parts of India. The existence of slavery in "heathen" nations was accepted as characteristic of their regimes from the first contacts made with them. It was also tacitly condoned as a convenient source of servants and labourers. Even after Britain was in a position effectively to control the economy of most of India there were upwards of half a million slaves of all nationalities on the Indian sub-continent. At the height of the campaign for international abolition, the Home Government found the Government of India extremely unwilling to co-operate. Orders were repeatedly issued between 1838 and 1841 to adhere to the general provisions for abolition. India agreed to stop overseas purchases but could not promise to do more than abolish slavery "by degrees". More vigorous action "would endanger the tranquillity of British possessions in India".

This tacit approval of a slave system was inherited from the original policies of the East India Company, which found a trading economy supported by slave labour and was happy enough to continue it. The trade with Arab merchants had always been lucrative, and slaves were always part of the merchandise. "John Company" became exceedingly touchy if European dealers trespassed on the Arabs' trading grounds, branding European and British ships as little better than pirates. But the rewards were so great that any adventurer considered the risks worth while. At the beginning of the eighteenth century it was claimed that ten shillings' worth of trade goods bought in London could be exchanged for one prime male slave in Madagascar, who could be sold in the New World for £15–£20. True, mortality rates were high. The pirates in the Mozambique Channel killed crews and slaves indiscriminately when surprise capture of the ship failed. The cold of the passage round the Cape killed Negro captives who had no clothing or bedding. Navigation in the South Atlantic was a hazardous enterprise, and contrary winds and calms added unexpected weeks to the passage. But even a 50 per cent survival rate was profitable in view of the low purchase prices. A curious advantage arose in offering a parcel of East African slaves. Buyers considered that those who had managed to live through the transit phase would survive the most exacting conditions of labour and were therefore well worth buying at a higher price.

The gradual run-down of supplies and the curb on West Coast slaving gave a further fillip to the East African trade, while the widespread penetration of European influences in the continent forced changes in the age-old practices of the Arabs. The market for slaves among the Arab buyers on the coast increased materially in the early nineteenth century, while the market for Arab trading goods declined through Western competition. The coastal nations had plenty of European goods, and Arab gee-gaws no longer proved attractive to them. Those inland tribes which had not been massacred, enslaved out of existence, or had survived by fleeing to the interior began to resist. They attacked the long lines of porters in order both to capture the goods they carried and to stop the

depredations on their food supplies caused by the Arab caravans, living off the country and consisting of several hundred
people. The result was more strongly guarded caravans, and
longer journeys into the interior of Africa. Arab traders reached
Lake Tanganyika in the 1840s, and in 1852 one caravan
achieved the crossing of the continent to Benguela on the
Angolan coast. En route it exchanged trade goods for slaves
and ivory, and continued west in the hopes of in turn exchanging these for European goods which, they were told, were
readily available in all the towns beyond Tanganyika. These
merchants were, of course, well aware that they might arouse
retaliation from the European powers if caught during slaving
activities, and the sale of slaves was not the main object on
these major expeditions. Slave purchase had by then become
for the Arabs a convenient system of transporting goods to and
from the coast. The slave was the cheapest and most readily
available beast of burden. Indeed human life was the cheapest
commodity for other purposes: not a little of the cannibalism
which existed was reputedly due to the fact that human flesh
was easier to obtain than that of any animal. The ritual eating
of a defeated enemy changed to using human flesh as a source
of nourishment.

Arab influence throughout East Africa remained very strong
till the time Livingstone was making his explorations. If the
Arab merchants had wanted they could easily have annexed
huge territories for their nations, but the Arab mentality did
not often range beyond commerce. One merchant who in fact
ruled an empire of his own but did so merely to further his
trade in slaves and ivory was Tippoo Tip. Born of an African
mother, he himself married an African chieftain's daughter.
By the late 1860s he presided over a commercial enterprise near
Lake Mweru on the Congo–Zambia border which was in
everything but name his private empire. He met Livingstone
and the explorers who later went in search of him, Cameron and
Stanley, providing them with porters who were almost certainly
slaves, whatever arrangements was made to pay Tippoo for
their services.

Later, when Tippoo's dormant political power was recognised by the European colonisers in Africa he was invited to
advise and help. Tippoo became governor of the Stanley Falls
area of the Belgian Congo in 1887. Soon afterwards Belgium

began a concerted campaign against the Arab slavers still busy in the Congo, and Tippoo retired with an enormous fortune to Zanzibar—one of the most ruthless slave merchants who ever battened on East Africa, and a man who, paradoxically, paved the way for European campaigns to destroy slave trading throughout the area his caravans had crossed.

Tippoo's guest, and arch enemy of all he stood for, Livingstone, had been sent by the London Missionary Society to found a mission station in Botswana in 1841. The explorer had been struck during his travels by the misery caused by Tippoo's agents. He saw signs of their depredations everywhere, and believed that physical security for the African would have to accompany, if not precede, evangelisation. Well-organised lines of communication and trading posts in which native products and natural resources were exchanged for European goods, would, he thought, pave the way for civilisation and minimise the traffic in human beings who were the only realisable assets of communities regularly on the verge of starvation. Christian Europe would, in effect, beat the Arab slavers and their African allies by successfully competing as traders.

Through Livingstone's inspiration, the Universities Mission to Central Africa was set up in 1857 in order to found mission stations in the middle of the continent. The missions would not only give religious instruction and general education but organise agriculture and trading activities.

This became the policy of almost all the Christian missions operating in Africa in the nineteenth century. While the reaction of stronger tribes, profiting from slaving enterprises with the Arab merchants, was hostile and frequently had tragic results, the missionaries undoubtedly played a vital role in stamping out a trade which was still flourishing long after slaving on the West coast had almost ceased.

Thanks to the abolition of slavery in the United States in 1863, the activities of philanthropic societies and missionaries could be concentrated almost entirely on the East African problem. Missions within reasonable distance of Zanzibar received British Government grants to help them house and feed slaves released from the island. A Catholic mission built villages in the vicinity of Pangani for several hundred converted freed slaves, who in turn taught other freed slaves crafts and agriculture. The Church Missionary Society set up a similar village near Mombasa. The Universities Mission built a freed slave village at Masasi in Tanzania.

The number of one-time slaves who actually benefited from these havens was, of course, infinitesimal compared with the tens of thousands of men, women and children in bondage or unable to succour themselves after being released. But the indirect progress was great. There was no restriction on a mission ward leaving the station to return to his own tribe; indeed those who had indicated that their conversion to Christianity was genuine were encouraged to do so. The word spread over many thousands of miles that the white strangers did indeed want to fight slavery; more, they were prepared to offer a means of livelihood in exchange for religious conversion. Tribes which had become nomadic or had retreated into infertile areas to avoid the Arab slavers took heart and settled down in their traditional districts. Slaves on the coastal plantations who saw no immediate advantage in claiming their freedom or running away knew that sanctuary existed should they ever want to enjoy liberty.

These efforts to weaken the hold of the Eastern slave merchants on an area of East Africa far greater than the European depredations in the West were minimised in their effect, not only by Arab mercantile interests, but by European powers with possessions in the Orient. Probably the most formidable resistance came from France.

Officially France vetoed slavery and slave trading in 1818, but until the end of the Bourbon regime little notice was taken of the law by French colonists and traders in the Indian Ocean. They were regular suppliers and agents for the Sultan of Zanzibar, who in turn sold slaves to the Arabian states. Under British pressure France reinforced her legislation by permitting British ships to stop and search suspected French slave ships in the Indian Ocean; this not only jeopardised the trade with Arabia but was particularly galling to French planters in the island of Reunion (the possession left to the French after Britain annexed Mauritius) and though only a small island it was an invaluable source of sugar. In Mauritius Britain staved off a sugar production crisis by approving the import of Indians to work on the plantations. The French believed, with some justification, that this was slavery in all but name, and indeed an outcry in England resulted in the scheme being suspended until stricter arrangements could be worked out.

The planters of Reunion thereupon announced a scheme to recruit labour in East Africa. As it was on much the same basis as the British scheme to bring in Indians no cogent protest could be made, though no one was in doubt as to the method of recruitment on the African mainland and in Zanzibar. Finally in 1859 the British Government authorised recruitment of Indian labour for French dependencies, and the French planters agreed to abandon their East African sources of workers.

The crisis in relations between Britain and France in the Indian Ocean was caused at least in part by the genuine desire of the former to stamp out the only major case of European-run trans-oceanic slave trading remaining. But the idealism conveniently supported the need to curb French attempts to retrieve some of their influence in the area.

At this time of vigorous anti-slave patrols by the Royal Navy the powerful opponent was the ruler of Oman, Seyyid Said, whose possessions and influence extended along the coastal area of East Africa and to Zanzibar, his great trading centre. Seyyid Said had signed a treaty with the Government of Bombay in 1822 under which trading in slaves between the subjects of the ruler of Oman and the subjects of any Christian power was prohibited. But the rights of a British naval officer to search Arab vessels was restricted by definition of areas where Arabs normally sailed on slaving trips to meet the demands of the domestic trade. Violation of the law was obviously easy by taking other routes, and to curb it the British insisted on a further treaty, signed after some argument in 1845, in which Seyyid Said vetoed all slave trading by sea and gave British ships the right of search of Arab vessels wherever they were met. An exception was made for dhows hugging the coast between Kila and Lamu, a stretch of more than five hundred miles, in order not to prevent the traditional transactions for "domestic slavery". As this stretch included Zanzibar once again the chances of evading the regulations were good. The four cruisers sent by the Royal Navy were comparatively easily evaded; slaves were still transported to the Arabian states and some, no doubt, were transferred at sea to vessels which eventually landed them in the Americas.

The town of Zanzibar had grown quickly in the first half of

the nineteenth century, the population of at least fifty thousand in 1850 being ten times the total prior to the Napoleonic Wars. The slave market in the centre of the town was reputed to handle twenty thousand slaves a year. It was a courtyard surrounded by high stone walls with an ancient banyan tree in the centre. The majority of the slaves were assembled under this tree in order to provide them with some protection of the sun. The Arab sellers haggled with buyers slightly to alter the prevailing prices which were graded according to age and sex. Cope Devereux, an observer with a British patrol vessel, said that in 1860 the prices ranged from a few shillings for old men and women to £3 for healthy young men. Children of about five years of age went for 10s. each.

This courtyard in Zanzibar is the origin of the so-called romantic accounts of an Arab slave market. Along the walls, which provided shade during the midday period, were the girls sold as concubines. They were as young as twelve years of age. The dealers kept jewellery and footwear with which to deck out the girls, but this finery was always removed when a sale was completed. The girls were carefully made up with kohl and massage oil. Their only dress was a piece of cloth draped round the hips. This was removed when the buyer approached. The most beautiful girls fetched as much as £125 in the 1850s. This blatant traffic in concubinage disgusted the Victorians, yet the girls had an infinitely better future than the ordinary slaves under the banyan tree awaiting the purchaser. The girls' high cost ensured considerate treatment on the journey to the Middle East. The worker slaves, on the other hand, endured appalling sufferings. Arab captains did not hesitate to run their dhows for the beach in order to elude British patrols. The crews could reach the shore through the surf. The slaves, chained to the decks, were left to drown as the surf broke up the dhow. If a dhow was becalmed the slaves' sufferings in the heat resulted in death from heat stroke. HMS *Moresby* found a dhow which had sailed with three hundred slaves on a trip expected to take two days. When it was becalmed for ten days only twelve survived.

Masters of incoming slave vessels from the African mainland threw the sick overboard because it was not worth while paying the Sultan's import duty on each slave if there was a likelihood that the slave died before a sale was completed. This destruction of sickly merchandise was so usual that the bones of drowned slaves glistened white on the seabed of the harbour approaches, and there were dogs on the seashore eating the washed-up corpses.

After the death of Seyyid Said the inheritance of his possessions in Africa and Arabia were divided, the former under the rule of Majoid, a younger—and weak—son who did nothing to curb the slave trade. He was succeeded by another son, Seyyid Barghash, an ambitious and intelligent man who had done his best to oust his brother by intrigue, murder attempts, and playing off the British against the French.

In 1871 the British Parliament sent a commission of enquiry to investigate the East African slave trade, as a result of which Seyyid Berghash was invited to close all slave marts and to forbid the export of slaves from any port under his control on the African coast. The Sultan grudgingly acquiesced and, encouraged by the presence of British warships off the coast at Dar es Salaam and supported by a British officer to command his personal bodyguard, issued orders prohibiting slave caravans moving from the interior to the coastal belt. He also stopped the practice of moving slaves in groups along the coast until they were just outside the Sultan's possessions.

The man who transformed a disregarded legal formality into a practical operation was a Lawrence of his time and place—Lloyd Matthews. For three years he had been a naval lieutenant on the ships concerned in the anti-slave patrols in the Indian Ocean. His naval training taught him strategy; his diplomacy and genuine affection for both Africans and Arabs were his virtues by instinct and choice. He hated the slave trade as greatly as he admired the Arab virtues of hospitality, honour, and courage. Moreover, he knew better than the abolitionists in London that slavery and slave trading were so deeply entrenched in East Africa and Arabia that a policy of gradualness was vital if the economy was not to be wrecked with all the consequences of civil disturbance.

The dangers of abrupt changes were demonstrated in 1894 when a crisis in the succession of the sultanate in Zanzibar provided an opportunity when Britain could enforce the complete cessation of slavery. There was consternation in the islands of Zanzibar and Pemba, some of the merchants and planters leaving immediately with their slaves for other areas—a rather futile move as even in Oman itself any slave arriving by sea was in theory able to take his freedom. The decree abolishing slavery in Zanzibar was issued on April 6, 1897, with freedom for every slave who required it and compensation for his owners. Immediately land values dropped. Only the most feckless of slaves appeared to have taken advantage of the law, turning to begging and theft when they were free.

Emancipation in Zanzibar did not do more than inconvenience the Arab merchants. Vast areas were still open to them to the north, and they had been exploiting them for more than a century in order to offset the competition from Europe and the restrictions of European legislation. The most lucrative source of slaves in this area was the Sudan.

This enormous territory, inefficiently supervised by Egypt, had in theory abandoned slave trading in 1857, but the proclamation was largely to quieten criticism in Europe. Nothing much was done to enforce the law, and indeed the local administrators were frequently conniving on Arab slaving expeditions in return for a share in the profits. Even after Europeans took over the most important administrative posts their corrupt assistants still concealed the extent of slaving in the remoter areas near the Red Sea coast and on the borders of Ethiopia. According to Sir Samuel Baker, who became Governor General of the Equatorial Provinces of Egypt in 1869, one slave trader, financed by a Khartoum merchant, had formed a private army of 2,500 Arabs, armed with muskets and led by deserters from the Sudanese and Egyptian armies. The country was divided into zones of operation to avoid clashes among the slave raiders, who would select a village, make an agreement with the leader to attack a neighbouring village, carry off the women and children for slaves, and take their cattle and sheep for food and to compensate the village allies.

Baker, given the task of fighting what was in effect a major war against a well-organised adversary, began by setting up strategic points manned by dependable troops who enforced peace in an area around each fort. Some Arab slave traders were caught and given an outlet for their martial fervour and spirit of adventure by being invited to fight on Baker's side. The well-nigh insuperable task of cleaning up the whole area was not complete when Baker's tour of duty ended, but he had laid the foundations for the campaign of Gordon, the darling of Victorian England and a strange mixture of religious piety and reckless courage. It was a mixture ideal for fighting a cunning and vicious enemy. Gordon embarked on the enterprise as a crusade. He was ably assisted by an American, Chaille-Long, a Frenchman, de Bellenfonds, and a German, Schnitzer (better known in Africa as Emin Pasha). At first Gordon found the tribes he wanted to help were suspicious and hostile, regarding all foreigners as menacing—an attitude justified by their experiences in the past and also by the fact that Gordon was pushing Egypt's influence farther south as well as trying to stamp out the slave trade. The vastness of the territory made complete success impossible; slave trading continued. The Sudanese tribes became resigned to the fact that they had to protect themselves. Thus the proclamation in 1881 of Mohamet Ahmed that he was the Mahdi sent by Allah to lead the Sudanese to freedom immediately resulted in tribal alliances on a scale never before known, and with Gordon back in England there was no one to face the Mahdi either with propaganda or force. Ahmed's conquest of the Sudan was the result of a holy war, but the tribal enthusiasm for it stemmed from the hatred of the Arabian slave merchants and the Egyptian officials who had condoned and fomented it.

In the slow and tenacious battle to stamp out East African slaving one nation has, perhaps surprisingly, a record which compares favourably with any other colonial power, not excluding Britain.

First World War propaganda created a general belief that Germany had been a ruthless coloniser in Africa. Objective examination of her record does not completely confirm this idea. In East Africa, at any rate, her policy had been an enlightened one. Perhaps at the outset Germany's main consideration had been to acquire territory to rank in power and size with those in Britain and other colonising nations. This policy did necessitate armed action against hostile tribes in order to develop the natural resources of the newly gained territories, but friendly or acquiescent natives were treated as well as anywhere in Africa.

Germany's ambition to run African possessions with Teutonic efficiency was pursued until the Allies deprived Germany of control. Where there was evidence of harshness it was the German form of well-meant instruction and discipline of the native population. German officials genuinely regarded African traditions and customs as repulsively barbaric, with their replacement by Kultur a moral as well as an economic necessity, and of benefit to all—black and white.

The energetic efforts advanced the economic condition of those natives who took advantage of them. Sisal, cotton, coffee, and rubber were grown on a large scale, and gave work both to labourers on plantations and in peasant holdings. Coupled with public works, the rationalised, large-scale agricultural production programme put labour at a premium, and there was a temptation to adopt forced labour or some similar euphemism for slavery. However, some earlier troubles with over-pressed tribes influenced the Germans to emulate their British neighbours, and contracts for work had to be explained clearly and set down in writing. To maintain civil calm tribal communities were strongly encouraged to go in for farming themselves rather than to become wage earners of German settlers.

Native education was lavish by the standards of the time. It was left largely in the hands of the missions, but the administration provided state schools where literacy and various crafts were taught.

Germany signed the Brussels anti-slavery treaty of 1890, and religious and anti-slavery organisations in Germany were vigorously demanding that slavery should be suppressed in German possessions even before that time; the campaign increased after the treaty was signed. By 1895 slave trading was an offence within the borders of Germany's African possessions, though not much was done to abolish slavery itself—largely because of the fear of civil upheaval unless exorbitant compensation was paid to the non-European slave owners. The colonial authorities therefore proceeded cautiously, authorising freedom by purchase and conferring freedom on all children born of a slave mother. It was a slow process but progress never halted till hostilities curbed finance and caused the withdrawal of officials and police.

Slavery lingered on until well after the end of the First World War. By then, however, the number of slaves working on plantations and as domestic servants had declined to such a small figure that the eventual abolition caused none of those economic and social troubles which the Germans had feared. Coupled with regulations for minimum wages, supervised labour contracts, duration of employment away from the tribal village, housing, food, and medical services when on government work, the change went smoothly. The standards for government work became automatically the usual ones in private employment.

It has been said with some justification that Britain colonised East Africa because of a desire to liberate the people from slavery and to protect them from the depredations of slave traders, while Germany went in solely to annex an empire. Yet Britain's method was to follow the old policy of setting up a commercial company, the BEA Association (later the Imperial BEA Company), while Germany was the first to declare herself the protector of the peoples of the area over which she was given influence in 1886.

Both nations, in their different ways, gave as much as they took from East Africa. Whatever criticisms African nationalists may make today about colonialism the fact remains that thanks mainly to Britain and Germany, the slave system established over nearly two thousand years was eradicated in less than a century.

Fourteen

After Britain's abolition of the slave trade more than three hundred treaties and international agreements were signed, chiefly at the instigation of the United Kingdom Government. Their defect was the weakness or absence of international supervision to ensure that the agreements were effectively enforced. This was remedied after the Brussels convention with the establishment of the Slavery Bureau in 1890. Its work ceased in 1914 with the outbreak of the First World War, and after the Armistice a fresh convention was made at St. Germain-en-Laye. The signatories were the victorious powers and the agreement applied particularly to slavery in Africa. To some extent the St. Germain-en-Laye agreement was a retrograde move. It appeared to abrogate the Brussels Convention, though thirty-seven years later, in 1956, the British Foreign Office, stated that it regarded the Brussels Act as still valid so far as the rights o visit, search, and detention of suspected slave ships was concerned.

The founding of the League of Nations on January 1, 1920, with twenty-eight wartime allies and fourteen neutral nations as members, offered the chance of re-creating an effective international anti-slavery organisation. The League's Covenant was not, in fact, greatly concerned with slavery beyond a vague gesture in Article 23 which supported fair and humane conditions of work. Not until 1922 did the League establish a temporary Slavery Commission. This resulted in the Slavery Convention of 1926. It was approved and signed by thirty-six members, and subsequently forty-six nations ratified the agreement.

The weakness of the League in other international matters in not having any means of effective law enforcement or inspection also applied to the Slavery Convention. Nations who wished to evade their responsibilities could find plenty of loopholes. The main value of the League's work was to formulate for the first time a description of slave trading and slavery.

Slave trading was defined as "all acts involved in the capture, acquisition, or disposal of a person with intent to reduce him to slavery; all acts involved in the acquisition of a slave with the view to selling or exchanging him; all acts of disposal by sale or exchange of a slave acquired with a view to being sold or exchanged, and in general every act of trade or transport in slaves".

Slavery was defined as "the status or condition of a person over whom any or all the powers attaching to the right of ownership are exercised".

There was no compulsion on the signatories to make regular reports on their domestic legislation designed to put the Convention's articles into operation; they were obliged to inform the League of the terms of any such laws, but no explanation was demanded of their failure to promulgate legislation.

The first major test of the value of the League's definition of slavery occurred in 1930, when a commission was appointed to enquire into allegations of slavery in Liberia. The United States, though not in the League, was responsible for suggesting the investigation, motivated by her paternal and traditional interest in the country ever since its founding by the American Colonisation Society as a refuge for freed slaves in 1821. From 1909 the US Government had provided advice and help as regards defence and economics, but the USA's policy of anti-colonialism resulted in what was perhaps an undue reticence in interfering with Liberian domestic politics. By 1929 the stories of slavery in various guises were so disquieting that the State Department made a direct charge in a note to the Liberian Foreign Office. The purport of this charge was that the export of Africans to the island of Fernando Poo had developed into a traffic which was "hardly distinguishable from an organised slave trade".

Liberia denied the charge of slave trading. She was a faithful and original member of the League of Nations and invited the USA and the League to supply two investigators, Liberia providing a third one.

The findings uncovered a situation which was doubtless not unique to Liberia, but would have applied to many other African and Asiatic territories had their governments permitted as detailed an investigation as Liberia authorised. There was inter-tribal slavery, partly because of the religious differences between the Mandingoes, who were Muslim, and the other tribes, who were pagan. The ancient African custom of pawning people survived. Forced labour for government works had been diverted to private enterprises; in neither occupation had the labourers been paid. Workers sent out of the country for work in French Gabon and Spanish Fernando Poo had been recruited under a system virtually the same as slave trading. But the American rubber company, Firestone, with vast concessions, was absolved from any taint of employing forced labour.

Liberia agreed to various reforms, financial aid was provided and experts were appointed as advisers. The worst exploitation of workers within the country disappeared, though up to 1939 Liberian subjects were being sent to work on the cocoa plantations in Fernando Poo much as before. The growing ineffectiveness of the League and the impossibility of approaching Spain during the Spanish civil war made international action futile. The semi-slave trade died away when Liberia's economy boomed during the Second World War, with American undertakings developing the country's defence system and trade.

When the United Nations Organisation took over the remnants of the League in 1946 it made no more definite attack on slavery than its predecessor. The only reference was in Article 1 (3) of the Charter: the promotion and encouragement of respect for human rights and for fundamental freedoms for all without distinction as to race, sex, language, or religion.

But on December 10, 1948, in the Declaration of Human Rights, Article 4 specifically prohibited slavery and the slave trade. Eight years later came the 1956 Supplementary Convention on the "abolition of slavery, the slave trade, and institutions and practices similar to slavery". To those peoples of the world able to read newspapers and to afford radio sets the need to set up yet another UN body seemed doubtful; slavery, in the general opinion, was an evil of the past. One reason for this fallacious belief was the inability of the enslaved to make their condition known, in contrast to other groups suffering from human injustice.

Political refugees have compatriots to fight on their behalf; racial minorities have majorities in other countries who are actual or potential allies; prisoners' names are given in courts or at least their disappearance after arrest is known. The infringement of human rights implies a deprivation of those rights from persons who, however briefly, have enjoyed them or know that international law enjoins that they shall enjoy them.

But a slave is a non-person. He is invariably illiterate, ignorant, and inarticulate. He has no vote. He may not even be counted as a cipher in a country's population. He comes into contact with no one who does not approve of, and conspire to, his enslavement. He is condemned because his plight will remain officially unknown. The government of his country will deny his existence and will probably have passed laws forbidding his enslavement. Estimates have been made that between one and two million people still exist in slavery today. The figure can at best be an intelligent guess, for it is quite certain that every nation, east or west, capitalist or communist, will deny that traffic in human beings exists within its borders, and every owner of a slave will exert every effort to prevent investigation. This was the situation when the UN embarked on a campaign to eradicate twentieth-century slavery.

Thanks mainly to voluntary bodies, notably the Anti-Slavery Society of London, the 1956 Convention covered systems of exploitation which were less obviously illegal than chattel slavery. Six types exist today.

The most widespread deprivation of individual freedom in the present century is in the form of forced labour. This is not, of course, slavery in the classic sense of the term, but serfdom is extremely difficult to define so that the dividing line between legality and illegality can be indicated. People forced to work are not, usually, the possessions of the employer; he cannot sell them; the type of work they do is specified and cannot be changed; the period of forced labour is normally defined.

It would be difficult, indeed, to prove beyond any semblance of doubt that the industrialists of Nazi Germany who employed —and indirectly killed—tens of thousands of men and women directed to forced labour were in reality enslaving them. The Jews, gipsies, "criminals", civilians from occupied enemy territories, and so on, remained under Nazi Government control, and a German steel master, for example, could not withdraw a dozen forced labour employees to cultivate his private farm, though of course he could easily apply for them at the nearest camp.

Britain's total conscription of the civilian population, emulated to a greater or lesser extent by every nation involved in World War II, approached closely to serfdom, despite all the safeguards to avoid dividing families, ensuring adequate payment, and rights of protest. But it was very obviously not slavery.

Forced labour and slavery both exact work from persons compelled to obey. In forced labour the State or private employers infer that they "own" the workers and can punish, discipline, and utilise them for their ultimate benefit.

No committee of the United Nations can expect any success in prohibiting a system of forced labour under State direction. It has to concern itself with the few cases of serfdom under private systems. Serfdom exists in the remoter areas of Ethiopia (which abolished chattel slavery in 1942) and in the High Andes of South America; it is alleged that a million serfs exist in Peru.

Serfdom is a relic of medieval feudalism, but it can re-emerge as a modern system of obtaining cheap labour. A typical instance occurred in 1966 when the forced employment of boys in Africa was revealed after the discovery of a smuggling organisation across the Kenya–Tanzania border. Men had been travelling through the villages in the bush country around Kisii, east of Lake Victoria, recruiting boys for forestry work at a wage of about £3 a month plus food, shelter and clothing. The boys were smuggled across the border into Tanzania and taken to maize farms and sawmills as many as four hundred miles from their homes. Both the Tanzania and Kenya authorities learned of the movement of these children and began investigating. The touts were Kenyans, and more than 250 boys were involved, ranging in age from seven to sixteen. Rescued boys told how no wages had been paid, clothing was rarely handed out, and food consisted of soya beans and maize. The boys worked twelve to fourteen hours a day and were whipped if they attempted to escape from the camp. These children had either volunteered for the work or their parents had authorised it. So long as the touts concealed details of any payment from employers, they could be prosecuted only for illegal entry and on infringement of laws on child labour and minimum wages. But some of the boys were doubtless sold by their parents. One man whose monetary transaction was proved was sent to prison for three years and given twelve strokes of the lash.

This type of forced labour of children is allied to the sham adoption practices prevailing in every part of the world where poverty and over-population exist. In the Far East it is known as Mui-tsai, and usually involves the sale of little girls. They may with luck live as drudges in a household; it is more likely that they will work in cafes, restaurants and dance halls until they reach puberty and can be forced into prostitution. One of the most horrifying facets of the sham adoption racket is the deliberate mutilation of children to enhance their value as beggars.

Another widespread custom stemming from poverty is debt bondage, practised in Asia for thousands of years. When a man incurs a financial obligation through debt or fine he (or a member of his family) pledges himself as security. In modern times the usual practice is for a man to offer as a substitute the services of one of his children in lieu of interest on the loan. Debt bondage cannot be utilised to pay off the actual loan, and in the likely event that the debtor can never repay the money the interest is then payable in perpetuity, being handed down from one generation to another. The child and his children are therefore in permanent debt bondage. The creditor, of course, prefers that the situation should continue, the work extracted from the slave being of far greater value than the orginal loan or the interest on it. This practice is a time-honoured one in India and though it has been illegal since 1947, it has proved difficult to stamp out.

The fifth form of modern slavery is really a problem of sex equality. While the female baby remains inferior to the male child, a wife is regarded as her husband's property, and a woman's sexual attractions have commercial value, the exploitation will continue. The attitude exists, in fact or by inference, in every country in the world, but is found in its most degrading guises in Arab and Muslim countries.

That an Arab woman is a "slave from birth to death" is today too sweeping a generalisation. Aid from both communist and Western sources—political, financial, economic, and scientific—has directly or indirectly encouraged the emancipation of many thousands of young Arab women. Both reactionary and progressive leaders are accepting that their women's brains can be as useful as their bodies. Whether they fundamentally approve of this situation or not, there is little chance of completely thwarting the hopes and ambitions of the youth of both sexes. But enlightenment will not easily permeate every dark corner where tradition is everything.

The Arab male's obsession with female virginity is at the root of the subservient position of Arab women. A moral virtue is protected by a cruel and inhuman evil. The ritualistic surgery of clitoridectomy is more widely practised in Arabia than most Western people realise. This operation, carried out by midwives, has no religious significance, even of a distorted kind. It is performed solely to destroy the Arab woman's ability to experience sexual pleasure and therefore is designed to defend her against temptation. If the operation is badly performed a nerve is exposed which will, indeed, make intercourse an agonising experience for the rest of her life. In any event the permanent tenderness is such that few girls would voluntarily permit intercourse. Thus she is forced into marriage, concubinage, or prostitution (the three vocations open to her) as a virgin. She is merely an object of pleasure or a child bearer.

As such she has a price whether she is on offer as a virgin or as a discarded woman of use to a brothel keeper. There are no other standards of value for an impoverished Arab woman who has the misfortune to be born into the social vacuum which is Arabia. Still bleaker are the prospects for the girl child who is the descendant of slaves or ex-slaves.

It is only fair to state that most of the rulers in Arabia have made efforts to eradicate slave trading and all forms of servitude beyond the domestic practices in the harem and the household. The formal prohibitions on slavery have been made mostly since the end of the Second World War, and the changes are too recent for the effectiveness to be assessed. But the status of the majority of women has not changed for centuries.

Love is not the exclusive monopoly of Christendom. A wife obtained for money and thereafter totally owned by her husband, is not necessarily unhappy, nor is a marriage system practised throughout the non-Christian world inevitably evil, either as monogamy or polygamy. It becomes enslavement only because it usually ignores the woman's wishes; she is the merchandise from which others profit. The ultimate degeneration of this contemptuous attitude to a woman is the sixth—and most shameful—form of modern slavery: prostitution.

The girl in the harem can count herself unbelievably fortunate if she remains there. The usual alternative is to become the girl in the brothel—a fate which awaits untold thousands of little girls growing up today. It is symptomatic of the West's self-interest that compulsory prostitution causes alarm mainly when it is "white" slavery.

The "white slave" is basically a moral problem because in most cases she is perfectly aware that her sexuality and femininity are to be exploited. She cannot know of the horror and degradation that the glamorous job in a dance hall, cabaret, or other place of entertainment will inevitably bring, but the problem is mainly to save her from her own stupidity rather than some gaoler.

The activities of the League of Nations, Interpol, and international welfare organisations have created the smug belief that the white slave traffic is no longer a major menace. So far as white girls are concerned, it is not. But goodly people whose fury is aroused when half a dozen European strip-tease girls disappear in the Middle East find no reason to ponder on the fact that most of the brothels of the world are run by exploiting girls who are coloured. No one has ever begun to calculate how many women are physically or financially imprisoned as owned prostitutes. They must number more than a million, and they are the greatest army of ill-treated serfs existing today. Nations which have laws to inflict swingeing sentences on any subject who tried to buy or sell a slave worker prefer to turn a blind eye to the traffic in women. Indeed, the trend of modern governments is to isolate their red light districts, with police supervision at the entries, but with no interference with the brothels' activities beyond checks on hygiene, fire hazards, and other factors affecting the girls' clients.

In an eadeavour to start on the tremendous task of at least exposing, if not curbing, those twentieth-century versions of slavery the United Nations in 1963 appointed a Rapporteur, Dr. Mohamed Awad of the United Arab Republic, who circulated a long questionnaire to member nations. At that time sixty-six nations had ratified the 1956 convention, which unfortunately left an almost equal number of countries within and outside the UN whose attitude to, and actions against, slavery could not be ascertained.

But from the evidence which provided the basis of the Rapporteur's report in the spring of 1966 it was obvious that slavery in every known form exists on a large scale. This ancient crime against humanity is actually involved in the modern science of atomic power. The facts emerged from a report to the United Nations originating from information gathered by two French teachers who went to Algeria under a bilateral aid programme between France and Algeria. Slavery is legally non-existent in Algeria, so any slave system is a hidden one, deeply entrenched in the family and tribal systems of the people who live largely independent lives deep in the Sahara. The Tuareg, who are, and regard themselves, as "white", nurse a fierce hostility on religions and racial grounds towards black Africans. The Tuareg have, of course, been slave traders from the days of the caravans trading between the Middle East/ Mediterranean littoral and Timbuktu. Sentimentalists portray these Berbers as a splendid anachronism, and they are glamourised in travel books and documentary films as the People of the Veil. They inhabit two distinct areas of the Sahara. Those in the south, living for the most part within the borders of the Mali Republic, have gradually turned from a nomadic life to agriculture, and with this change the old slave raiding and stock stealing activities have largely died away. The Tuareg of the Northern area of the Sahara maintain their traditional system of tribal society: the warrior and raider class; the farmers and camel breeders; the craftsmen in leather and other tradesmen; and slaves.

There is much to admire in their sense of independence and their skills as nomadic warriors and herdsmen. But their devotion to tradition has not prevented them from profiting from the West's lavish enterprises in atomic engineering. Those slaves working on the constructional work at the atomic base at In Ekkor were accepted and regarded by the French engineers as labourers freely entering into employment agreements and were paid. But their Tuareg owners lived on their earnings and were said by the French informants to take two-thirds of the slaves' earnings. As pay rates were generous a slave's purchase price was covered by a year's work. Thereafter the master's profit was 100 per cent.

Some of the Algerian slave traffic is alleged to be across the border to Mauritania. Slaves are needed for routine work, but there is also traffic in girls for concubinage and prostitution. Children of slaves remain the property of the owners; consequently there is a two-fold incentive to force girl slaves into prostitution: as a direct source of profit and for the eventual increase in the number of slaves.

Even a long established and wealthy government would find it a formidable task to stamp out slavery among the Tuareg of the Sahara or even to make an accurate estimate of the number of slaves who exist. The French teacher who had been employed in the Tamanrasset region, in the far south of Algeria, estimated that there were two thousand slaves in that area alone.

A thousand miles to the south of Algeria, in the Cameroon, which became independent on January 1, 1960, a Norwegian missionary with thirty years' experience of the social structure of the Muslim sections of the country has stated to the Anti-Slavery Society that slavery is condoned, particularly within the harems. In census returns details of the number of slaves in existence are hidden by their owners describing their activities under a variety of names.

In neighbouring Nigeria genuine and reasonably successful efforts have been made since independence to stamp out the long standing slavery and slave trading customs of the Northern region. Within the country the purchase of girls as brides is probably the most prevalent means of enslavement, but there is still a clandestine trade across the borders in the wider implications of traffic in human beings. One route is northwards to the Libyan ports; the other passes through Chad and across the Sudan to the Red Sea outlets. The enormous distances involved give a hint of the sufferings of the slaves. The expense and difficulty of moving captives for two thousand miles through the most terrible terrain in the whole continent are faced presumably because Muslim tradition dies so hard. These have been slave routes throughout the Christian era and probably long before. They are still followed despite the availability of slaves for Arab countries much nearer to the prospective purchasers.

Another ancient centre of slave trading, Sierra Leone, may contribute to this traditional Arab traffic. The supply area is among tribes living some three hundred miles from the coast and extends into the states adjacent to Sierra Leone among people hardly aware of national boundaries. The price of prime male slaves has soared since the days when a European slaver could obtain a Negro for a length of cloth. The cost is now £600. A woman fetches a lower price, the figure depending on her beauty and youth, and children are far cheaper because of the cost of feeding them till they are capable of hard work. Some of these slaves are bought by the Tuareg, but the majority are sold and re-sold on the trading route towards the Red Sea.

Little is known about the methods of obtaining these slaves. There is an unwritten law forbidding those who trade with the Arab slavers from kidnapping members of their own tribe, at least partly because of the possibility of complaint by the tribal members to the authorities. The most convenient victims are young people who for reasons of finding work or through family quarrels have left the locality of their birth and are therefore unlikely to be missed. Modern methods of quietening recalcitrants have been adopted. In 1964 a court case indicated that a drug had been used to deprive captives of the power of intelligent speech.

Slaving justifying intricate operations of this kind stretching right across Africa would not be profitable but for the existence of a large market for slaves in the Middle East. Whether an individual state in this area pays lip service to emancipation, genuinely attempts to bring slavery to an end, or simply ignores international enquiries and offers of assistance, the result is much the same: slavery continues.

Ruling Arab families have for centuries regarded the ownership of slaves as a status symbol. The Cadillac and the private aeroplane have not replaced them.

Time will remedy this situation; the new generation of Western-educated rulers have been bold enough to fight hidebound traditionalism. And the popular political movements of the larger Arab nations have had their effect so far as men are concerned. But the exploitation of women in conditions of serfdom will not disappear until the belief in female inferiority is destroyed by education, economic progress, and a restoration of the teachings of Mahomet, which were to restrain polygamy and concubinage rather than to encourage them.

Qatar abolished slavery in 1952. The worst conditions had been among the pearl diving slaves, whose health quickly broke down under the constant work at great depths and through respiratory troubles caused by the unnatural retention of breath for as long as three minutes. The oyster beds were more or less exhausted by the time of the discovery of oil in the country and the slave traders found a new market just in time to save their business. Investors in Britain and the USA who readily criticised the commercial interests of the eighteenth and nineteenth centuries which battened on the slave trade were content enough that their oil shares should rise thanks to slave labour. Most of the labour employed on the oil installations was enslaved, and supplied by Arab contractors. Until slavery became illegal on the order of Qatar's ruler, Sheik Ali Bin Abdullah Bin Jassim Al Thani, none of the Western oil companies prospering on slave labour saw fit to change the situation. With emancipation, the slaves continued with the same work, but for personal wages and with legal rights. No doubt shareholders deprecated the rise in running costs.

The majority of Qatar's slaves were in domestic employment. Most continued to work for their ex-masters, though gradually the improving economic conditions in the country encouraged them to start businesses of their own. As many of the slaves were the children of slaves, and had been brought up as companions of their masters' children, receiving the same education, they formed a new kind of mercantile class.

In the Federation of Southern Arabia, some of the sheikdoms and sultanates have formally abolished slavery. The slaves who exist are almost all children of slaves and are known as abd. They could in theory quite easily find sanctuary and freedom, but prefer the security of work for a ruling family to the rigours of their harsh desert lands. Whether these servants are in fact enslaved is disputable.

Much the same situation exists in the Trucial States, where slavery was supposed to end in 1957, and a formal declaration of its abolition was made in 1963. In the Yemen the republicans made slave-owning illegal as one of the reforms resulting from the revolution in 1962. Yemeni women, and probably the servants of the wealthier families, continued to exist in conditions similar to their previous slave status.

By reason of its size and its importance to Muslims, Saudi Arabia is in a unique position in tackling its slavery difficulties. Slavery was not legally abolished until 1962. Until then Saudi Arabia was the twentieth-century's stronghold of chattel slavery, a rich market for smugglers who were ready to defy the 1935 laws against the importation of slaves, strengthening an anti-slave trading agreement under the treaty of Jedda in 1927. In the quarter century covering the ban on imports and the abolition of slavery the price of an African slave trebled, and £2,000 was a not unusual price for a young girl. An estimate of the country's population at the time of abolition was 8 millions, of whom 250,000 were slaves.

Economic and political chaos would have resulted in the instant liberation of such a vast number of slaves, and while the government paid generous compensation to owners (with many others merely taking an oath that they had freed their slaves) many thousands continued to work for their owners as they, and their ancestors, had always done.

Slave trading still persists across the borders of Saudi Arabia, just as smuggling and illegal entry exist in more advanced and more populous countries. Its existence is not so much a reflection on the authorities as on Saudi Arabian families who cling to old ways. The traders have to work with great caution, and few would dare risk bringing in more than a dozen or so captives at a time. The traditional route was from Dubai, Muscat, and Buraimi to the market at Riyadh. Stories of slaves paraded for sale in Mecca at a "slave shop" called Dakkat al Abd (the slaves' bench) by Western writers must be taken with reserve in view of the government's campaign against the trade, but there are undoubtedly clandestine deals among the mass of pilgrims in the city.

Every Muslim should, of course, make the pilgrimage to Mecca at least once in his lifetime. Religious zeal may get him there, but worldly benefits of money are certainly needed to get him back home. Inevitably many pilgrims have no such resources. A pilgrim's only solution for survival may well be to accept slavery. More prescient pilgrims may take one or two children with them in order to sell them in Mecca. On a pilgrim caravan leaving Nigeria in 1964 an investigator was told that the children represented their parents' return tickets on the ship through the Red Sea and Suez to a Libyan port.

The simple method of eradicating the risk of a pilgrim being stranded in Mecca is for his own country to check that he has the resources needed for the return journey and to check re-entries against the numbers leaving. Nigeria has been active in taking these precautions. In 1962 eight thousand pilgrims were refused permission to embark on the pilgrim ships at Suakin in the Sudan because of their lack of a return ticket or the money to buy one, but with an ominous number of young girls accompanying their parents.

Most pathetic of all slaves in the mid-twentieth century are the simple and gentle Bushmen, the nomadic people of South Africa who probably brought Paleolithic culture from North Africa and for unknown ages were the sole human inhabitants of the south of the continent. Constantly attacked by more advanced races the Bushmen retreated to the Kalahari desert, where today perhaps as many as twenty thousand are managing to stave off extinction.

The Bushman bands, each consisting of a few families, occupy a large area of land over which they have exclusive hunting and foraging rights. Political boundaries, of course, mean nothing to them and the Bushmen exist in arid land north of the mountains of Cape Province and as far north as the Cubango river area. Thus they inhabit territory in South Africa, Botswana (Bechuanaland), South-West Africa, and Angola.

Reports of the killing and enslavement of Bushmen by both European farmers and Bantu are said to be "not infrequent". Thousands of them work as slaves for the Bantu, their complete ignorance of money and inability to understand any language but their own monosyllabic speech making them easy victims of exploitation. Political developments in the countries where they live make the future of these people an ominous one. Whatever tribes were virtually extinguished by slaving in the eighteenth century, civilisation's apathy over the Bushmen may well add another name to the list.

* * *

Time had not yet healed the injury inflicted by the white races on the black peoples of Africa. The hatred of colonialism is often unreasonable because the benefits it conferred do not allay the belief of Africans that it was a legalised version of slavery, the objects being identical: the exploitation of one race by another rather than the creation of a settlement for white immigrants.

Infinitely worse is the emergence of the myth of superiority and inferiority based on the colour of the skin. When Hawkins and his armed mariners rampaged along the coast of Africa in 1567 it is improbable that they would have regarded men and women of their own colour as merchandise. The blackamoor was described as an intelligent animal, though in the hearts of all the thousands of white men who emulated the sixteenth-century tradesmen in human beings there must have been the knowledge that their victims were human beings. The attitude of white superiority was a facile way of easing the conscience, and of suppressing every precept of Christianity and Western political ideals, fostering the theory of black sub-humanity until it became an accepted fact.

The past enslavement of Africans has produced the tragedy of racial discrimination. An accident of geography and economics has been perverted into a theory about a natural law, by, perhaps, millions of people.

When, a century ago, the anti-slave patrols in the Atlantic ceased for lack of slaving pirates, only part of the terrible bill owed by White to Black had been paid. The United Nations' International Year for Human Rights in 1968 is unlikely to be regarded by history as the final settlement.

References

(Unless otherwise stated, the works mentioned were originally published in the United Kingdom.)

General

The most comprehensive assembly of original material on slave trading—English, Portuguese, Spanish, French, and American—up to the time of abolition is in *Documents Illustrative of the History of the Slave Trade to America* by Elizabeth Donnan, 4 vols., 1930–5 (Washington).

These volumes include virtually all the published material by seamen, explorers, missionaries, and traders from the fifteenth century onwards, with numerous extracts from ships' masters' logs, agents' reports, statistics, and legislation. The majority of the documents are published in full.

Chapter One

Details of the legal position of slaves in Greece are well described in *Greek Constitutional History* by A. H. J. Greenidge, 1902.

The dependence of Rome on slavery, and the Empire's attitude to slaves, are documented in *The History of Rome* by T. Mommsen, 1862.

Chapter Two

The Golden Age of Prince Henry the Navigator by J. P. Oliveira, 1891 (Lisbon), (English translation 1914), is a detailed survey of the exploration of the coast of West Africa and the development of trade.

Azurata's "Chronicles" were published in *A New General Collection of Voyages and Travels* by Thomas Astley, 1745. A translation by C. Raymond Beazley and Edgar Prestage was prepared for the Hakluyt Society, 1897.

The trading and political developments of Spain and Portugal in the early phases of the African and American explorations are given in detail in *Ferdinand and Isabella* by W. H. Prescott, 3 vols., 1857.

Chapter Three

The Principal Navigations, Voyages, Traffiques, and Discoveries of the English Nation by Richard Hakluyt is the general source of all accounts of the maritime activities of Hawkins and other English sailors of the sixteenth century.

An excellent version of the Hawkins' expedition is *The Hawkins Voyage* (for the Hakluyt Society) by C. R. Markham, 1878.

English Seamen in the 16th Century by J. A. Froude, 1895, contains further material.

The adversary's view of Hawkins is available in *Spanish Documents Concerning English Voyages to the Caribbean 1527–1568* for the Hakluyt Society, 1929.

James Barbot's "Description of the Coast of North and South Guinea" is in *Collection of Voyages and Travels* by John Churchill, 1732.

Chapter Four

The Journal of the African Society and the Court Minutes of the East India Company provide extensive material on the official trading policies of the Government through chartered companies, and illustrate the financial ramifications of the slave trade in the seventeenth and eighteenth centuries.

The Case' of the Royal African Company describes the illicit competition on the African coast and indicates the early moves to defend and develop concessions on the African mainland, 1729.

John Barbot, James Barbot, and James Barbot, Jnr., published several accounts of their voyages; they were used in abstract form in much of the subsequent material attacking the slave trade.

Chapter Five

The economic situation of England is meticulously covered in *A History of England in the 18th Century*, vols. 1–8, by W. E. H. Lecky, 1883.

John Atkins's *A Voyage to Guinea, Brazil, and the West Indies* was first published in 1737. Extracts were widely reprinted in subsequent propaganda material.

Chapter Six

The History, Civil and Commercial, of the British Colonies in the West Indies, 3 vols., 1801, by Bryan Edwards is a first-hand survey of the plantations, slave markets, and general economy of the British West Indian possessions. The period covered is 1760–90.

Memoirs of Granville Sharp, 1820, records the author's campaign for the liberation of slaves brought to England.

The impact of the slave trade on Liverpool is described in *A General and Descriptive History of the Ancient and Present State of the Town of Liverpool*, 1798.

Details of the petitions for and against the slave trade are recorded in the Calendars of State Papers.

Chapter Seven

The basis of all biographies of William Wilberforce is *The Life of William Wilberforce* by R. J. and S. W. Wilberforce, 1838.

The *Zong* case is recorded in *Memoirs of Granville Sharp*, 1820.

The Minutes of Evidence in the Parliamentary Enquiry into the slave trade are covered by vol. 1 for 1789, vols. 2 and 3 for 1790, and vol. 4 for 1791. Thomas Clarkson prepared a digest of these in *Abstracts of the Evidence*, 1791.

The Impolicy of the Slave Trade by Thomas Clarkson, 1788, is a typical example of the literature in the anti-slavery campaign of the period.

William Pitt's speeches appear in *Parliamentary Speeches*, 1808.

Chapter Eight

French works on the country's West Indian possessions and the St. Domingue insurrection are numerous; the background to the disturbances and the emergence of Toussaint l'Ouverture are well described in the modern standard work *Histoire de Toussaint l'Ouverture* by P. Sannon (Paris), 1920.

The actual civil war is covered by *Histoire Militaire de St. Domingue* by De Poyen (Paris), 1899.

The development of Sierra Leone as a slave sanctuary is described in *The Life and Letters of Zachary Macaulay* by Lady Knutsford, 1900.

The conditions in Sierra Leone have a vivid treatment in *A Voyage on the River Sierra-Leone on the Coast of Africa* by Lt. John Matthews, RN, 1788.

Travels in the Interior Districts of Africa by Mungo Park (1799) and *The Guinea Voyage* by James Stansfield (1807) are well-written travel books with objective accounts of slave trading at the time of the abolition campaign.

Chapter Nine

A comprehensive and official account of the international diplomatic moves by the British Government is contained in *Some Account of the Trade in Slaves from Africa as Connected with Europe and America* by James Bandinel of the Foreign Office, on behalf of the Earl of Aberdeen, and issued by the Stationery Office in 1842.

The controversy of the right to search US ships is recorded in detail in *American Abolition from 1787–1861* by E. G. de Fontaine (New York), 1861.

The adventures of the *Cyane* appear in *Reminiscences of the Old Navy* by Edgar Maclay (New York), 1898.

Chapter Ten

Bryan Edward's book, referred to in the notes on Chapter Six *supra*, provides details of the life of slaves in the West Indies.

Chronological History of the West Indies by Thomas Southey, 1827, is full of anecdotes, mostly with a maritime flavour.

A History of the West Indies (3 vols.) by Thomas Coke, reproduces material from earlier histories and has personal accounts of Methodist missionary work on behalf of the slaves (1811).

Chapter Eleven

A Nation of Immigrants by President Kennedy (1964) is a concise survey of American policy on immigration, white and coloured, free and enslaved, from colonial days to the present time. It is excellent as a guide to the campaign for abolition and emancipation.

History of the United States by George Bancroft, records in detail the history of individual states with voluminous notes and reproduction of legal moves against and for slavery, 1883 (New York).

American Abolition from 1787–1861 by E. G. de Fontaine surveys the campaign for the Negro up to the civil war, and despite a pro-slavery bias is a graphic account of an involved situation (New York).

The concept of a slave-run empire is contained in *Sociology for the South* by George Fitzhugh, 1854 (Richmond, Virginia).

The clash over slaves between north and south can be understood from the material in *The Fugitive Slave Law and Its Victims* by S. R. May, Jnr. (1856), and *The Underground Railroad for Slavery to Freedom* by Wilbur Silbert (1899) (both published in New York).

Slave smuggling is described in *Twenty Years of an African Slaver* by Captain Canot and Brantz Mayer, 1854 (New York).

Chapter Twelve

The suppression of the slave trade on the African coast from a semi-official American view is contained in *Journal of an African Cruiser by an Officer of the U.S. Navy* by Horatio Bridges, edited by Nathaniel Hawthorne, 1845 (New York).

The modern definition of slavery, and the international methods of suppression, are all based on the General Act for the Repression of the African Slave Trade, 1890 (Brussels).

Chapter Thirteen

A Three Years' Cruise in the Mozambique Channel for the Suppression of the Slave Trade by Lt. Barnard is an early work on the East African situation, 1848.

Richard Burton's *Zanzibar* (1872) and *The Slave Trade of East Africa* by Edward Hutchinson (1874) were among the first books to reveal the dimensions of the Afro-Arabic slave trade.

Six Months on a Slaver by Edward Manning, published in 1879 (New York) and *Slave Catching in the Indian Ocean* by Captain Colomb (1873) are colourful and presumably authentic records of post-abolition slave trading.

Chapter Fourteen

General Act for the Repression of the African Slave Trade, 1890 (Brussels).

Reports of the Slavery Convention of the League of Nations, 1926 (Geneva).

The Supplementary Convention on the Abolition of Slavery, the Slave Trade, and Institutions and Practices Similar to Slavery— United Nations, 1956 (Geneva).

A world-wide survey, and evidence resulting from a questionnaire, in the United Nations Economic and Social Council's reports from the Special Rapporteur on Slavery. 1966.

The annual reports of the Anti-Slavery Society and the periodic publication of the *Anti-Slavery Reporter* (which first appeared in 1823) record interesting material from missionaries, travellers, social workers, etc., as well as details of contemporary legislation.

Index

214